Telecommunications Regulation

Much has been written on telecommunications regulation, but little has focused on the actual processes used in regulation. Using unprecedented access to the key actors inside the UK Office of Telecommunications (Oftel) and supporting interviews, this book explores how telecommunications regulation works from the inside, providing a novel insight into the dynamic process of regulation in the United Kingdom.

Telecommunications Regulation includes a significant re-evaluation of key regulatory issues including:

- the role of information in regulation
- the interdependence of regulators with others
- accountability
- the comparative roles of individuals and organizations within regulation.

Drawing on direct observation, this volume also highlights the importance of cultural and social variables, alongside the more recognized parameters of legal and economic conditions in shaping effective regulatory action.

The concluding chapter stands back from the detail of UK telecoms regulation to consider the wider implications of the study for:

- understanding the limits to effective regulation
- the development of regulatory policy, institutions and decision-making
- the future of telecoms regulation internationally.

Clare Hall, Colin Scott and **Christopher Hood** are, respectively, Research Fellow, Senior Lecturer in Law and Professor of Public Policy and Public Administration at the London School of Economics and Political Science.

Routledge Advances in Management and Business Studies

1 **Middle Managers in Europe**
Yves Frédéric Livian and John G. Burgoyne

2 **Marketing Apocalypse**
Eschatology, escapology and the illusion of the end
Edited by Stephen Brown, Jim Bell and David Carson

3 **Relationship Marketing in Professional Services**
A study of agency–client dynamics in the advertising sector
Aino Halinen

4 **Job Design and Technology**
Taylorism vs anti-Taylorism
Hans D. Pruijt

5 **Regulation and Organizations**
International perspectives
Edited by Glenn Morgan and Lars Engwall

6 **Information Technology, Organisations and People**
Transformations in the UK retail financial services sector
Jeff Watkins

7 **HRM, Technical Workers and the Multinational Corporation**
Patrick McGovern

8 **The Internationalization of Small to Medium Enterprises**
The Interstratos Project
Edited by Rik Donckels, Antti Haahti and Graham Hall

9 **Neo-Industrial Organizing**
Renewal by action and knowledge formation in a project-intensive economy
Rolf A. Lundin, Hans Wirdenius, Eskil Ekstedt and Anders Soderholm

10 **Perspectives on Public Relations Research**
Edited by Danny Moss, Dejan Vercic and Gary Warnaby

11 **Resources, Technology and Strategy**
Edited by Nicholai J. Foss and Paul L. Robertson

12 **Telecommunications Regulation**
Culture, chaos and interdependence inside the regulatory process
Clare Hall, Colin Scott and Christopher Hood

Telecommunications Regulation

Culture, chaos and interdependence inside the regulatory process

Clare Hall, Colin Scott and Christopher Hood

ROUTLEDGE
Taylor & Francis Group

London and New York

First published 2000 by Routledge
11 New Fetter Lane, London EC4P 4EE

Simultaneously published in the USA and Canada
by Routledge
29 West 35th Street, New York, NY 10001

Routledge is an imprint of the Taylor & Francis Group

Typeset in Sabon by Florence Production Ltd, Stoodleigh, Devon
Printed and bound in Great Britain by T J International Ltd.,
Padstow, Cornwall

British Library Cataloguing in Publication Data
A catalogue record for this book is available from the
British Library

Library of Congress Cataloging in Publication Data
A catalogue record for this has been requested
ISBN 0 415 19949 2

Contents

PART IV
Decision-making

PART V
Lessons learnt

Figures

Tables

Preface

Early in 1994, the newly installed Director General of Telecommunications, Don Cruickshank, invited us to conduct an independent 'inside' study of the working of Oftel, the UK telecommunications regulator. We jumped at the chance, since it gave us a not-to-be-missed opportunity to produce the first in-depth inside study of one of the new breed of utility regulators in the UK. One of our number, Clare Hall, was physically located in Oftel for two years and spent four days a week observing, interviewing, questioning, reading and functioning as a participant observer in Oftel's work. The remaining day was spent at the LSE talking over observations and case studies and arguing about methods, patterns and tactics with the armchair generals in the rest of the team.

Our methods for this study reflect our disciplinary biases, in anthropology, socio-legal studies and public administration respectively. Mixing these approaches together exposed us to the risk of 'horse-designed-by-committee' jokes, but we found an emphasis on culture fitted well with an analysis of the gaps between formal legal provision and administrative practice. As well as direct participant observation and case studies, we interviewed many key players – in Oftel, other parts of UK government, the EC Commission, telecoms firms and user groups – to build as complete a picture of the world of telecoms regulation as possible. The book is a hybrid between 'pure' ethnography – trying to understand regulation from the viewpoint of the telecoms tribes under observation – and institutional-theoretic approaches which try to locate observed patterns within a framework of general propositions about public law and organizational practice.

With unprecedented freedom of access within Oftel and, within the bounds of commercial confidentiality, solid support from the telecoms industry, the main constraint on the project was the formal access agreement with Oftel and the Department of Trade and Industry. That agreement prevented us from gaining access to official advice to ministers and allowed us to see documents relating to other exchanges between the DTI and Oftel on a case by case basis and with explicit permission. Our findings need to be interpreted with this constraint in mind. In practice, however, everyone was very frank during the two years we spent immersed in Oftel's affairs and we were given the opportunity to conduct a series of interviews within the DTI which broadened our perspective and prevented us from being too Oftel-centric in our view of the regulatory process. Even so, we cannot pretend that this book is more than a partial snapshot of a particular period in the 150 year life of telecoms regulation in the UK. In particular, the constraints on access led us to leave out of our research the major issues facing UK communications regulation in the face of the convergence of broadcasting, telecommunications and computing.

One of the themes of our book is an attempt to identify and assess the various decision styles and organizational processes that could be observed in telecoms regulation. So the reader may fairly ask what decision styles and forms of organization we adopted for our research. Like Oftel itself, we worked largely through a meetings culture – not exactly debating every issue once drunk and once sober, as the ancient Goths are said to have done, but certainly revisiting and re-evaluating our ideas over time. Like Oftel's own processes, part of the way that we worked could be described as 'adhocratic-chaotic'. Serendipity and x-factors certainly played their part in what could be politely described as a dynamic learning process with highly permeable boundaries. As with Oftel's own decision processes, the adhocratic-chaotic style was mixed with what we later term 'Cartesian-bureaucratic' and 'bargaining-diplomatic' styles. The first was represented by systematic fieldwork rooted in a tightly defined set of research questions and the conventions of cumulation represented in normal science. The second consisted of the push and pull of our various disciplinary and personal biases as we argued endlessly about the nature and significance of what we had observed. We leave it to the reader to judge whether that combination shows all a hybrid's failings or a creative combination of approaches.

We owe an enormous debt to Don Cruickshank and to all the Oftel staff for a helpful mixture of unstinting support and frank criticism of our work as it developed, and for the degree of openness to meetings, files and people that we enjoyed. Though we were dependent on Oftel for access, responsibility for the conclusions of the study lies with the authors alone. The main telecoms firms and the DTI also kindly gave their consent to the study and were unfailingly helpful to us. We thank the many people who gave up their time in interviews to improve our understanding of the regulatory process and exposed us to their thinking and ways of working. Many of our interviews produced a rich combination of shrewd observation, in-depth knowledge, and positions about policy or organization expounded with remarkable articulacy and passion. Many of our interviewees also kindly read and commented on draft chapters and though we did not always agree with their comments, they certainly helped us to improve the book. By convention we do not identify them here or in the text.

Research costs money as well as time, and we gratefully acknowledge financial support from the Leverhulme Trust, the Centre for the Study of Regulated Industries (CRI), the Suntory and Toyota International Centre for Economics and Related Disciplines (STICERD) and the LSE staff research fund. Additionally Colin Scott was able to develop some of the ideas and add a comparative dimension to the research while a Visiting Fellow at both the Law Program and the Reshaping Australian Institutions Program of the Australian National University, and with financial support from the Society of Public Teachers of Law.

We are pleased that we can publicly thank numerous academic colleagues who read part or all of the book in draft or provided other assistance: Robert Baldwin, David Coen, Richard Collins, Bruce Doern, Imelda Maher, Richard Rawlings, Tony Prosser and Mark Thatcher. We are particularly grateful to our colleague Robert Baldwin who shared in the design of the project and gave us considerable assistance in developing ideas at our regular meetings, but elected not to participate in the writing of this book.

Clare Hall
Colin Scott
Christopher Hood

LSE, September 1999

Part I

Introduction

1 Ducts, poles and holes in the ground: the inner world of telecommunications regulation

> Every public action, which is not customary, either is wrong, or, if it is right, is a dangerous precedent. It follows that nothing should ever be done for the first time.
>
> Francis Cornford, *Microcosmographia Academica* (1908: 28).

INTRODUCTION

This book explores the inner world of UK telecommunications regulation as it operated in the middle and late 1990s. It was a world where bureaucracy, technocracy and econocracy came together in not always harmonious ways as the regulatory structure coped with a changing political, technical and business environment. This book reports what we learned about 'life among the telecommunications tribes' during the course of a two-year process of participant observation, and discusses the implications of what we learned for conventional accounts of how regulation works (or fails to work) and how it should be reformed.

REGULATOR-WATCHING: THE OUTER AND INNER LIFE OF REGULATION

Regulator-watching became a major preoccupation of academics, business analysts and financial journalists in the late twentieth century, with the development of a regulatory state (Majone 1994; Loughlin and Scott 1997) replacing a previous emphasis on nationalized industry or public enterprise. Nowhere was this development more dramatic than in telecommunications regulation, involving as it does a major and dynamic formerly publicly-owned utility sector at the heart of the information age. It is not surprising that telecommunications regulation has attracted many academic commentators and analysts (e.g. Gist 1990; Hills 1986). Hitherto most academic regulator-watchers have concentrated on observing the outer life of regulation, working as if from a helicopter hovering above the heat of the regulatory fray, or looking at the hands of a clock from a distance (Neunreither 1998: 262). From these vantage points such observers are well placed to track and assess events in the outer world of regulation – the major players, the public statements the players make and the broad outcomes of regulatory policy (see, for example, Veljanovski 1991; Vickers and Yarrow 1988; Armstrong, Cowan and Vickers 1994; Graham and Prosser 1991; Prosser 1997).

There is much to be said for this approach. Distance can lend perspective, even if it does not always bring enchantment to the view. We can tell the time without needing to get inside the clock, and a helicopter approach can be as useful in regulator-watching as it is in traffic management. Indeed, the regulators themselves, and their courtiers and hangers-on, may be all too like drivers caught in heavy traffic – too concerned with the details of their tussles with those immediately surrounding them to see themselves in context or grasp the bigger picture of the whole traffic system.

Watching the outer life of regulation also has its limitations, because it cannot convey anything about the inner life of the process. If we want to understand what makes a clock tick, we cannot do so by just looking at the hands, but need to get inside to examine the mechanism (Neunreither 1998: 262). Nor can helicopter-borne traffic cops see what is going on inside the vehicles whose movements they can observe – what the drivers are doing, how they perceive and respond to other drivers, how they interact with their passengers or back seat drivers. Our aim in this book is to bring out what can be learned from inside the regulatory clock or vehicle – the view of the passenger or inner clockwork, so to speak – and to contrast it with the external or helicopter perspective on regulation. In doing so, the book aims to bring out three features of regulation, none of which can be easily illuminated from the external perspective. One is the exploration of how office and inter-office cultures regulated regulation in this case. A second is how regulatory 'absolutism' played out in practice. The third is how the process of regulatory decision-making worked.

HOW CULTURE REGULATES REGULATION

Looking at the hands of the regulatory clock from the outside, culture is visible only as it comes out in organizational behaviour, for example in disposition to prosecute or invoke sanctions; but from an inside perspective, culture is what regulates regulation and hence is all-important to understanding the process (Meidinger 1987).

The notion of culture as a regulator of institutions is far from new. Mary Douglas (1985: 3) has written of culture as 'a general regulatory mechanism for human behaviour'. Hugh Heclo and the late Aaron Wildavsky (1974), in a famous study of the British civil service a quarter of a century ago, observed that if anything regulated the upper reaches of that bureaucracy, it was a shared ethos and set of mutual rating mechanisms, not formal controls from ministers or Parliament. They identified a 'village world' with a slowly-changing population of a few hundred people, whose denizens were regulated by shared attitudes and beliefs and a 'stock market' of reputations for cleverness, 'soundness' and ability to deliver departmental commitment. The system was regulated by its internal 'conversations' more than by law and formal rules and by reputation-mongering against a set of distinctive values and beliefs. The telecoms regulation village of the mid to late 1990s was different from Heclo and Wildavsky's village in several ways – the village population turned over more rapidly, the villagers were more heterogeneous and culturally self-aware, and policy frequently triumphed over community – but it too was regulated by culture in ways this book tries to bring out.

How did culture regulate regulation? We identified at least three ways. First, as Heclo and Wildavsky showed for their (now long-retired) Whitehall mandarins, culture defined boundaries, social and cognitive. Culture was what fixed – and took away – the limits of the thinkable (as against the unthinkable), what set the boundaries between remembering and forgetting and between people considered to be useful, helpful or on board and everyone else. Sue Wright (1998: 9) sees culture as 'a contested process of meaning making', a contest over the meaning of key terms and concepts by differentially positioned actors seeking to contest and redefine core meanings, and this process of meaning-making was central to the regulatory process.[1] Since institutional life without any boundaries – even in the highly cerebral world of 1990s telecoms regulation – is cognitively impossible, this regulatory function of culture was unavoidable: it established the mental short cuts that no computer, programmed to work through all possible options, could have taken. An example of the way that culture defined regulatory boundaries is the outcome of legislation passed by the government in 1992, intended to toughen up Oftel's responses to customer complaints. The background to the legislation was political dissatisfaction with the way the utilities regulators generally responded to customer complaints by adopting an informal 'good offices' role in mediating between service providers and customers. The legislation empowered Oftel formally to determine the outcomes of a range of disputes between consumers and telecommunications providers; but during the period of our study the exercise of such formal powers had not shifted into the realm of thinkable regulatory actions within Oftel. A cultural preference for informality, which pervaded not only the handling of customer complaints but also breach of licence conditions, was only gradually eroded, as we will show in later chapters.

Second, and related, regulation was to some extent stabilized by a clash of microcultures which served to check policy runaways, preventing any single regulatory microculture from dominating the process. Wright's definition of culture cited in the previous paragraph stresses the contestation going on in the process of meaning-making, and it is that contestation which (albeit unintendedly) has a regulatory effect. This theme is also familiar in institutional analysis, and Michiel Schwarz and Michael Thompson (1990) have shown in another context (the development of a lavatory rim-block by a multinational corporation caught between orthodox scientific attitudes and dark-green environmentalist worldviews) how products can be shaped – and in their view, improved – by a clash of culture. Conflict of microcultures also seemed to be a central process in regulating UK telecoms regulation in the 1990s. For instance, within Oftel, we found a meetings culture in which the different microcultures inside the organization – legal, technocratic, econocratic, bureaucratic – came together in what seemed like endless dialogue. Another key fault-line in the wider telecommunications regulation system was the pervasive tension between a commercial, market-minded and expert outlook represented by Oftel and the politics-dominated, brokerage culture of its parent department, the DTI. Indeed, we discovered that each of the key government organizations in the telecoms regulation world – the DTI and Oftel – found the other more difficult to deal with than the chief regulatee, British Telecom (BT), or foreign multinationals. Yet it was precisely the tension between the two public service cultures that prevented telecoms regulation from becoming 100 per cent econocracy or 100 per cent brokerage.

Third, regulatory change was mediated by culture in the sense that major adaptation was preceded by cultural change. Richard Chapman and John Greenaway (1980), writing about long-term processes of institutional reform in the British public service, have observed that reform programmes tend to take effect only at the point where there is some shared view that change has to come and of the direction it should take. Something similar seems to have been at work in regulating telecoms regulation. In that sense, culture functions both as a shock absorber, shielding institutions from unlimited exposure to changes seen as alien, and as an incubator, producing the conditions for long term change. For example, in the mid 1970s the notion of telecommunications customers having the right to plug their own equipment into any BT socket was considered so unthinkable that an elaborate and now quaint-seeming regulatory apparatus of officially approved fitters was devised for the purpose. A decade or so later 'the right to plug in' at will had become generally accepted, heralding a new regulatory era in which the setting of standards for terminal equipment became a major regulatory factor.

Each of these three cultural processes – cognitive boundary-setting, clashing microcultures, shock absorption and incubation of change through culture – were central to the regulation of regulation in the telecoms world of the 1990s, although each of them is almost invisible to the external analyst.

REGULATORY ABSOLUTISM: 'SELDOM PURE, NEVER SIMPLE'

Seen from the helicopter, most regulatory encounters are dominated by a few high profile individuals commanding media and public attention. The analogy is with the sort of high school history of the age of absolutism in which attention is focused on the kings and emperors to the exclusion of all else. And indeed the structure of the UK's 'OF-type' regulators is such that the various director-generals appear – from the outside at least – as absolute monarchs, with more than a passing resemblance to eighteenth century enlightened despots like Catherine the Great or Frederick William II. The contemporary history of utility regulation was written in terms of their edicts and treaties, and the media painted regulatory policy as the product of their personal styles. Many writers on regulation fiercely attacked this absolutism as inherently limited in democratic accountability (Veljanovski 1993a; Hansard Society 1996), while others (notably Foster (1992)) defended the enlightened despotism the OF-type regulators were said to represent – in a similar spirit to Jeremy Bentham's conclusion that benevolent despots might prove more receptive to his views on rational policy making than an oligarchic or parliamentary regime (Everitt 1931: 150).

Both sides of this argument are based on a shared premise that this book seeks to question – namely that regulatory director-generals were in fact relatively absolute in their decision-making power. That underlying premise looks less robust from the ground-up perspective than from the external perspective, in at least two ways. First, when the perspective shifts from the helicopter view to an inside examination of the 'royal' organization, the limits on directorial absolutism, even within Oftel, become more readily visible. When we observed the courtiers and other hangers-on wrangling over policy within Oftel, we could see what absolutism actually amounted to. Our conclusion is (with apologies to Oscar Wilde) that regulatory absolutism in the court of Oftel's Don Cruickshank was seldom pure and never simple. As historians and sociologists have often pointed out, even theoretically absolute monarchs cannot be everywhere, and have limited resources for keeping track of all decisions going through the royal apparatus.

Second, the assumption that OF-type director-generals were absolute implies that the organizations they headed had sole mastery in their regulatory realm. The perspective we offer here is rather different. Rather than a single dominant player, Oftel was one of a number of interdependent actors within a regulatory space (Hancher and Moran 1989). The regulatory space or habitat it occupied included other regulatory actors, notably the DTI, a range of industry players with different interests and other organizations, such as consumer bodies. Oftel could not shape its habitat at will, but had to manoeuvre among the other actors within the regulatory space. If there is any parallel with the age of absolutism, it may lie more in the way the supposedly absolute monarchs of the eighteenth century German states had to deal with powerful neighbours abroad and rival claimants to authority at home (such as the church, the nobility and the free towns). Viewing the activity of Oftel as that of one of a number of interdependent players in a complex regulatory space not only alters the conventional picture of what such regulators are like; it also has implications for the analysis of how utility regulators might be reformed. An agenda for reform based on assumptions of absolutism may be rather different from the prescriptions that are appropriate for an interdependent regulatory space.

REGULATORY DECISION-MAKING: CARTESIAN-BUREAUCRATIC, ADHOCRATIC-CHAOTIC OR BARGAINING-DIPLOMATIC?

From the external perspective regulatory decision-making can only be observed in terms of outcomes or public events where formal statements are made; but many questions about how organizational decision-making works in general, and regulatory decision-making in particular, can only be pursued by looking at the process from the inside. The literature on social and organizational decision-making is too vast to be easily summarized or surveyed, but we can contrast three broad views of how the process works, which can be loosely termed Cartesian-bureaucratic, bargaining-diplomatic and adhocratic-chaotic. Our analysis suggested that dominant decision-making styles among these three varied according to the background conditions.

In what might be called the Cartesian-bureaucratic view, the regulator is an enlightened strategist, applying reason and special expertise to 'create public value' (Moore 1995) and solve market-failure problems for the public good. An example of the Cartesian-bureaucratic style is Oftel's review and revision of the price control contained in BT's licence conditions in 1995–6. This decision process concerned a policy issue perceived as relatively discrete (though it also acted as a magnet for other policy concerns, notably the decision to introduce new licence controls over anti-competitive conduct and to supplement the established retail price control with a wholesale or network price control). A second element underpinning a Cartesian-bureaucratic decision style in this case was a perceived match between the data required by the regulator (on such matters as rate of return and cost of capital) and data developed by licensees. It was in the one central domain where good data was apparently not readily available, the projection of future market shares for BT and other licensees, that the Cartesian-bureaucratic style seemed most threatened. A third element underpinning the Cartesian-bureaucratic style was that with the use of readily available data, the subject under debate was amenable to economic modelling for a range of assumptions, using methods that reflected a reasonable consensus among professional economists within the regulatory community, and an acceptance by other professionals that the econocrats' models should dominate the decision process.

In contrast to the Cartesian-bureaucratic style of decision making, the bargaining-diplomatic view sees regulation for 'grown-ups' as about inescapably political negotiation and doing deals, making and breaking alliances and coalitions, power-broking and diplomacy among major players. The bargaining-diplomatic decision style is exemplified by the determination of interconnection conditions between public telecommunications operators (PTOs) between 1992 and 1995. The key characteristic here was that regulatory decision-making effectively substitutes for what would otherwise be determined in the market by commercial negotiation between firms. While the objective of the decision process – fair market access in the case of interconnection – was relatively uncontroversial (a feature shared with the Cartesian-bureaucratic style), what was meant by this objective was contested and inherently contestable. Oftel approached the issue by using industry workshops and working groups to bargain over the possible outcomes and to dilute the bargaining power of BT. Though senior Oftel staff presented the process as one of gathering the information to enable the regulator to make a rational and informed decision (Cartesian-bureaucratic style), it seems more plausible to view the process as a way of moving the bargaining positions of the various telecommunications licensees closer together so that the eventual decision made by Oftel had a degree of legitimacy within the industry, in terms both of process (all the firms had had their say) and of substance (the deal was struck on terms which enabled new entrants to secure market access without bankrupting BT).

In the adhocratic-chaotic view, complex interdependencies and high-dimensional dynamic systems, linked to limited cognitive capacity at both individual and organizational level, means that decision-making is shaped to a large extent by happenstance and chance interconnections beyond anyone's conscious control. Issues are processed in an adhocratic-chaotic style when neither the input information nor any agreed conception of the outputs being sought are available within the cultural frame within which decisions are made. Setting out on a decision-making process in such conditions involves an attempt either to develop input information or output objectives. As the boundaries of the issue for determination are blurred and permeable, the range of actors may be large and changeable, providing considerable scope for new issues to be brought in. Such a decision style is exemplifed in the process by which Oftel decided to introduce a new condition into BT's licence to control anti-competitive conduct. In this case senior staff had a ready solution, in the form of the proposed licence modification, but little data to indicate that there was a problem to solve. The early decision-making process on this licence modification was characterized by fluidity in participation and a lack of clear input data or clear objectives. The outcome of the process, however, was an imaginative solution to a problem of authority and effectiveness in enforcement of BT's licence conditions.

Each of these accounts of decision-making seemed to capture part of what we observed in telecommunications regulation in the mid to late 1990s. All of these styles of decision-making can be argued to have a necessary and even beneficial role to play in the process (though the idea that an adhocratic-chaotic decision style might have its advantages is a controversial one that we develop later). Oftel's self-image, as we shall show later, was very much of a Cartesian-bureaucratic decision-maker in this sense in contrast to the bargaining-diplomatic view and particularly to the adhocratic-chaotic view, which was strongly resisted as an image by the analycentric Oftel culture. Oftel was not always able to be Cartesian-bureaucratic, given that the background conditions linked to that decision style were often lacking, which meant that the organization's behaviour frequently failed to match its ambitious self-image.

However, issues for decision are not static. They do not necessarily retain the same characteristics throughout the life of the decision-making process. If decision-making is initially adhocratic-chaotic in style because neither input information nor output objectives are readily available, subsequent sorting out of input information may shift the process towards the bargaining-diplomatic style. If at that point a broad consensus is achieved on output objectives then the process may shift further towards the Cartesian-bureaucratic style. An example of a shift from an adhocratic-chaotic to a bargaining-diplomatic style was the way Oftel went through the process of incorporating a new condition prohibiting anti-competitive conduct in BT's licence in 1996. The first phase of the policy process (noted above and described in further detail later in the book) was poorly focused as Oftel sought to extricate itself from the administrative difficulties of supervising compliance with highly specific and detailed licence conditions. Problems of poor quality input information and poorly-focused objectives for the licence modification process were never overcome. In the later stages of the modification procedure, the shape of the likely outcome had become fairly clear, and Oftel and BT bargained extensively over much of the detail. In spite of the apparently chaotic character of much of the decision-making in this case, and difficulties experienced in enforcing the new licence conditions that resulted, Oftel was able to use the shift to proclaim that it was changing from a traditional industry regulator to a competition authority and demonstrate its continuing relevance as a regulator of a liberalized telecommunications sector.

Later in the book we try to bring out the chameleon character of the telecommunications regulatory process as it shifted among these different decision styles. How far and how often did Oftel's self-image as a Cartesian-bureaucratic decision maker match the reality of its behaviour? Were departures from that style invariably associated with inferior policy outcomes, or could they bring unintendedly beneficial effects? Is there a single all-purpose style for regulatory excellence?

THE PLAN OF THE BOOK

After the next chapter, which briefly sketches out the history and institutional landscape of the world in which our telecommunications regulators operated, this book develops each of the three themes sketched out earlier. Chapter Three develops the theme of culture as what regulated regulation. Mainly from an Oftel perspective, it explores the way culture and microcultures operated as a boundary-setting, equilibrating, shock absorbing and incubating process. It pays particular attention to Oftel's meetings culture as a process which fostered the interplay of microcultures at the heart of the process of meaning-making, serving to test information with a variety of internal and external players and continually probing the limits of what was thinkable.

The next two chapters critically examine the idea of regulatory absolutism as discussed earlier. Chapter Four looks at the way Oftel as an organization interacted with its director-general, and explores the extent to which policy and practice was shaped by the 'royal apparatus' as well as by the will and opinions of the director-general, and considers the external relationships of the Director General of Telecommunications (DGT). Chapter Five broadens the analysis to examine the relationship between Oftel more generally and the other institutional players in the telecommunications regulatory space, looking at the scope and limits of Oftel's ability to shape its world by fiat, and the extent to which it was dependent on other powerful actors to gain its objectives. We conclude from the analysis in these two chapters that the popular perception of regulatory absolutism in the hands of the OF-type director-generals was not only a distorted view of the power of Oftel's DG, but also leads to policy prescriptions for reform that may be irrelevant if the true picture is one of complex interdependence among a range of actors.

The four chapters in the fourth part of the book examine how the decision-making process worked, drawing on case-study material we accumulated during our two years' immersion in the telecoms regulators' world. The aim is to bring out the mixture of Cartesian-bureaucratic, bargaining-diplomatic and adhocratic-chaotic elements in different regulatory decision processes. For each of the three decision styles we offer a negative and positive case, or relative success and failure in the outcomes of the processes. Chapter Six offers a more developed characterization both of the types of decisions made by Oftel and the processes used to make them.

Chapter Seven aims to demonstrate the Cartesian-bureaucratic theme at work, using case material to show how Oftel's technocrats and econocrats aimed to use their analytic expertise in policy development. The deployment of decision-making processes close to the Cartesian-bureaucratic model was frequently found in the most established policy domains. The deployment of the Cartesian-bureaucratic decision-making style could lead to poor decisions where the quality of information was poor, a fact sometimes recognized by senior Oftel staff, leading to a switch in style, and sometimes not recognized, with adverse consequences.

Chapter Eight uses case study material to explore the conditions under which decision-making within Oftel tended towards the adhocratic-chaotic model through the elements of chance, happenstance, accidents of history and limits to rationality that no organization, even (or perhaps especially) one as cerebral as Oftel can altogether eliminate from its working. It was often with the more novel problems which required decisions from Oftel that adhocratic-chaotic decision making was most in evidence. This chapter shows that for such a regulatory bureaucracy, key information problems include not only the classical and much-emphasized element of information asymmetry between regulator and regulatee, but also the obstacles that can lie in the way of information moving freely across parts of the regulator's own organization and are retained from one time-period to another. Contingencies such as the existence of staff who have stayed in post longer than the average or informal discussions (for instance over lunch or in the smoking room) may be crucial in determining how effectively regulatory organizations can use the information that they do have. In some instances the adhocratic-chaotic style was deliberately adopted by Oftel as the best means to reach a creative solution. The case for such an approach is evaluated.

Chapter Nine seeks to bring out the bargaining-diplomatic element in the telecommunications regulatory process, in the form of the (not always acknowledged) give-and-take processes that took place in the course of policy development and enforcement. Here the decision-making procedures deployed are linked to the powers and capacities of other actors in the regulatory space. The choices made by Oftel to develop diplomatic-bargaining models were a product not only of such constraints, but also positive decisions to exploit the participation of others both to promote formal legitimacy (through participation) and also secure better information to guide decision-making.

The final chapter stands back from the earlier analysis to consider the 'so what?' question. First we assess the implications of our study for broader regulatory science. We suggest that the observation of contingency and interdependence within the telecoms regulatory regime places significant limits on the capacities of individual regulators to act instrumentally in controlling or regulating regulatees. Given the widespread character of such limits to instrumental regulation we suggest a less narrow approach to the design and reform of regimes which focuses on all the relationships within a regulatory domain, and exploits the potential for modest shifts in the balance of capacities, rather than focusing exclusively on the capacities of regulatory agencies. For regulatory policy we suggest that the limits to rational policy making which we identify in the case of UK telecoms regulation may be pervasive within regulatory regimes. However we observed distinctive approaches by Oftel, both to exploit those limits and to reduce their impact, which might be more widely adopted.

The final chapter concludes with a consideration of the prospects for telecommunications regulation, asking whether the institutional arrangements for transition to competition in telecommunications observed in this study are demonstrably necessary, whether distinctive sectoral regulators are necessary for the next stage of competitive markets in telecommunications, and whether globalization of markets and internationalization of telecoms policy is likely to lead to the creation of supranational regulatory institutions.

2 The archaeology of a regulatory regime

> Government is getting more powerful, not through owning, but through regulation.
>
> Peter Drucker, *Financial Times* 27 April 1999

SEVEN AGES OF TELECOMMUNICATIONS REGULATION?

Since the advent of the telegraph and telephones in the nineteenth century, the state has been closely involved in the regulation and control of telecommunications. Max Weber, writing in 1911, saw control of telegraphs and mails as a crucial feature in the development of the modern Western state (Gerth and Mills 1948: 213). But regulatory form and institutions were not the same everywhere; nor did they remain unchanged over time as technology and politics changed. As with Shakespeare's account of the life of man, UK telecoms regulation has gone through seven ages over the century and a half that the telecoms industry has existed to date. It is important to understand something of the archaeology of the regulatory regime described in this book, because of the capacity for ideas and institutions to exert influence over the present day long after they have apparently been displaced by new ideas and institutions.

Regulation is a term which does not admit of an agreed meaning in studies of telecoms, and consequently has the capacity to obscure as much as it illuminates (see Baldwin, Scott and Hood 1998: 2–4; Daintith 1997: 3–5). When we refer to telecoms regulation in this book it is to indicate the processes by which standards or rules (whether formal or informal) are made (for example relating to price or quality of or access to telecoms services), compliance with such standards or rules is monitored, and behavioural modification sought for those who do not comply. Responsibility for administering these processes does not necessarily reside with one organization, and in practice in the UK responsibility has shifted between institutions and frequently been fragmented.

The first age consisted of state oversight of the pioneer companies in the early days of telegraphs, heavily influenced by imperial and military considerations as well as domestic electoral politics. Telegraphs were state-run from the start in India and other parts of the empire, but at home were provided at first by competing companies, subject to regulation from bodies like the Railways and Canal Commission (since telegraph wires tended to run along railway lines and canals). This age ended in nationalization of the telegraph companies on the eve of an election in 1868. A Conservative government was seeking to woo rural voters by ensuring that their telegraph costs were subsidized by more profitable urban telegraph traffic. The new universal-service regime was to be run by the Post Office, a UK-wide central government department under a minister, the Postmaster-General (Foreman-Peck and Milward 1994: 48).

The second age, from 1869 to 1912, was one of hybrid state involvement – part-nationalization in the form of Post Office operation of telegraphs and part-regulation, as a new and more powerful telecoms medium, telephones, grew up alongside telegraphs and was developed by private or local authority enterprise. A period of telephone company competition in the 1880s was followed by nationalization of the trunk telephone network in the 1890s, leaving only local telephone services in the hands of private or independent enterprise for the following two decades (Pitt 1980; Foreman-Peck and Milward 1994: 108–111).

The third age was one of blanket nationalization and began in 1912 when all remaining local telephone companies (apart from the municipally-run local service in Kingston upon Hull) were nationalized and operated together with postal services as part of the Post Office – in contrast to the use of statutory boards operating nominally at arm's length from Ministers which became the standard administrative formula for the running of nationalized industries later in the century. This third age, in which regulation and service provision were combined in a single overarching ministry, lasted over half a century, making it by far the longest age to date in the history of telecoms. Telephone technology, based on electro magnetic switching, changed relatively little over this era, although radio and later TV developed as a separate and technologically distinct medium, with its own set of regulatory and service-providing institutions overseen by the Post Office.

The fourth age began in 1969. The Morrison formula for nationalization finally caught up with posts and telecoms, and the Post Office was changed into a statutory board operating at arms length from its parent department, according to a framework then standard for UK nationalized industries. Regulation of telecom operators and consumers was shared between the Post Office corporation and the overseeing department, which retained some powers carried over from the second age. Telecommunications and post continued to be run under a single administrative roof. The fourth age gave way to the fifth little over a decade later, in 1981, when posts and telecommunications were split into two separate public corporations, with British Telecom assuming a separate identity within the public service (Thatcher 1993)

The sixth age, beginning in 1984, involved the transformation of BT from a statutory publicly-owned corporation into a limited-liability company. The government sold stock to private investors in three stages between 1984 and 1993.[1] Regulatory powers were reconfigured and dispersed among old and new state organizations. The Office of Telecommunications (Oftel) was created as a non-ministerial department headed by a semi-independent Director-General to oversee the now privatized BT while a ministerial department, the DTI, retained some of the regulatory powers once possessed by the Postmaster-General. This sixth age, a landmark of the 'Thatcher revolution' in UK public services (and subsequently copied to a greater or lesser extent for other utilities in the UK and for telecoms in many other countries), has been much more documented and discussed than any of the preceding five ages (Vickers and Yarrow 1988; Graham and Prosser 1991; Foster 1992; Armstrong, Cowan and Vickers 1994; Levy and Spiller 1996; Vogel 1996; Prosser 1997). To borrow a phrase deployed to describe the effects of policy change in the water industry over a similar period, telecommunications policy was transformed in its sixth age 'from backwater to goldfish bowl' (Maloney and Richardson 1996: 166). The central institutional structure of the sixth age was a *menage à trois*, in the sense that the regulatory regime involved three major players, the DTI, Oftel and BT. BT survived into the privatization era as a single company rather than being broken up into several companies, as happened to AT & T in the USA after an anti-trust suit in 1982 (Huntley and Pitt 1990)), plus an additional 'bit-player' in the form of Mercury Communications Ltd (MCL). MCL was created as a subsidiary of another formerly government-owned telecommunications utility (Cable and Wireless, formed in 1928 to develop telegraph and telephone services in the overseas empire). Cable and Wireless was privatized in 1981 (Bradley 1992) and was encouraged by the government to snap at the heels of BT as a not-too-threatening competitor expected to capture only a few per cent of BT's monopolistic market by operating as an alternative supplier of voice telephony (the DTI expected MCL to secure a market share of about two per cent by 1990 (Baker 1993: 79)). BT's power derived from its size and market position, within which it faced little threat of serious competition, and from its virtual monopoly on the sort of market expertise which a regulator seeking to provide a surrogate for a competitive market would need.

In the sixth *menage à trois* era, Treasury and DTI concerns to maximize government revenue from sales of further tranches of BT stock served to protect BT against radical restructuring or competition from anything more dangerous than the MCL 'gnat'. The telecoms market (up to the point that mobile phones began to develop) consisted entirely of organizations created by the UK government, and Oftel functioned essentially as the regulator of a single company, concentrating mainly on price control through the use of an RPI – x formula of a type adopted for all the privatized utilities and intended to minimize regulatory micromanagement of those industries (Littlechild 1983).

After 1992, during the time that our study was going on, the telecommunications regime was in the process of moving to a seventh age, characterized by a number of features: all the former government stock in BT had been sold (meaning that Treasury concerns to maximize revenue from future BT share sales no longer overshadowed the regulatory process); the elephant-and-gnat duopoly of BT and MCL in the early privatization era had been replaced by a multilateral regime in which more players (including US telecom companies accustomed to a quite different culture of regulation) entered the expanding UK telecoms market; global mergers of big telecommunications corporations overshadowed national regulation; domestic telecommunications regulation was attracting increasing interest from supranational bodies within the EU and beyond; and the boundaries of the telecom sector were changing as the advent of digital broadcasting and the widespread take-up of the internet undermined conventional boundaries between telecommunications, broadcasting and other media.

However, as Oftel and the other players in the telecoms regulation regime sought to adapt to the shift in the telecoms world after the duopoly review of 1991–2, many of the institutional and cultural features of the earlier ages of telecom regulation remained. Even at the time of writing some of the key players in the regulatory space have careers going back to the age of public monopoly and are part of a common diaspora of former Post Office or BT people straddling the public-private divide. Not only did Oftel have to find a way of handling the seventh age with regulatory powers largely designed for the sixth, but some of the people and much of the mind-set and habitual ways of doing business that had become established in that era (including within BT, which itself retained strong traces of public service attitudes, as well as contacts and experience, inherited from the fifth age) did not disappear overnight. As has often been observed for the working of government and complex institutions more generally, the regulatory regime we observed retained both cognitive and structural traces of the earlier eras and its dynamic was path-dependent, in that it was shaped by the key regulatory events and responses of an earlier era.

THREE LIFE-STAGES OF OFTEL?

Though Oftel has existed through two of the seven ages of telecoms regulation sketched out above, it can itself be seen to have gone through several developmental life-stages as a regulatory organization (somewhat similar to the well known life cycle approach developed by Bernstein 1955, and Downs 1966). Here we briefly discuss three life-stages: Oftel's complicated birth, its repressed adolescence in the *menage à trois* era and its confident youth as a maturing organization aiming to reposition itself in the regulatory firmament as a high-status competition authority. As with the telecoms regulation regime more generally, earlier ages of Oftel influenced its later ages, particularly the legal framework it acquired at its complicated birth. Some of the main features of the framework are summarized in schematic form below.

Complicated birth

The statutory and organizational form that Oftel acquired at birth as part of the sixth-age regulatory regime were the product of a distinctive set of political concerns linked with a search for legal powers and institutional frameworks to read across from other sources and adapt for telecom regulation.

The distinctive political concerns included a search for regulatory arrangements embodying commitment to a privatized telecom sector subject to relatively light regulation that a subsequent government hostile to privatization or disposed to more state intervention would find difficult to reverse overnight. Commitment in this sense has been highlighted by Murray Horn (1995) as a key issue in institutional design, and it certainly figured large in this case (Department of Trade and Industry 1984: cl. 1). In the early 1980s telecom privatization was a controversial and untried idea, strongly opposed by BT trade unions and by the Labour Party which was then in opposition. The Conservative government of that time had good reason to fear that commercial investors would be deterred from venturing into the privatized telecoms sector unless some degree of continuity in the regulatory regime could be guaranteed. That meant rejecting the option of locating all the regulatory powers with DTI ministers, on the grounds that such an arrangement would be seen by investors as a recipe for rapid policy reversal on a change of government; constant political interference of the kind that had been an everyday feature of the nationalized industry regime in the fourth and fifth ages discussed above.

Instead, concerns for commitment led to the adoption of a regulatory system that combined a semi-independent agency with day-to-day monitoring and enforcement powers (heavily circumscribed by procedural protections for regulatees) with a regime of 25 year operating licences for private telecom companies issued by DTI ministers. Those licences could only be modified by the regulator through specified procedural mechanisms (see Figure 2.2) and could not be instantly revoked on a change of government. Levy and Spiller (1996: 100–106) argue that the device of multi-year licences served as a functional substitute for alternative institutional means of securing commitment to the goals of the enacting coalition, and see 25 year licences as a more credible way of conveying commitment to investors than setting down the regulatory rules in specific legislation which, within a Westminster style system, might be modified by current or future governments.

However, apart from considerations of commitment (and in some tension with that political requirement), the government did not want to hand over all control of telecoms policy to a strong independent agency at the outset. As mentioned earlier, a political need to secure substantial revenues from the sale of government stock in BT, which was part of a broader political strategy both to address public sector expenditure problems and to secure re-election through tax cuts financed from the proceeds of privatization, meant that government had stakes as an owner or part-owner of BT that would not have been served either by breaking up BT into separate companies before privatization or by unleashing an aggressive fully independent regulator on BT before the government stock had been sold. Hence government's fiscal needs in practice outweighed the rhetoric of competition and efficiency that surrounded the politics of privatization (Moon, Richardson and Smart 1986: 351). Reflecting this political imperative, BT was moved into private ownership as a massive and dominant vertically integrated monopoly (subject to very gradual liberalization), and the regulatory regime imposed on it was intended to be light.

As noted earlier, that regime involved ministers in determining and issuing multi-year licences for telecoms operators, albeit with the advice of Oftel staff. The retention by the DTI of the formal licensing power meant that the arms length regulator was only able to monitor and enforce those licence conditions, or negotiate over modifications. Moreover, government settled on an organizational model for a semi-independent regulator – based on the Office of Fair Trading, established as a national consumer protection agency under the previous Conservative government in 1973 – that had proved not to be too threatening to ministers,[2] and constituted Oftel as a non-ministerial department within the ambit of the DTI. Non-ministerial department status, as opposed to that of an independent quango (a model which was apparently rejected early in the deliberations over the organizational form Oftel should take), meant that its head was not entirely free to make independent pronouncements about government policy[3] and that the fledgling organization could be subject to a greater measure of Whitehall control through key staff appointments and exchanges under a common 'pay and rations' regime (in the conventional civil service jargon) than would apply to an independent quango. Moreover, the Secretary of State had a back-stop weapon in the form of a legal power to give general directions to the DGT about functional priorities and matters to which he should have regard in determining whether to exercise his powers.[4] This big stick power (reminiscent of the ministerial direction powers under the fifth age nationalized telecoms regime) has never been exercised but it is part of the background of DTI-Oftel relationships, meaning that a DGT who was completely out of step with ministers would be in an untenable position.

A third political concern, also in some tension with the previous two, was to counter the charge being made by the numerous critics

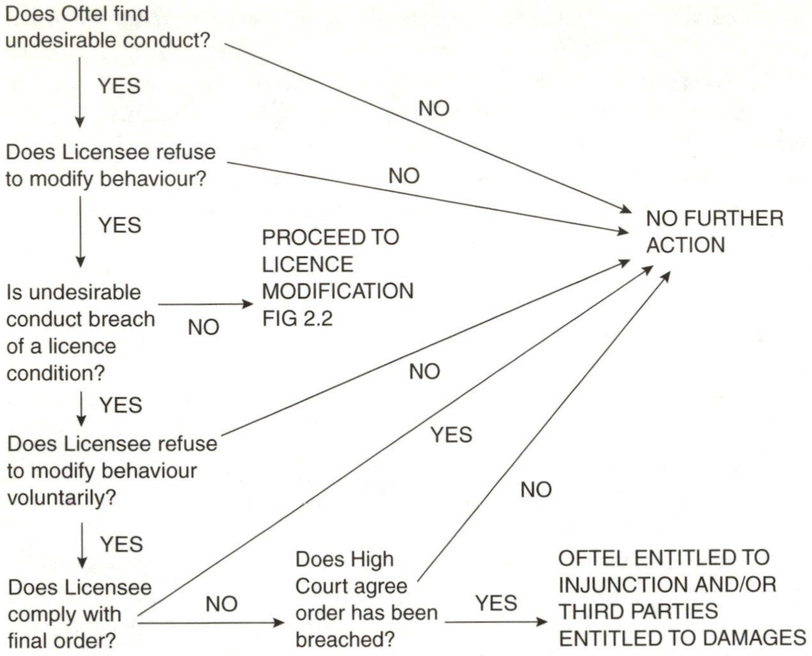

Figure 2.1 Licence enforcement process – handling a complaint or Oftel-initiated investigation

of the new policy of privatization at that time, to the effect that any regulatory regime would be readily captured by BT. The expectation of such critics was that regulation of privatized utilities in the UK would follow a pattern of producer capture that public-choice analysts argued to be typical of the US model of independent regulation (Peltzman 1976; Foster 1992). The apparatus of capture reassurance included the avoidance of an independent multi-person regulatory commission structure along the lines of the US Federal Communications Commission. These create several possible entry points for industry lobbying and were claimed by the government (perhaps disingenuously, since entrusting the issuance of licences and the specification of the conditions that went with them to Ministers hardly provided a cast-iron protection against capture) to be the type of organization most vulnerable to producer capture (Department of Trade and Industry 1984: cl. 1).

Several other mechanisms of capture reassurance were deployed. These included the separation of monitoring and enforcement from the granting of licences, the appointment of 'great and good' figures

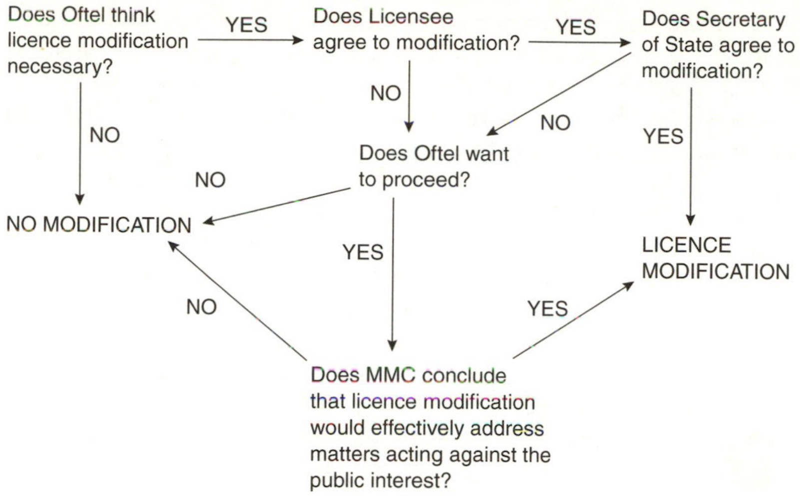

Figure 2.2 Licence condition modification procedure

from outside party politics, Whitehall or the telecoms industry to exercise the monitoring and enforcement role through direct statutory powers, and the attempt, reflecting the concerns of the government's adviser, Professor Stephen Littlechild, to develop a system of regulation based largely on a form of price control which was designed to reduce to a minimum the degree of discretion exercised by the regulator (Littlechild 1983). The procedure for licence enforcement envisaged by the legislation is shown in Figure 2.1. Another way of providing capture reassurance was a provision written into the rules for modification of telecom operators licences that entitled DTI ministers to veto licence modifications agreed between the regulator and the regulatee (on grounds of national security) or to refer them to the Monopolies and Mergers Commission (on any grounds), and to require the DGT to make a licence modification if the MMC made a ruling implying that such a modification was in the public interest (Figure 2.2). Again, such capture reassurance provided no guarantee that DTI ministers would not be lobbied by powerful producers, and did not even formally bind the DGT to observe MMC recommendations, since he had a wide discretion in what modifications to introduce in such circumstances (see Scott 1997).

The regulatory regime that emerged in response to these political concerns and the delicate balancing of the rival considerations in play was characterized by the combination of multi-year operating licences on terms set by ministers, with monitoring, enforcement and bargaining over licence modification by a body with independent statutory powers but not constituted as an independent quango. Within this broad structure legal and organizational detail had to be added. Much of the institutional detail came from copying legal and organizational forms that could be adapted to the new regime – a common theme in institutional change and engineering (Scott,W.R. 1995: 44–5) – and some came from last-minute improvisation and *ad hoc* additions to make the new regulatory regime more politically palatable as the legislation went through Parliament, for example in respect of consumer protection. Both of these processes, and the combination of the two, created unintended effects, mainly in providing Oftel with more discretion and regulatory power than seems to have been originally intended.

Copying came largely in the form of adaptation of provisions from the former Post Office Act 1969 (the legislative framework for the fifth telecom regulation era), for instance in obliging the DGT to ensure universal service and to take over the complaint-handling role from the statutory Post Office Users National Committee under the previous public corporation regime, and also through copying and adaptation of the legislative framework for competition regulation embodied in the 1973 Fair Trading Act which gave powers to ministers, the Monopolies and Mergers Commission and the Director-General of Fair Trading in handling issues of competition and fair trading. Such copying, a standard feature of bureaucratic behaviour under time pressure, had several unintended effects which will be discussed further below. In what was portrayed as a landmark policy development by a government which became a global byword for doctrines of market liberalism, it based the regulatory framework heavily on the statutory obligations of the previous public-enterprise regime (Gist 1990; Graham and Prosser 1991), associated by some with the style of '1970s industrial policy' (Veljanovski 1993a: 14 cited by Prosser 1997: 63). Moreover, in reading across legal and institutional arrangements from the Office of Fair Trading to the new telecommunications regime, it assigned to the DGT discretionary power (especially over the treatment of recommendations from the Monopolies and Mergers Commission) that was unusually wide for a non-ministerial office. By copying key parts of the DGT's powers from the configuration of ministers' powers under the Fair Trading Act 1973, the 1984 Telecommunications Act almost accidentally gave greater autonomy from ministers to the DGT over telecoms regulation than the Director General of Fair Trading was given in competition policy.

Last-minute improvisations in order to smooth the passage of the 1984 telecoms legislation through Parliament included the addition of extra protections for consumers and vulnerable users, such as explicit protection of the interests of rural users and of call-box services (Thatcher 1993: 85–6). Social concerns, which had hardly figured in the original econocratic and finance-led deliberations over the design of the regulatory regime by Ministers, advisers and civil servants, were hastily bolted on to the telecoms legislation late in the legislative process, and unintentionally added to the spread and ambiguity of Oftel's regulatory powers, by creating duties that were too many and too contradictory to minimize discretion (Graham and Prosser 1991: 186–8).

The combination of these two politico-bureaucratic processes associated with the birth of Oftel created a regulatory structure that was far from the simple formulaic price-control regime envisioned by Stephen Littlechild, producing a sprawling and partly contradictory set of provisions that gave Oftel substantial opportunities to manoeuvre and made the DGT a potentially more powerful figure relative to government than the Director General of Fair Trading on which Oftel had originally been modelled.

Repressed adolescence in a *menage à trois*

Designed on the political and bureaucratic lines discussed above, the young Oftel found itself working with older and better-established players in a regulatory environment in which the regulatory powers were carefully dispersed. The new player lacked the experience of the others, but possessed untested powers (cf. Bernstein 1955: 79). The first DGT, Bryan Carsberg, took up his appointment on a three-year contract in August 1984, the day on which BT was converted into a public limited company. Before his appointment, Carsberg had been a professor of accounting at LSE, and had been an adviser to the government on the liberalization of the telecoms sector and the privatization of BT (Oftel Press Release 1/84). The 1984 Telecommunications Act (s.1(5)) gave Carsberg as DGT the formal power 'to appoint such staff as he may think fit, subject to the approval of the Treasury as to numbers and as to terms and conditions of service', but at the outset these statutory powers were something of a fiction, since a shadow Oftel had been established within DTI before Carsberg's appointment and its staff were simply transferred from DTI to Oftel's new quarters at Holborn Viaduct. Hence the organization Carsberg headed was closely linked to DTI through an umbilical cord of staffing and bureaucratic housekeeping.

The regulatory culture that developed in the early Carsberg era was heavily conditioned by the fifth and earlier ages of telecom regulation, as described earlier. The culture included a style of informal negotiated compliance between BT and the regulators, building on the shared experience of the fifth age, which included assumptions on the part of regulators that BT comprised reasonable people and on the part of many BT staff that the regulators were part of an extended Whitehall family, divided but not wholly dissolved by privatization. Hence a style of enforcement that avoided the use of its apparently draconian but procedurally cumbersome enforcement powers and worked through more informal means of securing compliance was established early in Oftel's life.

Oftel during the Carsberg era could be said to be a repressed adolescent in three senses. It was tied to DTI's apron-strings for its administrative management, meaning it was not in practice a wholly autonomous organization in managerial terms. It faced the daunting task of regulating a giant bureaucracy that had been in the UK telecoms business for over 70 years and commanded most of the information and expertise that the newly-established regulator needed to make effective decisions. And its scope for policy development was overshadowed by Treasury concerns to maximize revenue through BT share sales. Nevertheless, it found scope for manoeuvre in three ways. First, new concerns and issues, outside the formal framework of the 1984 Telecoms Act, gave it opportunities to pursue new themes. Second, the ambiguity and contradictory nature of the DGT's powers which emerged from the complicated birth of the organization gave it scope for manoeuvre, such that Carsberg was able to give explicit priority to the promotion of competition over the many other priorities that could have been read into his powers under the 1984 Act without challenge (see Oftel press release 12/85). Third, the rapid political recognition that price control over BT could not be allowed to lapse altogether after five years (the sunset provision built into its licence in 1984), meant that Oftel had to become involved in major licence modification negotiations early in its life.

Confident youth: Oftel's third phase as aspiring competition authority

In 1993, after a brief hiatus, Sir Bryan Carsberg was succeeded by a new DGT, Don Cruickshank. Thus it fell to Cruickshank to foster a fully competitive market in the post-duopoly period. In contrast to Carsberg's academic and policy-adviser background, Cruickshank had had a managerial and business career path, including time working for the influential management consultants McKinseys, which is commonly said to be an entrée to a well-developed 'McKinsey network' of influential figures across a range of major organizations.[5] He had also gained managerial experience at the sharp end of the public sector as Chief Executive of the National Health Service in Scotland from 1989 to 1993, a task which he often declared to have been much more demanding than his role as DGT.

Cruickshank arrived at Oftel at a time when the sixth age of telecoms regulation was beginning to give way to the seventh, creating more opportunities for repositioning Oftel than had been available in the early days of its repressed adolescence. As noted earlier, Treasury and DTI concerns to protect BT's market position to increase revenue from share sales had disappeared by 1993. A growing number of players in the market, notably cable TV companies backed by US and Canadian money, began to move the regulatory regime away from the *menage à trois* style and had a marked effect on the competitive environment. Cruickshank himself came in with new ideas about opening up telecoms markets. Accordingly, after 1993 Oftel sought to use its powers more actively to create competitive conditions, involving greater formality, a greater willingness to test the limits of its statutory authority and a general aspiration to move from being an industry regulator to a competition authority.

While Oftel's environment and policy settings were changing, it changed as an organization under the mercurial and managerially-conscious Cruickshank. While it continued to draw a substantial number of staff from the DTI (including its Deputy Director-General, whose role as a go-between between Oftel and the DTI is discussed later), Oftel became managerially self-sufficient and the calibre of its staff was judged by most of the observers we talked to, to have markedly increased since its early days, meaning that Oftel came to have more clout within Whitehall as a policy shop (cf. Bernstein 1955: 89). The regulatory space was changing as new firms entered the telecommunications sectors, convergence between telecommunications and broadcasting brought new issues and regulators within Oftel's mileu, and international firms and supranational public authorities, such as the European Commission, took a growing interest in the UK telecoms market.

Cruickshank seized the opportunity to reposition Oftel as a competition authority as a solution to the growing problem of regulating network competition. This shift towards competition rules in place of detailed sectoral regulation is a trend in policy in a number of jurisdictions, however, either as a response to technological or economic change or because of a perceived incapacity to deliver competitive policy outcomes by detailed regulation (Scott 1998b). Perhaps, however, the most distinctive contribution of Don Cruickshank to telecommunications regulation was not at the level of substantive policy but rather in developing processes. By using novel and transparent mechanisms for the development of policy he effectively broke with the Whitehall culture of secrecy, while simultaneously addressing an important regulatory problem, the need to test regulatory information supplied by regulatees. The commitment to openness caused difficulties both for licencees and for other government departments and regulatory agencies.

INHERITANCE, CHOICE AND UNINTENDED EFFECTS

It is a commonplace – indeed a truism – of institutional and political analysis that policy and organizational choice tends to be sharply circumscribed by structures and mind sets inherited from the past. Oftel and the regulatory regime around it was no exception. Just as traces of the fifth and sixth age of telecoms regulation persisted into the seventh, Oftel's third phase as an organization was heavily conditioned by some of the conditions of its birth. Three of those conditions, noted earlier, are worth repeating.

First, the effects of the political calculus surrounding the institutional form of BT and Oftel in 1984 lived on long after the political considerations that led those organizations to be shaped in the way they were had disappeared. The decision by the Thatcher government not to restructure BT on privatization in 1984 and not to orient the regulator towards active promotion of competition and attacks on BT's anti-competitive conduct (Gist 1990), for the political reasons discussed earlier, lived on to the seventh age in the shape of the regulatory problem Oftel faced and the instruments it had to use to deal with that problem.

Second, the 1984 Telecommunications Act continued to be the source of Oftel's formal powers long after the Act had become seriously outdated, because of the high costs in political energy and parliamentary time in modifying any such framework. (In Australia, major legislation on telecommunications has been introduced every two years following the 1989 reform process which saw the introduction of a duopoly policy and creation of a new regulator (Armstrong 1990–), while in the UK the same legislative framework has remained in place for a decade and a half with only minor modifications.) Hence Oftel was faced with an obsolescent statutory framework (which may have become outdated faster than many other major statutes because of the rapid technological transformation of telecommunications since 1984), which had several consequences. It meant Oftel had to develop methods of implicit regulation to deal with circumstances where it was expected to act but had no formal power, for example over service quality in 1986–8 (Scott 1993b; see also Armstrong, Cowan and Vickers 1994: 360). It meant Oftel was formally obliged to continue – or at least make a show of – performing functions it no longer considered central to its regulatory mission, such as the complaint-handling function inherited from the fourth and fifth ages of telecoms regulation. It also meant Oftel had to find ways of adapting formal powers intended for another purpose to the regulatory tasks of the seventh era of telecoms regulation. A notable example, which we consider later in the book, is the use of licence modification procedures originally intended solely to modify BT's behaviour, in order to steer a newly multilateralized telecoms sector as a whole.

Third, the origins of Oftel (and the two senior members of the original regulatory *menage à trois*) as part of a common civil service culture stretching back to the fifth and earlier eras of telecom regulation continued to have an effect even in Oftel's post-umbilical phase.

The effects of cultural and institutional baggage inherited from the past are not simple. Sometimes such baggage provokes reaction – a Cultural Revolution-type revulsion against the styles of the past – while at other times it produces continuity, with adaptation of past practices taken as a low-cost way of coping with change. Oftel exhibited elements of both patterns, though continuity is perhaps the more marked trait. However, within the constraints of its inheritance Oftel sought to manoeuvre in ways that enhanced its policy responsibilities and influence and took it up-market in the policy world.

Indeed, Oftel was more able to manoeuvre for itself within the policy space than might have been expected from its modest origins as the minor player in the regulatory *menage à trois* of the early 1980s. As indicated above, this outcome, almost certainly unintended by the architects of the 1984 Telecommunications Act, derived from the multiple and contradictory powers laid on Oftel as the 1984 Telecommunications Act took its final shape, enabling the organization to exercise substantial discretion in the relative weight to lay on those powers. The apparently unintended creation of incentives for BT and Oftel to come to a negotiated agreement over licence modifications rather than (as seems to have been originally expected) have most such modifications determined by the MMC gave Oftel, when headed by a resourceful DGT, a more central position in changing the telecoms regulatory regime than had been expected. The way that the politico-bureaucratic process served to lay additional duties and expectations on Oftel once it had been created (a normal feature of bureaucratic behaviour) enabled it to expand and reshape its policy role.

Hence, following a commonly-observed pattern of entrepreneurial bureaucratic behaviour, Oftel consistently (though sometimes belatedly) responded to changes in its environment by seeking to shape those changes in ways that increased or enhanced its responsibilities or influence. Thus it took a lead in mapping out potential policy developments associated with technological convergence between telecoms, broadcasting and other media, perhaps mindful of the possibility of a merger with the broadcasting regulators (Oftel 1995c). It also eventually developed a European orientation, aiming to sell the UK model of telecommunications regulation to the EU as the latter developed directives for the liberalization and re-regulation of member states' telecoms sectors. Such sales activity and involvement in EU policy making not only served to reduce the disruption that might otherwise have occurred to the UK's telecom regulation regime from new EU directives (Hunt 1997), but also lifted Oftel's policy profile at home and overseas and increasingly took it – not without conflict, as will be explained later in the book – into realms formally confined to the DTI and Foreign Office.

This chapter has briefly sketched out the archaeology of the telecoms regulatory regime so that readers can place our analysis of regulatory culture and institutions into a larger historical context, and grasp the formal rules of the game within which Oftel and the other players in the regulatory space had to operate. The remaining chapters of this book examine in detail how the telecoms regulatory culture worked, how the DGT functioned within his own organization and in the larger regulatory space of which Oftel was only a part, and the different forms of regulatory decision-making that could be observed during Oftel's third phase as a confident youth adapting from the sixth to the seventh age of telecoms regulation.

Part II

Culture and regulation

3 Peculiar place, peculiar culture: organizing and structuring the regulatory office

> The innocent view of culture is that we don't have it at home . . . One way to overcome culture blindness is to be attentive to the way that claims of authority and solidarity are being treated.
>
> Douglas (1990: 4)

In Chapter One, the first theme we introduced was the way culture regulates regulation – a process that is invisible from a 'helicopter' perspective on regulation and often to the participants too. We suggested culture regulated regulation in three ways – by fixing social and cognitive boundaries, holding rival worldviews and micro-cultures in tension and mediating change. In this chapter we focus on the culture of Oftel to probe further into the way culture regulated the conduct of that organization. Oftel was only a part of the wider telecoms regulatory community, as the last chapter showed, but it was the primary focus of our study.

The last chapter sketched out the formal rules of the regulation game as UK telecoms moved from its fifth to its sixth age of regulation in the 1980s, and identified some of the major players, particularly the *menage à trois* of the DTI, BT and Oftel that was established in the sixth age. But to understand how particular meanings were attached to the key words and phrases that dominated regulatory parlance – 'effective competition', 'undue preference', or Oftel's own corporate mantra of 'the best possible deal for the consumer in terms of quality, choice and value for money' – we need to look at the inner workings of the organization. How did the denizens of Oftel's immigrant-and-emigrant culture learn what they were supposed to do? What were the tensions and internal boundary lines within the organization? How did Oftel people see the other players in the regulatory space? Our interest here is not only (perhaps not so much) in the formal structure as represented in official organograms and the like, but also in all the unofficial or informal ways in which transactions were conducted and conduct regulated within the organization (Machado and Burns 1998: 380).

Three related features of the way culture regulated the regulator are explored in this chapter. First, the Oftel population to be regulated kept turning over. Thus the regulating culture had to be like the culture of childhood, insofar as it related to an ever-changing group of immigrants and emigrants (it was also a largely oral culture, another feature that it shared with the culture of childhood).

Second, there were distinct subcultures and social fault lines within the organization. Those fault lines were associated with different professional specialisms and rival groupings within the Oftel structure, particularly of functional branches and project task forces, each reflecting a different management microculture. Oftel when seen from outside (for instance by DTI observers) was often perceived as a monoculture, but from inside it was an organization whose culture embraced tension among different sets of attitudes, assumptions, management doctrines and views of the world.

Third, and closely related to the other two features, Oftel was dominated by a meetings culture. Meetings were a central mechanism in shaping the relations between the DGT and his 'court' within Oftel; this will be discussed further in Chapter Five. But they were also ways of 'Oftelizing' new recruits, sharing information within a bureaucracy of strangers, establishing a pecking order, building consensus and received views, and working round (if not fully resolving) tensions between Oftel's competing subcultures. Meetings were a central part of the process of attributing meaning to the regulator's working vocabulary and the glue that held the office together.

A CULTURE OF IMMIGRANTS AND EMIGRANTS

As noted in the first chapter, the best known account of how culture regulated the conduct of the senior civil service in Britain was given by two US observers, Hugh Heclo and the late Aaron Wildavsky (1974) some 25 years ago. Heclo and Wildavsky saw Whitehall as a small village world, quite different from the government of strangers that characterized the US federal structure (on a bigger scale, with lateral appointment for the 'spoils' appointments at the top and a Presidential-Congressional divide). Heclo and Wildavsky's villagers were regulated less by formal rules or oversight from ministers or

Parliament than by common norms and ways of working learned in a closed-career structure in which most people stayed for three decades or so. Within a permanent closed-career structure, mutual checking processes established the dominant values, received views and methods of doing business, and mutual rating processes (for the valued qualities of cleverness, soundness and clout) were the key control over individuals.

The telecoms regulatory village could only partly be regulated by such mechanisms. It is true that, as noted in the last chapter, there was a diaspora of fifth-age telecoms era people extending across Oftel, the DTI and BT with common backgrounds, known 'form' and experience of doing business with one another. That network cut across the new administrative lines that had been drawn across the telecoms map in the 1980s. It is also true that about half of Oftel's staff were career civil servants subject to some 1990s equivalent of the mutual rating and checking processes within the Whitehall village that Heclo and Wildavsky described in the mid 1970s. Such people (at the higher levels, at least) tended to have a personal network extending beyond Oftel into other parts of Whitehall and could expect a reputation for competence or expertise (or its converse) built up in Oftel to follow them into their new job when they moved on.

Oftel itself differed sharply from the sort of organization Heclo and Wildavsky had described. To some degree it was a bureaucracy of strangers, and becoming increasingly so at the time of our study. Everyone had come from somewhere else, including the DGT (who came from a minority tribe as an outsider with a management background and was appointed by lateral entry for a fixed term in contrast to Heclo and Wildavsky's job-for-life mandarins of the early 1970s). Most people stayed in Oftel for no longer than the classical Chinese three year term of office. It was an immigrant and emigrant culture. These immigrants had come from very different backgrounds, including business and City law firms as well as the Whitehall village. The office was physically located in a no man's land between the City of London and Whitehall and the cultural regulator for such an organization had to be rather different from that described by Heclo and Wildavsky.

Oftel's history as a deliberately (if perhaps somewhat carelessly) crafted hybrid was briefly described in the last chapter. Its geography also signified a hybrid status. The office was outside the square mile or so of Whitehall that compassed the world of Heclo and Wildavsky's villagers. Nor was there any of the Victorian or

Edwardian pomp of much of Whitehall about its quarters, inside or outside. It was housed in two floors of an anonymous modern commercial office block (albeit one rented entirely to government agencies) within the City of London, close to the financial markets, the headquarters of BT and other telecoms companies and the big city law firms. But if Oftel was *in* the City in a physical sense, it was not exactly *of* it in cultural or social terms. It deliberately held itself aloof from casual contacts and communication with business was carefully managed, for example in a Prussian restraint over *Hospitality and Principles of Propriety* (Office Notice 4/96).[1] People within the telecoms industry (including those with an industry background who worked in Oftel) often declared the organization's greatest weakness to be a poor understanding of how business and commerce worked.

The hybridity signified by Oftel's location was also a characteristic of its staff composition. Of the 160 or so people who worked in Oftel, few saw the organization as a permanent home and they were heterogeneous in background and experience. The features of Oftel as an immigrant and emigrant society, as noted earlier, meant that working relationships tended to be temporary and knowledge was segmented. For example, 39 per cent of Oftel's staff left the organization during 1997. Most branches experienced staff changes from month to month. An unscientific staff survey suggested that the number of other people within the organization Oftel staff knew (however casually) ranged from four-fifths at the top end to only one-fifth at the bottom of the range.

Oftel's immigrants brought different understandings about standard operating routines and ways of working from their different backgrounds. That diversity increased the tendency for adhocratic-chaotic styles of decision-making (introduced in Chapter One and to be discussed further later in the book) and meant there had to be a process of 'Oftelization' if the organization was not to become a Tower of Babel.

All of Oftel's staff were employed as civil servants, but only about half of them came from a previous civil service position. Most of those came from the DTI, Oftel's parent department, and an increasing number from other government departments. Typically they were on loan for a fixed period of three years (the standard term of office in Imperial China, also commonly found in the UK civil service tradition) after which they expected to return to their home departments. These civil service people, ranging over all grades or levels, were diverse in professional terms as well as departmental backgrounds. They included not just the policy generalists, but also lawyers, economists, engineers, statisticians and information officers from a range of government departments. However, they shared some common administrative *lingua franca* and ways of working that marked them off from the other half of Oftel's staff, who did not come from a civil service background. The fact that many of Oftel's staff came from the DTI (and in many cases returned thither) produced important social networks and channels of communication and mutual influence.

The people with a civil service background had particular professional knowledge, such as how to write a briefing document for a Minister. They shared assumptions about how to distribute responsibility and authority in an organization. The Director General of Telecommunications (DGT), Don Cruickshank, observed that those from a civil service background: 'understand particular words such as "policy", "advice", "management" and "executive" to have a particular, given meaning' and these meanings shaped their actions within the Office. But such words did not carry the same nuances of meaning for the other half of Oftel's staff – those who did not come from a civil service background. They were internal boundaries marking one 'world' or one set of tribes from another.

Those with a civil service background saw much of their professional knowledge as lying in an understanding of 'how Whitehall works, which door to knock on'. They drew on a personal network extending across different government departments for work and personal support. Such behaviour corresponded to the *modus operandi* of Heclo and Wildavsky's Whitehall villagers, carefully keeping track of colleagues in a small world where paths might well cross at different points in a career. One senior policy adviser commented: 'I went to one meeting . . . and the first forty-five minutes were spent establishing who knew whom, where people had worked together before. Then we got down to business . . .'

The remaining seventy or so people in Oftel, including the DGT himself, were recruited on fixed-term contracts from outside the civil service, either to bring in specific expertise (especially for technical branch staff, who often came from the telecoms industry) or to provide an alternative point of view. Most of these people did not feel themselves to be civil servants (although they were all employed as such),[2] did not share the traditions and experience of those who came from a civil service career background and often had different values and ways of working. For instance, one respondent from this group expressed puzzlement about what the 'expertise' of those with a civil service background amounted to, particularly for the civil service generalists ('I don't know where they are coming from, what they know . . .'). One senior staff member saw 'a huge gulf between civil servants and people with experience outside'.

Those who came from a specialist background outside the civil service often used the terms 'arrogant' and 'naive' to describe the civil service culture. By arrogant they meant exaggerated confidence in the ability of staff to solve abstract and conceptual problems of a novel and complex kind, combined with an 'inability to admit mistakes'. By naive, they meant in particular a lack of commercial experience. A senior staff member declared, 'I am absolutely convinced that experience of working in industry is essential for this job', whilst one specialist, from outside the civil service, commented of the civil service culture: 'I don't think they have much to teach me . . . My first impression was of the ignorance of finance and accounting practices, business strategy. Oftel is commercially naive – but then, so is BT'.

The diversity of background and operating styles within this immigrant and emigrant culture was if anything increasing during Oftel's third life-stage in the Cruickshank era, as discussed in the last chapter. As noted there, during the organization's first and second life-stages staff recruitment had been handled by the DTI. The consequence was that Oftel structure and culture tended to replicate that of the DTI and Oftel was treated as a DTI satellite over staffing, with the needs of the child sometimes sacrificed to that of the parent department. One Oftel administrator observed

> DTI had an interest in a strong and effective regulatory authority so it did its best to support Oftel but it could, in the past, also recall staff at very short notice and Oftel had very little, to no say at all in staff appointments. Oftel was not in control of its own people and had only marginal control of recruitment.

During Oftel's third life-stage, as described in the last chapter, the apron strings were cut as Oftel established its own management structure, including the handling of its own recruitment. Such changes reflected a change in the broader civil service structure at that time, where there was increasing emphasis on a cost centre approach to public service management[3] and more delegation of hiring, grading and recruitment powers to individual departments subject to general merit-appointment rules and running-cost controls (see Hood, Scott *et al.* 1999, Chapter 4).[4] Those broader background changes in public management chimed with at least two Oftel-specific factors. One was a critical internal audit report in 1992 that recommended Oftel should create its own administrative capacity separate from that of the DTI. A second was the advent of a managerially-minded DGT, Don Cruickshank, who had distinct views about how the office should be organized and who placed heavy emphasis on the need to recruit higher-quality staff, in terms of expertise and intellectual calibre, to improve the quality of Oftel's work and thereby increase its status.

The consequence of managerial autonomy for Oftel (which established its own personnel section in 1993 and thereafter controlled its own recruitment) was that the organization moved further away from DTI structure and culture. An internal auditor subsequently observed:

> It is now true to say that Oftel is developing its own culture, related to its tasks and duties, rather than merely importing DTI culture with DTI staff. The DTI culture, formal and hierarchical,[5] may therefore be challenged.

This largely (and increasingly) cerebral organization of immigrants, growing away from the structure and culture of its parent, inhabited by people from many different backgrounds, and with an ever-changing population, posed particular challenges for cultural integration. Personal relations could be problematic. 'I don't know anyone here; they are always changing,' commented one civil servant, who saw himself as merely passing through Oftel on his way to another civil service post. 'There is no loyalty, there is no sense of identity,' commented another. The flux and flow of people also meant organizational memory and information transfer could be erratic. When staff left they took most of their acquired knowledge and skill with them. Moreover the ever-changing body of new recruits took time to become fully effective. There was repeated reference to 'the steep learning curve' in the organization; 'You have to ask and ask again and again. There is so much to learn,' according to one recruit. It was recognized that it took about six months for a new person to 'get up to speed' and to become really 'useful'. Getting 'up to speed' and becoming 'useful' meant tuning in to the regulatory culture as well as absorbing the technicalities.

A CLASH OF MICROCULTURES

The way this diverse and ever-changing population went about its work of regulating telecoms was itself regulated by Oftel's office culture in several ways. There were integrating processes of general 'Oftelization' which worked largely through a meetings culture which will be described later, and the meetings culture linked up with informal networks of a type commonly observable in organizations. But culture also regulated the regulators in another way, by a clash of competing microcultures that prevented the values or assumptions of any one of Oftel's managerial or professional tribes from going unchallenged.

As we noted in the first chapter, such processes of mutual checking among rival entrenched tendencies within or around organizations have been identified by several theorists of culture and organization as a central control mechanism for checking policy runaways and modifying single-perspective product or policy designs. Andrew Dunsire (1978) has even seen such countervailing tensions as affording strategically-placed individuals with an opportunity to shift the balance among rival forces by throwing their weight in one direction or another. Certainly Oftel senior staff told us that the various 'fault lines' within the organization were not there by accident. The cleavages were understood and deliberately retained by management, they claimed, because the divisions contributed to a creative tension that helped Oftel find original solutions to novel problems. In other words, they seemed to see the clash of microcultures as valuable precisely because of the tendency of that conflict to promote what we call the adhocratic-chaotic issue-processing style, briefly referred to in Chapter One and discussed further in Chapters Six and Eight.[6]

Microcultures clashed inside Oftel in several ways. One was its character as a Babel House – a term used by Andrew Dunsire (1978: 175–8) to characterize a bureaucracy that includes a variety of professional specialisms with their own characteristic attitudes, working languages and ways of looking at the world. Oftel could be considered as a Babel House in a sense that goes beyond Dunsire's classic characterization of the relationship between different professional specialisms in a bureaucracy, because cutting across those professional differences were differences in background, particularly between the staff who came from industry and those who came from the public service. The other way microcultures clashed was through a tension common in many organizations in the 1990s between a functional branch structure (the traditional way in which work had been divided up in the civil service), and cross-cutting project teams. The resultant matrix structure (following the experience of many private and public sector organizations) created another source of tension and perhaps predictably the system tended to operate in branch mode as the default model. However the branch/project team divide also cut across some of the other fault lines within Oftel and gave Oftel's top brass another way of steering the structure through its inbuilt tensions.

Competing professional subcultures

Cutting across the tension between those with a civil service background and those who were new to the civil service was the division between different professional 'tribes' within Oftel. Three of those tribal identities – of lawyers, 'techies' (that is, technical specialists in telecommunications) and economists and statisticians – were built into Oftel's branch structure, with advisory branches devoted to each of those specialisms, as can be seen from the organizational chart shown in Figure 3.1. Other professionals were scattered throughout the organization, working in the various policy branches shown on the left-hand side of Figure 3.1. For example, formal legal opinion came only from Branch 7 but there were numerous lawyers working within the policy branches (both legal secondees from City law firms[7] and civil servants with a legal background).

This staff mix meant that competing professional perspectives were built into the policy branches and the project teams, while the advisory branches remained as relatively pure repositories of particular professional expertise. The mingling of skills was seen as part of a distinctive Oftel culture and was valued by many of those who worked within the organization as a source of a peculiar range of knowledge and skills. For instance, one legal secondee commented on 'how useful it was to have a team of economists at your side'; equally the econocrats and policy staff needed the perspective of the legal branch (Branch 7), to arrive at policies that were workable and not vulnerable to reversal through judicial review. The legal branch was important not only in advice over policy proposals but also in shaping the management of Oftel, since irrationality in decision-making was a justiciable ground for challenging regulatory decisions. Its input was seen by the DGT as so fundamental that the legal branch head was effectively the third most senior staff member in Oftel.

When expertise was needed for a specific project or problem, for instance in accountancy methods, consultants were brought in to add to Oftel's melting-pot of specialisms and backgrounds. Consultants generally reported directly to the DGT as they passed through, although not all were birds of passage and some consultants

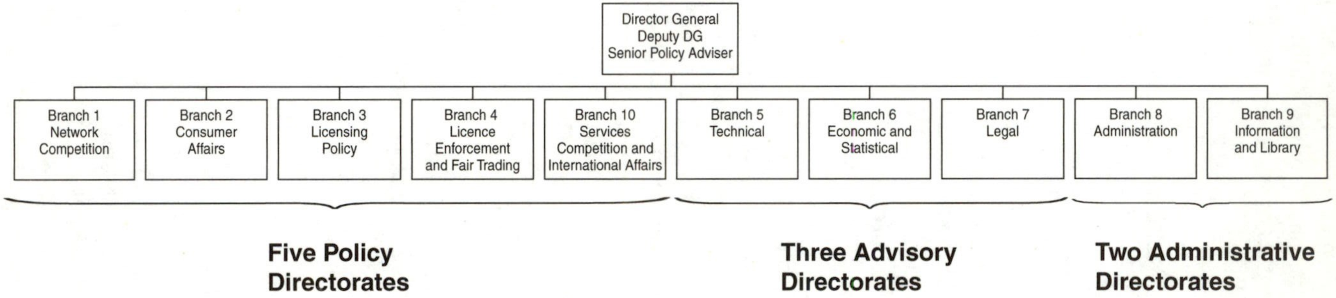

Figure 3.1 Oftel organizational map (March 1997)

– many of them senior figures in their fields – worked within Oftel on a long term basis, such that they were around for a longer time than some of the regular employees, and played a significant role in shaping policy. They amounted to another hybrid in the organization, and in some cases were able to provide institutional memory that was lacking among the regular employees in Oftel's immigrant/emigrant society.

The diversity of background, skills, experience and expectations held within the several professional subcultures was reflected in professional linkages that went across branch or project boundaries and extended to the professional world outside Oftel. For instance, members of professional groups often ate lunch together in the canteen even if they never worked together on projects or case-work. And such links extended outside Oftel, into other parts of government, the professional bodies and elsewhere. For example, Oftel's legal staff continued to follow professional development training and their professional career structure within the Government Legal Service. They saw themselves as part of a wider professional grouping with special obligations to uphold the rule of law, natural justice and notions of democracy or fairness, in contrast to ordinary commercial norms. For instance, the Head of the Legal Branch acknowledged the professional pride that went with being a member of the government legal service, noting that:

> . . . government lawyers have a different role from commercial ones. They must defend what is legal and work to sustain the boundaries whilst a company lawyer might be seeking to challenge or circumvent and push against these boundaries.

As issues went through the Oftel machine, there was an interplay between technical and analytical competence during meetings, across the personal social networks and between the professional collectives. What each of the various professional cultures contributed was a different way of looking at problems and priorities, potential actions, risks and effects. In the constant policy dialogue that went on in Oftel's Babel House structure, external professional obligations differed and occasionally brought conflict. For instance, accountants and lawyers clashed over their conflicting interpretations of companies legislation from time to time, and Oftel was one site for a broader set of battles for turf going on among warring professionals (Dezalay 1991). Hence the contest and dialogue among professional subcultures was one of the basic mechanisms shaping regulatory activity within Oftel; and though power was by no means evenly distributed among those subcultures, the conflict and dialogue modified policy as it developed and served to prevent any one group from possessing a cognitive monopoly over regulation.

The branch structure/project management fault line

In addition to the way regulation by Oftel was shaped by tension and dialogue among different professional subcultures was another source of tension shared by many organizations in the 1990s, that between a functional branch structure and a project management structure. The latter cut across the tribal divisions of the different professions within Oftel and served as another cultural melting-pot. This tension between the branch and project management structure offered a point of leverage for the DGT over the organization, but in management there is no free cultural lunch and the branch-project team tensions created problems as well as solving them.

On one side of this divide was Oftel's structure of functional branches, the traditional way of dividing up policy work in the UK civil service. This structure was partly inherited from the DTI and partly copied from the OFT on which, as was noted in the last chapter, Oftel was originally modelled. Hence the various duties of Oftel under the 1984 Telecommunications Act were distributed among the different branches shown in Figure 3.1, with the branch structure constituting a set of letter boxes and repositories of particular expertise and routines for matters like public relations, network competition or consumer complaints. By 1997, as Figure 3.1 shows, there were ten branches. Headed by a senior civil servant – properly 'the Director' but commonly called 'the Branch Head' – each branch was subdivided in classic bureaucratic fashion into further sections each led by a Section Head.[8]

Branches were defined by specialized knowledge of policy domains or professional fields. Within the branch structure, the tradition was that specialists offered advice and generalists sorted out policy. Sections and branches were often reluctant to move across clearly marked boundaries of responsibility, branches could be jealous of their relative status and staff could be sensitive to marks of status or distinction. Particular tasks or individual work packages were allocated from above, often with more regard to the grading or hierarchical level deemed to be appropriate to a given work package than to the background or ability of any individual. The branch culture was a mixture of collective and individualist orientation.

It was collective in so far as it tended to emphasize shared perceptions and shared responsibility among peers – a traditional way of dispersing risk in public bureaucracies. But this collective focus was combined with a degree of personal autonomy and responsibility within the hierarchical structure. In standard bureaucratic fashion, tasks were passed down the hierarchy and difficult problems worked their way upwards to be handled by senior staff. Authority came from the top and dispersed downwards. This pattern was part of a long standing civil service culture designed to be resilient in the face of political uncertainty and change. Branches also owned the standard routines of line management and 'pay and rations'. Within the branch structure the line manager (or Reporting Officer as this position came to be termed in Oftel-speak) wrote assessment reports on junior staff, set their work objectives and generally looked after their welfare. 'If you go off sick, you phone up the Line Manager'.

In addition to the branch structure, and in some tension with it, was a project management structure that cut across branch boundaries and was introduced to Oftel by Don Cruickshank almost as soon as he arrived as DGT in 1993. Project management structures had been introduced some years before into BT, were fashionable in both the public and private sector at that time (cf. Parry, Hood and James 1997) and often figured in doctrines for reform of public bureaucracies. Project management skills are frequently declared to be in particularly short supply in traditional public service structures. But the project team structure also fitted with the new demands on Oftel as the organization began to move from the sixth to the seventh age of telecoms regulation. The regulatory issues associated with the emergence of a competitive telecoms market were different from those Oftel had faced in the sixth age of telecoms regulation, and called for an interdisciplinary approach that could not have been delivered readily – or at all – by the functional branch structure. Don Cruickshank recognized the need for a project management overlay within Oftel's structure in these conditions and imposed such an overlay on top of the branches in 1993 in a deliberate attempt to break the rigidity of the branch structure and modify the civil service culture.

This project team structure, imposed from above, was used to exert greater management discipline on Oftel by the DGT. Under the organization's annual management plan,[9] published deadlines were set for completion of projects. There was then periodic assessment and consultation to set priorities, to define new projects and improve the quality and effectiveness of work done within Oftel.

Internal benchmarks for quality of service were introduced, and the project structure was thus part of a whole management style recognizably related to modern management doctrines of quality management and strategic management.

Projects were led by individuals designated as project managers by the DGT or DDG. The DGT or DDG was conceived as the client for the project teams' work, and also took an active part in project work. The project managers were almost invariably Branch Heads, but they were able to go outside their own domains in selecting members of their teams from across Oftel, cutting across the boundaries of branch-held knowledge. The criteria for selection were knowledge, availability and personal character traits, including the ability to work well in a particular team. Team members were expected to bring their individual competence and knowledge to bear on the problem, not to act as representatives of branches. A team was changeable and could shrink or grow as members moved in or out. Some remained at the core until the project was completed – or fell apart through lack of interest or changing circumstance. This flux contrasted with the greater stability of the branch structure. In some cases people found themselves to be team members on projects they had not been told about. In other cases people who might have seemed obvious choices for a project team were not selected because their interest in the topic was not appreciated by the project manager organizing the team.

There had been opposition from some quarters in Oftel to the introduction of the project management style, using familiar arguments against this approach to organization in the public service. One former Branch Head had commented:

> Project management, originating in building construction, does not really translate into policy making areas of the sort addressed in the civil service . . . There are many examples of attempts to set performance indicators for the civil service, but they all hit problems where tasks change and grow.

Even after the initial battles over imposition of a project management overlay on top of the branch divisions had been won and lost, tensions between Oftel's branch and project structures remained throughout the period of our study. The two structures embodied different cultures, sets of values and expectations. The project team structure often fitted with the values and expectations of those immigrants who came into Oftel from outside government, who frequently had experience of project team work in their previous employment, and were less comfortable with the traditional civil service norms of grade hierarchy and group responsibility built into Oftel's branch structure. The team-based approach, involving a combination of individualism and collectivism that contrasted with the public service traditions embedded in the way the branches worked, chimed with Don Cruickshank's aim to 'leaven the civil service culture'.

However, the branch structure, and the civil service culture it embodied, did not crumble away at the first whiff of project-management grapeshot. Branches remained within Oftel as an alternative pole to the culture embodied in the project team structure. Projects came and went but the branches were more permanent. The branch structure was the default mode into which most Oftel people fell if uncertain or insecure. A branch head commented:

> Possibly we do have a branch culture. Don [Cruickshank] hopes it will wither and become just pay and rations and that project management will replace it. But the branch structure helps people to feel at home.

Tensions between the branch structure and project team structure created a number of difficulties familiar in organizations with matrix structures. There were inevitable confusions about lines of authority and reporting. For instance, project managers were supposed to participate in the (branch-based) staff appraisal procedures for members of their project teams. But often (if the project manager was from a different branch) they played a limited role, leading to feelings by some staff that their project-based work was discounted or ignored if they were not working closely with the Reporting Officer who conducted the appraisal. There were also underlaps between junior staff within branches who were allocated project work as a work package, without explanation of its context or importance, and those who had more opportunity to participate in project discussion or policy formulation. Indeed, the project structure could be seen as a way for a few key individuals at the top of Oftel to impose fairly tight control over the organization by keeping the overall threads of policy within their own hands.

However, the tensions between the branch structure and the project teams could also be seen as regulating the regulator by introducing tensions that prevented either the traditional civil service culture, embedded in the branches, or the alternative managerial culture, embedded in the project teams, from achieving unchallenged dominance within Oftel. It pitted long term functional perspectives against limited term focus on specific problems, the grade hierarchy style of the branches against the team style of the project groups where all members of the team had their seat and voice, individual initiative on the part of team members against the collective views embodied in the branch cultures. It could be argued that the elements of each of these cultures was necessary for Oftel to function effectively in the emerging seventh age of telecoms regulation. Without the project groups it would probably have been too sclerotic and compartmentalized to deal quickly with rapidly developing problems demanding expertise that cut across its traditional subdivisions. In fact, it seems unlikely that it could have survived at all with an exclusive reliance on such a structure. But without the branches, as organized repositories of expertise and orderly procedure, Oftel would probably have been too eccentric in its decision-making to survive as an organization expected to possess the traditional virtues of bureaucracy, in terms of some minimum level of consistency, predictability, collective memory and stability over time. Because the two institutionalized cultures were kept in tension, neither achieved complete dominance. Such cultural balancing acts are hard to sustain, and the tension between the two elements was certainly experienced as painful by those working within Oftel. In 1998 the official doctrine of Oftel's top brass that the juxtaposition of branch and project structures produced creative tension came into question. Discussion began about a new organizational structure to overcome the branch/project group conflict and indeed, shortly after the accession of a new DGT to succeed Don Cruickshank, such a structure was introduced after the period of our study (briefly described in the Epilogue at the end of this book).

OFTELIZATION AND THE MEETINGS CULTURE

If one of the cultural mechanisms through which regulation was regulated within Oftel was the push and pull of competing micro-cultures, another was what we came to call a meetings culture, involving both meetings within the organization and meetings between Oftel and outside groups. Much of the daily activity within Oftel was conducted through various types of meetings: internal meetings, external meetings, meetings with visitors, working meetings, strategy meetings, workshops, seminars, brainstorming, team meetings, branch meetings, conversations.

Oftel's meetings culture was developed to an extent unusual outside organizations like the Treasury (where it is often said that senior policy officials spend all day in meetings and only begin their individual work at the end of the office day). The degree to which it operated through a meetings culture differentiated Oftel from the *modus operandi* of its parent department, the DTI – a difference which sometimes led to conflict and failures of understanding between the two organizations, which will be discussed further in the next two chapters. Immigrants to Oftel often commented on the number of meetings within the organization. For instance, one Policy Adviser observed: 'Oftel has more meetings than anywhere else I worked. I used to ask if they were all necessary but I do now think that they are'.

Indeed, such was the demand for meeting space within Oftel that the DGT made perhaps the ultimate sacrifice by allowing his personal toilet to be turned into yet another meeting room for the organization.

Why were there so many meetings and what functions – intended or unintended – did all these meetings fulfil? Formally, the meetings served the purpose of solving problems, brainstorming issues, clarifying thinking, arriving at agreed solutions and gaining final approval for completed work. They also served as forums within which the meanings of key terms were developed, cognitive boundaries (of what counted as unreasonable or unthinkable) were set or removed, status and power relations were established and common values or expectations emerged. In that sense the meetings were functioning as a central regulator of telecoms regulation.

Internal meetings within Oftel

Despite the publication of office policy, frequent consideration of how meetings might be better managed and training programmes, the many meetings inside Oftel were frequently surprisingly ill-disciplined, even chaotic. One staff member commented with surprise on the informal style of meetings – taking off jackets, relaxed body language, participants coming and going – which contrasted strongly with her previous experience in the Department of Employment. Generally there was no formal agenda, no minutes were taken and very few people even took personal notes. Another senior staff member said 'When things are definite and have an agenda then you can do minutes. Where meetings aren't structured you can't really do minutes. This is an Oftel thing as it is *not* Civil Service training'.

The senior person present, by default, usually chaired the meeting regardless of other interests or knowledge. Meetings frequently started and finished late. They often overlapped, with participants moving from meeting to meeting, sometimes with no appreciation why they were even asked to attend. Preparatory papers had a tendency to appear too late to be useful. So we need to understand not only why Oftel had so many meetings, but also why they appeared relatively ill-disciplined in comparison with meeting cultures in other bureaucratic settings.

Oftel was a cerebral, top-heavy, policy-heavy organization with relatively few routine processing functions. It was an organization largely composed of general staff officers deliberating policy and strategy rather than of front-line battle troops of the kind that staff social security or tax offices. Moreover, tasks and roles were frequently ill-defined, outside policy domains like statistical analysis, telephone numbering policy or the handling of consumer complaints. So it is not suprising that meetings were a marked feature of Oftel's internal organizational style. Given that the organization dealt heavily in non-routine rather than standardized issues, there was a need for brainstorming meetings that allowed free flow of thought. A narrowly functional explanation of the number and style of meetings in Oftel's distinctive meetings culture could be couched in these terms.

However, in addition to problem-solving and policy closure functions, the frequent meetings within Oftel also served to establish, reinforce or modify the culture of regulation. They served as a melting-pot for the transient members of Oftel's immigrant-and-emigrant population to learn about priorities, practices and cultural meanings of the language of regulation. They served as a glue or cement, a means for bringing together the different perspectives and preoccupations of the various professional tribes within Oftel and the two managerial cultures embodied in the project and branch structures (as discussed in the last section): and they established a pecking order of status or authority within Oftel's internal organizational space.

First, the meetings culture served to introduce Oftel's immigrants into shared attitudes and beliefs, meanings of key terms, and the relationship between apparently conflicting principles or precepts. Meetings were the main fora in which newcomers learned about the peculiar culture of Oftel and indeed the wider environment of the regulatory space. They may have been all the more important because Oftel had very limited space where informal social contact could be made. The smoking room was available only to those who could tolerate the atmosphere but it could be a significant contact point for information transfer, as we show in Chapter Eight. Kitchen areas had deliberately been placed as meeting points in central locations, but the boiling water was available on tap so there was no need to linger in them waiting for a kettle to boil. So casual contact was relatively unusual. People were too busy.[10]

Hence Oftel's many immigrants had to attend meetings as part of a process of building up a personal network of contacts. In Oftel, as in many other organizations, a newcomer had to learn who really counted in the office, who had useful knowledge, who was open and approachable. The route to effective integration lay through the construction of a network of personal contacts as sources of information, practical advice and emotional support. Everyone had such networks to a greater or lesser extent, including the top brass who needed them to prepare for meetings with limited or no briefing papers. Meetings were important as one of a number of ways of building such networks. As Oftel's immigrants became culturally acclimatized and developed their own informal networks, they learned which meetings were essential, useful or merely a waste of time, and so became more selective about attendance. The many papers and e-mails streaming around the office were handled in the same way as attendance at a meeting and the development of networks helped new arrivals to assess their significance. 'At the start I was copied into everything . . . even highly technical papers . . . Now I have learned to be brutal and not respond to everything', said one relative newcomer.

Meetings were thus a crucial element in the process of 'Oftelization' of new arrivals. They paralleled or complemented the formal staff training and induction activities arranged by Oftel for new recruits. Given the diversity and relative transience of the staff combined with a changing environment and the complexities of the policy issues with which Oftel was grappling, the organization offered an increasingly formal induction programme run by training officers,[11] followed up with regular internal workshops and awaydays, which were themselves part of the meetings culture. Inevitably the formal induction activities were only part of the cultural Oftelization of the organization's new recruits. As one staff member recalled:

> It was eight weeks before I got my induction course. They had one the week I joined . . . but no-one in my branch knew about it . . . I was lucky and I had information from my room-mate about the internal machinations, how to do things without treading on anyone's toes.

Second, apart from its melting-pot functions for Oftel's immigrants, the meetings culture also served as an information exchange and a means of juxtaposing and reconciling the conflicting microcultures described in the last section. Given the divisions of perspective among the different professions and the structural divisions of the organization, meetings were the only way to bring the different players and pieces of information together. Meetings were an accepted means to work in both the civil service tradition embedded in Oftel's branch structure (with its associated strategy of diffusing risk through establishing consensus and a common view) and in the project management culture in which exchange of ideas was the driving force for effective work.

Third, the meetings culture was key to the status and authority structure of Oftel. Senior staff attended more meetings than junior staff and (to anticipate a theme that will be developed further) many meetings functioned as a royal court for the DGT. Meetings were a way of identifying the useful people and establishing status. They allowed the top staff of the organization to reach down into it, talking directly to a variety of ranks rather than only to the company commanders.[12] Given that the DGT was personally responsible for regulation of the industry under the 1984 Telecommunications Act and that the bulk of Oftel's activity was policy work, the scope for delegation and autonomous work was less than in a structure where the top brass could stay out of many decisions. For that reason, Oftel could not have functioned as a professional bureaucracy (in Mintzberg's (1983) classification) with a high degree of decentralization in casework activity[13] and its environment was not sufficiently stable for it to function as a machine bureaucracy.

Within these constraints, the meetings culture established a way for Oftel to operate in a manner coming somewhere between that of a simple structure (with all activities overseen by a dominant chief) and an adhocracy (with lateral processing but little decentralization). It allowed some space for deliberation and exchange of ideas that would not have been available in a traditional bureaucracy, where many responsibilities are delegated downwards and never emerge into the sight of the people at the top. It also allowed the DGT to break through the information asymmetries that he might have faced within Oftel had he eschewed the cameral style of group deliberation. Nicholson (1994: 72) has observed that there can be 'demonstrable benefits in confusion and uncertainty which give managers room to manoeuvre. The dynamics of chaos can be used either to personal or organisational advantage, or both in different situations'. The meetings culture, together with the tension he introduced between the branch and project management structures, was central to the way Don Cruickshank managed the dynamics of chaos within Oftel. We discuss Cruickshank's management style further in Chapter Five.

If the meetings culture is seen as part of a process by which regulation was regulated, it is easier to understand why the apparent chaos noted earlier continued to be tolerated. The meetings were not just about orderly processing of decisions, but information exchanges, stages on which talent could shine, fora in which different cultures mingled and clashed, and ways of marking status and power. Minutes, orderly chairing, briefing papers and stable participation were not necessary to fulfil such functions (and would in fact have worked against them). In addition, the informal meetings culture had its advantages in serving as a potential way of liberating imagination and intellect, outside the conventional bureaucratic division of labour, within an organization facing a changing environment. But these advantages did not come free. The price Oftel paid for its semi-chaotic meetings culture included weaknesses in its institutional memory sometimes reflected in a tendency to reinvent the wheel (as noted in the hotel phone pricing case discussed in Chapter Eight), and a failure to engage the talent and knowledge of the (mostly junior) people who did not attend or participate in the meetings.

The high-level meetings, however, generated other meetings as specific policy ideas worked their way up from junior staff working on work packages to the large, inclusive meetings at which the final product was 'signed off' by the DGT or DDG. Those policy ideas tended to develop through conversations across social and e-mail networks. People thought issues through, had conversations with their peers or their immediate boss and then the completed analysis, conclusions and policy options went to a meeting for presentation. So the meetings culture also generated a pre-meetings culture, which perhaps represented a response by the civil service culture to the dynamics of chaos management strategy discussed earlier. According to one staff member:

> We now have pre-meetings for meetings as [the DDG] has made it clear that she doesn't want dissenting voices at meetings. We are supposed to come up with a common line that she can say 'yes' or 'no' to.

Meetings between Oftel and outside bodies

Many of Oftel's meetings were held with outside bodies, including telecoms firms, other UK government organizations, overseas bodies, EC officials, and consumers and interest groups.[14] Meeting styles ranged from very formal to casual exchanges between colleagues of long standing, though most external meetings were more tightly managed and better recorded[15] than meetings taking place within Oftel. Large-scale meetings like industry workshops, formal meetings with industry groups or discussion with new players in the regulatory space were generally set up well in advance, with prepared agendas, background papers and briefs prepared for the DGT or another chairperson. By contrast, arrangements for bilateral working meetings were made at the request of either side, sometimes at very short notice over the telephone. Such arrangements were possible between BT and Oftel because of the physical proximity of their respective offices in the City of London, as noted earlier.

There were informal but distinct rules of the game[16] about these industry meetings that were most marked where personal relations were likely to persist long after the particular problem or project under discussion had been resolved. When a bilateral working meeting was organized the expected participants would be identified and then later confirmed. This practice was more than a security requirement (though security requirements had to be met, since all visitors had to be signed into the building at the front desk, following standard civil service procedure). According to one Oftel staff member:

> There is a kind of etiquette about it. Oftel tries not to smother visitors. Sometimes a small company may only send a couple of people. BT has the bureaucracy and size to send four or five. There have been times when I have been at a meeting with an Oftel lawyer and several BT people. Normally we try to keep things balanced. And there is no point in sending in visitors [to Oftel] unless they are necessary.

BT confirmed this view:

> We have a policy of not out-numbering Oftel. We usually ask how many people are going to be at a meeting. If Oftel is fielding all economists and accountants we know we should do the same. It also gives us an indication of the sort of discussion we are likely to have. If Oftel fields a lawyer, which it does increasingly, then we do too (Williams, not dated).

The inclusion of lawyers apparently imparted an extra degree of importance to any meeting with the regulator; 'If Oftel field a lawyer, I know they are serious,' commented one telecoms company executive. The character of individual participants would also be taken into account as far as possible when arranging a meeting. Personality was recognized to be significant for the conduct of bargaining and, within the limitations of available staff, efforts were made to avoid putting known antagonists together in the same meeting. One constant in most meetings between Oftel and BT was that a member of the BT Regulatory Affairs Department (RAD) would attend.[17] RAD was set up by BT to act as a gatekeeper for all dealings between the organization and regulators and, consistent with recognized good practice for regulatory affairs offices within firms generally, attempted to manage the flow of information between the two bodies (Coen and Willman 1998: 35). However, Oftel staff generally felt they got better quality information when they dealt with operational people within BT and often identified both a functional and cultural gap between RAD and BT's operational staff that was linked with tensions inside BT.

Why did all these meetings take place between Oftel and other bodies? The official purpose of the meetings was to exchange views and solve problems. Beneath these issue-specific functions, the meetings seem to have fulfilled broader functions of network maintenance, negotiation of meanings and appropriate behaviour. Oftel's openness and accessibility to other bodies within the regulatory space, the many meetings and the extensive public consultation helped to promote consensus, in the form of common perceptions about issues and acceptable behaviour, and thereby helped define culturally acceptable boundaries to regulatory activity. The meetings provided fora in which Oftel's formal and substantive legitimacy as a regulator was developed, challenged and negotiated, as we shall see in Chapter Eight. The meetings and consultation provided opportunities for the many actors to identify roles, establish their authority and state their interests. The meetings also allowed issues involving novelty, ambiguity, imbalance or unfairness to be debated widely across the telecoms world.

CONCLUSION

This chapter has focused on some of the distinctive features of the inner world of Oftel as a regulatory bureaucracy, with only occasional glances beyond the office world to the wider regulatory space or policy community within which Oftel operated. In the next chapter we look more closely at the role of the individual Director General, and the extent to which he was able to function as a 'regulatory monarch', before going on to look at the nature of the wider regulatory space in Chapter Five.

This chapter has argued that culture served as a regulator of Oftel's work in defining meanings, setting boundaries and keeping contradictory attitudes and beliefs in tension. Some of this cultural regulation could be seen as deliberately contrived by management. A recurring strain of management thinking, epitomized in Peters' and Waterman's (1981) best-selling *In Search of Excellence*, sees organizational culture as malleable and ownable, capable of being shaped and altered at will by managerial leadership. Don Cruickshank, with a background in professional management, was certainly well aware of the importance of organizational culture. He talked about it a great deal, often trying to characterize and compare the distinctive cultures of BT, the civil service and Oftel. As we have seen, he tried to re-engineer Oftel's culture by changing the structures and the people, in particular by introducing a project management structure that was designed to pose a frontal challenge to traditional civil service practices and attitudes.

The microcultural tensions within Oftel tended to be explained away by Cruickshank and his lieutenants as products of deliberate choices. If their accounts are to be believed, branch structures and project management were consciously kept in a finely tuned creative tension comprising the 'collibration' style of organizational control expounded by Andrew Dunsire (1996), as discussed earlier. Collibration refers to the manipulation of tensions between actors for the purposes of achieving a form of control. The balancing of tensions can occur both within an organization, as in this case, or between organizations, as we discuss in Chapter five.

However, anthropologists reject the notion that organizational culture is owned or alterable at will by management (Wright 1994; Alvesson 1993)[18] – though they concede that a manager with an appreciation of cultural constraints is likely to meet with more success in changing an organization than one who lacks such an appreciation. Some of the cultural regulation to which Oftel's activities were subject seems to have been spontaneous, unintended, dysfunctional – or all three. The underlaps between the rival microcultures embodied in the branch and project structures created gaps in information transfer, as we will see later. And the intendedly proactive style of the project teams was often substantially diluted in practice by the default style of consultation and consensus-seeking that serves to diffuse risk of error in bureaucratic decision-making. The style of Oftel's meetings culture, as suggested earlier, contributed to institutional memory lapses and put grit into the *menage à trois* relationship between Oftel, BT and the DTI within the regulatory space.

Accordingly, it seems safer to conclude that the cultural regulation that was shaping Oftel's behaviour in telecoms policy was a mixture of consciously-contrived, management-engineered culture and a deeper less manipulable set of attitudes, beliefs and working practices that were rooted in coping strategies, inheritance, inertia and reactions against changes engineered by management. Views about the balance between the two varied among participants, with the top brass predictably veering towards the cultural engineering end of the spectrum and other individuals bringing out the immanent features of the culture. Whether we split the difference between those two views, or incline towards the implied view of one camp rather than the other, it is impossible to understand how Oftel worked without taking into account the culture that shaped it.

Part III

The absolutist myth in regulation

4 'Oftel, *c'est moi*': the role of the DGT

> The finest plans are always ruined by the littleness of those who ought to carry them out, for the Emperor himself can actually do nothing
>
> Bertholt Brecht, *Mother Courage* (1935) sc.6.

A REGULATORY *ROI SOLEIL?*

As noted in the opening chapter, the OF-type regulators set up in the UK during the privatization era of the 1980s and 1990s seem at first sight to have an absolutist character. Statutory powers to regulate were vested in individual director-generals together with a power to appoint staff, meaning the DGT was a statutory creature but Oftel was not. And the OF-type director-generals became the visible public face of state regulation. This apparent personalization of regulation was one of the distinctive features of regulation UK-style, in contrast to experience in North America and Australia. In contrast to the traditional anonymity of senior civil servants in Britain, the regulators made regular media appearances and their names became widely known, at least during times when the politics ran hot in their regulatory domains.[1] This statutory and media personalization of the OF-type DGs created an impression of regulatory monarchs who were masters of all they surveyed, and whose imperious whims could affect the fates of giant corporations and millions of consumers.

This cult of the individual in utility regulation came partly from predictable media pressures to find a human face or talking head to associate with the abstract rules and frameworks within which the former nationalized industries worked. But it also stemmed from a deliberate strategy by the senior civil servants responsible for establishing Oftel in the early 1980s. They chose to play up the telecoms regulator as an individual person of great consequence, rather as the absolute monarchs of early modern Europe liked to be portrayed in impressive equestrian statuary, larger-than-life portraits and similar power signatures. The human face of regulation was thus a conscious PR device designed to shape the image of the new organization and gain legitimacy for it. According to a former Oftel press officer:

> BT is a high-profile company. Oftel was much smaller then and everyone was saying it was a paper tiger – so we had a deliberate policy to build (the DGT) up as a real force. We succeeded, and in a sense over-succeeded, so that we began to draw back towards the end, with Carsberg . . .

This judgement was shared by a former very senior Oftel official, who observed: 'It was only about six years later that we came to realize that the image had gone too far and the whole issue of personality cults and individual powers had arisen by then.'

As that remark implies, this PR strategy to personalize utility regulation, together with what appeared to be wide powers giving individuals the capacity to make arbitrary decisions, produced consequences far from those intended by the bureaucratic architects of the policy. It led to what Sam Sieber (1981), in a well-known analysis of reverse effects in social affairs, terms 'exploitation' – a mechanism in which devices intended to achieve a given effect come to be used by opponents for a purpose diametrically opposite to that for which the mechanism was originally conceived. In this case, the regulatory cult of personality, intended to buttress the legitimacy of the OF-type DGs, came to have a delegitimating effect. Representatives of the regulated industries and their advisers used it to portray the regulatory regime as suffused with large concentrations of arbitrary power in the hands of unaccountable individuals.

Academic discussion also reflected concerns about what was seen as over-personalized power and accountability deficits (Veljanovski 1993b). The two most widely canvassed solutions to the *roi soleil* problem were constitutional-monarchy approaches, involving greater use of formal procedural rules to constrain the regulators' discretion (Foster 1994; Veljanovski 1993b; Helm 1994) and putting the regulators' royal powers into commision, replacing individuals with collective decision-making by regulatory boards (Veljanovski 1993a; Corry *et al.* 1994: 85; Hansard Society 1996: 7; Prosser 1997: 299).

Others saw the relative freedom of individual director-generals from bureaucratic and other constraints as a strength of the UK regime in contrast to the structures adopted in North America.[2]

Our study of one regulatory director-general (Don Cruickshank as DGT) suggests that the deliberately-cultivated and much-criticized *roi soleil* image obscured as much as it illuminated. As noted in the first chapter, the scope for arbitrary exercise of public power by the DGT was sharply limited in two ways, by the organizational process of Oftel functioning as the king's court and royal apparatus, and by other powers and principalities within the regulatory space, particularly the DTI with which Oftel shared regulatory power under the 1984 legislative regime briefly described in Chapter Two and in our account of regulatory space in the next chapter. This revisionist analysis of the DGT's power, going against the grain of most academic and practitioner analysis of the personality problem in UK utilities regulation, has implications for policy prescription to which we return in Chapter Ten.

EXTERNAL LIMITS TO ABSOLUTISM: THE OFTEL-DTI RELATIONSHIP

Even (and perhaps especially) the supposedly absolutist monarchs of early modern European history were frequently checked in their capacity to exercise power by other institutions sharing their 'authority space' – like the Pope, the Holy Roman Emperor, the guilds, free towns and landed gentry (Henshall 1992). A parallel can be drawn with the case of the DGT and his role in the regulatory space. The carefully-contrived media image of *roi soleil* concealed a structure (described and analyzed in Chapter 2) in which regulatory powers over telecoms had deliberately been divided between the DGT and DTI by the architects of the 1984 regime – precisely to limit the former's absolute power. That division, and particularly the DTI's role in telecoms regulation, attracted much less attention and discussion by academic and media commentators than the supposedly absolute powers of the DGT.

As noted in Chapter Two, though the DGT had statutory power to enforce and modify licence conditions for telecom undertakings, the DTI retained major policy-making powers, notably to issue national and international operating licences and to represent the UK in international negotiations in the EU and World Trade Organization and with key trading partners like the USA. Though the DGT also had some role in all these matters, thus checking the DTI's policy monopoly in some domains, the reverse checking role – of the DTI over Oftel – was perhaps even more pronounced. Given the considerable interest by DTI, Treasury and government ministers in Oftel's activities for the first decade or so of its existence, because of the financial considerations over privatization discussed in Chapter Two (which were in turn linked to a larger political strategy), the capacity of the DGT to reach individual decisions was heavily constrained by the need to keep the DTI informed and to persuade the DTI that his 'line' was correct and politically defensible. To pursue the baroque-age analogy, the power of the DTI and the Treasury relative to the DGT was much more than that of the Holy Roman Emperor and the Pope *vis-à-vis* the house of Hapsburg or Hohenzollern.

Indeed, the position of Oftel as quasi-independent yet still part of the government was central to understanding the limitations of the DGT's power. The ambiguity of the DTI-Oftel relationship was the root of a contested area of process and policy, and that ambiguity was most marked where the policy environment was changing, relevant information and experience within the bureaucracy was limited or non-existent and novel responses were needed. In such situations, where did responsibility lie? Who was to take the lead role in decision-making – regulatory agency or ministry? Within the DTI, one senior official spoke of a 'higher density of interaction' between DTI and Oftel than with other utility regulators, and attributed this 'dense interaction' to 'the fast-moving nature of the market, historical process and the way it was set up'.

Strategic-level stuff: absolute monarch or petty princeling?

Strategic issues in telecom regulation (such as the speed of market liberalizatation, the opening of the UK market to overseas competitors, and development of the UK line on European Community policy making) constituted a key policy domain in which any pretensions of absolutism the DGT might have harboured were heavily circumscribed by the rival claims of the DTI. Indeed (in contrast to the line their predecessors had taken in public in launching the 'cult of personality' for the DGT), senior staff in the DTI told us they had retained effective control of strategic policy issues. On this view, if Oftel was to have any role in setting telecoms regulatory strategy, it was because the DTI permitted and encouraged it, not because the DGT could unilaterally decide to do so. In the words of a senior DTI official: 'DTI is doing strategic-level stuff. When I ask the question, "Why do we issue licences?" – as I often do, my staff reply, "Because Oftel might get it wrong and ministers are concerned." '

Another senior DTI official declared:

> The department's role is strategic in relation to the regulatory framework. The licensing responsibility enables ministers to take the lead in the pace of liberalization. Maybe this began in 1984 as an acceptable [limit on the] degree of freedom for the DG at that time, but it has allowed ministers to pull the levers to control the pace of changes for political presentation.

In reality, in spite of the bureaucratic theology of strategic and other matters, there could be no strict demarcation between the province of the DTI and that of Oftel in the rapidly changing and highly coupled world of telecoms regulation policy. Even though the DTI had its own distinct formal responsibilities within the regulatory framework (notably licensing and international affairs), it was deemed necessary to work closely with Oftel so as to have 'efficiency in regulation'. Such co-operation, according to a DTI official, was: '. . . not a formal relationship; we need sensible rules and good relations with industry, not too onerous, so we need to have reasonably close relations with Oftel . . .'

Then there were other matters which fell outside the formally-specified responsibilities of ministers but on which the DTI could 'give advice on the political impact or consider regulatory consistency'. Overall, this particular respondent felt there was: '. . . a healthy dialogue with proper regard to people's ultimate responsibilities . . . This, in the end, is a question of personal relationships; individual character and the value placed upon informal relationships.'

In short, far from the monarchical figure that he appeared to the media and some academics, the DGT and his office were seen by DTI insiders as in an inextricably (and often conflict-laden) Siamese relationship with the DTI, with the two bureaucratic bodies joined hip and thigh, like Siamese twins.

Foreign affairs: a contested role?

The limits of the Sun King metaphor for the figure of the DGT in telecoms regulation shows up most clearly in the foreign policy dimension of his activity. Far from being a plenipotentiary in the foreign policy dimension of telecoms policy, the DGT's role was an ambiguous and contested one. Only the DTI, as a ministerial department, had the legal capacity to operate in the European and international theatre in relations with foreign governments. While the DGT and Oftel could not in practice be excluded altogether by the DTI from a foreign policy role (despite the formal demarcation of responsibilities), that role was one of sharing power, mostly as a junior partner, not monopolizing it.

Oftel could not be excluded from a foreign affairs role both because it had specific expertise that DTI lacked and because Oftel was expected to have an international voice by other players in the global telecommunications regulatory space. Other national governments and agencies engaged in telecoms privatization and re-regulation actively sought to draw on the knowledge and experience Oftel had gained as an international pioneer in that field. Moreover, Oftel actively sought a foreign affairs role, especially in the development of the EU regulatory regime for telecommunications: EU Directives had a direct impact on Oftel's domestic activity and it wanted to ensure that those Directives were as far as possible compatible with its regulatory regime and followed the UK way of thinking. Hence during Cruickshank's reign as DGT Oftel sought to go beyond the limitations of its formal role as a purely domestic power with no foreign-affairs dimension. While Oftel and the DGT might have had some (understandable) imperial ambitions as a player in the international telecoms regulation arena, its role in that dimension was limited, tentative and friction-laden – at best a minor partner in an uneasy *de facto* condominium, far from the Sun King image.

Both the DGT and DTI officials testified to the limits of the DGT's role in foreign affairs and the degree of bureaucratic friction it generated in Whitehall. According to a senior DTI official:

> Oftel wants a role in influencing the EU as the Directives directly impinge on what Oftel is doing. . . . There is a problem in the Commission as only the ministers can represent the UK Government in council and the other [European] NRAs [National Regulatory Authorities] report directly to a minister which Don doesn't. For the sake of the EU, Don would have to submit to a minister and that just doesn't work. Don is frustrated by what he sees as bureaucrats with little understanding of Oftel doing a job in which he thinks he should have a role.

While accepting that Oftel had acquired sector-specific experience and expertise relevant to the foreign-affairs dimension of telecoms regulation that the DTI did not possess in-house, DTI officials nevertheless tended to see themselves as far more experienced, worldly (and consequently, effective) in European and international negotiations. The DTI official quoted above suggested: 'DTI is more cynical through longer experience. Oftel has a very different set of priorities, a different set of thoughts . . .'.

The ambiguous boundary line between the two organizations in the foreign-affairs dimension, with the DTI as the *de jure* policy monopolist and Oftel as an important *de facto* player because of its knowledge and the way it was perceived by overseas governments was seen both by Oftel and the DTI as a frequent source of conflict and difficulty. In the words of one DTI negotiator, in international bargaining: 'DTI skate on the surface and glibly say whatever we want to be the truth. Oftel will then go naked into the chamber and expose all the weaknesses of DTI arguments!'

He saw a conflict between what he saw as Oftel's narrow and often naive econocratic viewpoint in international negotiations and DTI's broader political view, suggesting that:

> The economics are very simple in this area. But the correct answer, from a technical point of view, might not be the intuitive answer and Oftel might correct the DTI perspective. But Oftel sometimes misses the broader, negotiation point. . . . It is the disingenuousness of the technocrat or the technical expert and it is not appreciated in DTI . . . DTI are after broader interests – such as GATT. Oftel are more focused and will go around the houses. . . . The difference is in institutional experience. In Oftel the international ramifications are not appreciated except on a technical basis . . . DTI can be economically incorrect because we know that international negotiators are economically illiterate. You use different arguments in a trade negotiation from dealing with the economists in the FCC and Oftel is not aware of this difference.

Cruickshank himself was well aware of the politico-bureaucratic frictions and limitations that surrounded his foreign affairs role. As he put it:

> The Government is very nervous that relations with sovereign states, and member states in the EU, should be handled by

> officials reporting to ministers. But Oftel is a non-ministerial Government Department, and I, as head of the department, am part of the Government – as the Treasury is always telling me.

He related several examples of the form that those frictions and limitations took. In one case:

> I attended a G7 meeting . . . all the countries had their Minister, senior Civil Servant and National Regulator sitting in threes around the table – except the UK. I was actually sitting *behind* the Minister and the Civil Servant. . . . I did have to point out that all the others were acting as a team and we weren't. This is gradually changing.

He also noted that:

> When I go to a foreign capital I have much higher levels of access, to politicians' dinners *et cetera* than the DTI because I am treated as a Minister. I have said, 'Come on, let's make use of this access,' but the DTI don't like it – it is a complex status thing.

In short, in the international arena the DGT's role was formally one of a subordinate functionary, not any kind of monarch, and any role that he managed to achieve in that arena was a limited and unofficial one, constantly running up against the sensitivities of those who did possess the formal power in international negotiations, saw the DGT and Oftel as at best an agent and could be jealous of Oftel incursions in that domain.

Absolutism – or checks and balances?

In contrast to the public perception of the DGT as wielding uncontrolled arbitrary powers, Don Cruickshank declared: 'I actually had more discretion when I was running the NHS in Scotland than I do as a regulator – with all its panoply of independence.'

Hardly the words of the regulatory *roi soleil* of media imagery. Cruickshank was not suggesting that his work was frequently subjected to egregious political interference over issues in which the statutory framework gave him unambiguous policy ownership, though he did suggest that one of the important reasons for government preferring individuals to commissions for utility regulation was not so much the orthodox managerial-efficiency arguments of rapid decision-making and clear leadership as the opportunity that individual responsibility gave for the government 'to get him alone in a dark room and beat him up!'[3] Cruickshank saw his main weapon against such interference as the sovereign power – or threat – to publish policy documents. In the nature of real-life politics such a 'nuclear' threat could be used only sparingly to ward off ministerial interference. But, according to a senior DTI official:

> It was rare under the Conservative government for ministers to interfere in a DG's responsibilities but fairly common for Don [Cruickshank] to have an opinion on ministerial responsibilities. Ministers didn't criticize Don. The regime was set up to remove political influence from economic decisions and by criticizing [they would] actually undo the structure.

Nevertheless, there were at least three ways in which the DGT's discretion was limited. One was the 'black letter' statutory framework, as described in earlier chapters, which defined his powers and duties. A member of staff in Oftel observed

> Don is really concerned about what his powers actually are and he often sits in meetings with his copy of the T[elecommunications] Act beside him and he refers to this frequently, saying, 'I can't do that,' or, 'I must do this . . .'.

However, the constraints on the DGT's discretion were not simply – or even perhaps mainly – those contained in the words of the Telecommunications legislation. A second key source of restriction of the DGT's discretion arose in relations with the other telecoms regulator, the DTI, and were the product of bureaucratic custom and political *realpolitik*. After all, if the DGT was entitled to immediate access to DTI ministers, those ministers also had ready access to the DGT. As Cruickshank put it, the notion of independence of the utility regulators had been:

> . . . interpreted by some . . . to mean 'thin relations' with only limited contacts between Directors General and the rest of Government and this continues to a degree in electricity, in gas – but I think this is a mistake . . . I don't actually have the discretion that the law says because being out of step with the Government is untenable; it goes back to my thing about, well

> legitimacy I suppose. So I spend a lot of time working through issues with DTI. . . . I am very keen, however gritty, that in the end we don't do anything that the Minister doesn't know about or can't live with. It is . . . part of the unwritten UK constitution that there are limits to the number of confrontations with ministers that are possible and this limits [everyone's] behaviour.

Respondents in the upper reaches of the DTI expressed a similar view of the unwritten code of consultation governing the DGT's behaviour and overlaying the formal words of the statute. According to one DTI official:

> Oftel is the typical British compromise. In legislation Oftel is independent but it must accede to ministers or be challenged by [statutory] Orders. So in practice there needs to be give and take, close personal relationships – though frustrations and tensions are inevitable.

Put in a slightly different way (again from the DTI):

> It is not effective to have a constant falling out with ministers. There are the statutory duties on the regulator and there is also a personal preference for informal discussion with ministers. Then there are some areas which are not so clear and this is where the lobbying occurs.

Third, when political trouble or potential trouble blew up over issues for which Oftel and the DTI had overlapping responsibilities and Oftel had been left with the discretion to develop policy, the DTI could exercise political *force majeure* in snatching back responsibility for policy.[4] Universal Service (to telecommunications consumers) was a case in point, where the DTI resumed the initiative of policy leadership at short notice. According to the DGT:

> Universal Service is a potential hassle with the [potentially conflicting/overlapping] roles of the Secretary of State and the Director General, Conditional Access is another . . . I cascade these issues down by meeting [the Minister] . . . [But] On Universal Service – I missed the legal *vires* issues [i.e. jurisdictional questions] and so put it back three months. The USO [Universal Service Obligation] as a tax [on BT] became an issue with the DTI legal department and it ended up having to go to the Cabinet

> Office. The change in the tone of exchanges between one day and the next was extraordinary; one day Oftel was doing it, the next the Secretary of State; the next it was Oftel again.

The monarchical metaphor completely fails to capture these three key restraints on the DGT's discretion and the functional necessity and political imperative for the DGT to manage a delicate and ambiguous pattern of interdependence between Oftel and DTI as joint authorities in the telecoms regulatory space. Cruickshank and Oftel managed this relationship in a number of ways, but rarely from a position that approximated to absolute authority. Like any streetwise senior civil servant with a well-developed nose for political sensitivity and embarrassment, Cruickshank stressed the importance of having an acute sense of political timing ('issues are often about timing rather than substance') and trying to head off trouble by anticipation and discussion with DTI ministers over delicate issues where Oftel and DTI's domains intersected.

Second, Cruickshank often sought to encourage joint working with the DTI, in order to reduce conflict between Oftel and the DTI. He set up a series of quarterly summit meetings between Oftel and the DTI, in which the DGT and the head of the Communications and Information Industries Division in the DTI met together with their various lieutenants, in order to fulfil 'a moderating role' in exchanging information and limiting the tendency of the lieutenants on each side to pick fights with one another and push the conflict up to their respective bosses (another standard feature of bureaucratic behaviour).[5] Rather than encouraging such privateering activity to push out the boundaries of his empire by pinpricks aimed at the DTI's policy possessions, he often stressed the need for teamwork between Oftel and DTI:

> I also suggested joint working teams – some of which work and some don't, though I'm not certain why. These [teams] deal with areas of joint interest, Conditional Access, International Licences. On Conditional Access what went through Parliament was what we wrote [as a joint working team] ... The middle ground [between DTI supervision of Oftel and total independence] is the joint working parties. Then we have shared work, shared ownership.

Third, Cruickshank and Oftel were often in a position to 'manage upwards' even in circumstances where formal policy responsibility clearly lay with the DTI and Ministers, and had several resources for doing so. Since the DGT was accountable in part to the Secretary of State for Trade and Industry, he had immediate access to ministers, which could be used for lobbying over policy. A senior DTI official suggested: 'A non-ministerial department is in a similar position to a private company and so will lobby ministers by various means; in private discussions or by engendering public conditions . . .'

In addition, as has already been noted, Oftel increasingly possessed information that was not readily available to the DTI, especially as the quality of Oftel's staff improved dramatically following Oftel's administrative independence from DTI in staffing matters,[6] and telecoms technology and business structures changed. For example, over matters such as radio spectrum (telephony) for fixed access or international liberalization, we were told that 'Oftel did the work'[7] and that there was close co-operation between the DTI and Oftel. A DTI official noted:

> Oftel has increasing expertise that is not available anywhere else in government, for example the effect of windfall tax [on the privatized utilities, introduced by the Blair Labour government after its election in 1997] . . . so it is not an individual [sector] regulator but a resource that the government must use.

Oftel also had other other resources (such as its transparent policy style and perceived quasi-independence from government) that might on occasion be politically useful to the DTI and ministers. For instance, Oftel's Deputy Director General suggested:

> There are times when Government finds us useful, when Don can do things they can't. Rebalancing and ADCs for example. BT was running rings around us. . . . The risk was that if regulatory control was reduced then BT would increase line rentals and this was politically very difficult for the Government.

Rather than an absolute monarch, Don Cruickshank as DGT is better understood as a skilful public manager – managing upwards, downwards and sideways in his organizational environment – whose effectiveness lay in persuasive power and political acumen as much as unchallenged legal authority, because many of the cards in telecoms regulation – in legal authority and ultimate political and legislative power – were in the hands of the other regulatory authority, the DTI. As the comments and opinion cited earlier indicate, precise limitations on the degree of independence and interdependence between the regulator and the ministry were not clearly defined. The statutory framework described in Chapter Two provided some checks and balances between the two organizations and others had evolved through custom and practice. Some of those checks and balances took the form of cultural constraints – the 'complex status thing' commented on by Cruickshank in his reflections on his foreign-policy role quoted earlier – both in what was seen as appropriate behaviour in various contacts between government departments, the DTI and Oftel and also in the definition of acceptable or tolerable regulatory action by either side. These blurred boundaries of responsibility and authority were constantly under negotiation through a process of action and reaction. The authority of the two sides was established both through ties of trust and confidence constructed over time within the tight professional collective of senior Oftel and DTI civil servants and through interpretation and reinterpretation of the formal powers in the 1984 Telecommunications Act. Beneath the Sun King public image of the DGT's role lay the reality of a culturally complex balance of power, co-operation and conflict between the DGT and the DTI – one of the most hidden features of the telecoms regulatory regime, discussed further in the next chapter, since both sides preferred to present a united face to the wider world.

INTERNAL LIMITS OF ABSOLUTISM: THE DGT-OFTEL RELATIONSHIP

Just as the absolutist power of early modern European monarchs was typically checked by other external players in their 'authority space', so was it commonly checked by the court apparatus that surrounded the monarch – the chamberlains and chancellors and the wrangling that went on among the royal courtiers and hangers-on, in councils and committees in the crucial organizational space between expressions of the royal will and detailed policy execution. Oftel, the DGT's royal apparatus, was not exactly a Byzantine court, though it was culturally diverse, as has been shown earlier. But nor was it simply an automatic implementation machine for the DGT's royal edicts. As shown in Chapter Three, it was a complex policy-deliberating and policy-shaping organization that acted as another checking influence on the DGT in at least two ways, to be explored below. One was through the role of deputy director-general as a key influence over the DGT and a pivotal figure in the Oftel-DTI nexus. The other was through the interdependence between the DGT and the rest of Oftel.

Spy, double agent, safe pair of hands? The pivotal role of the deputy director-general

Within Oftel a key figure during the period of our research was the deputy director-general (DDG), an experienced mid-career senior civil servant from the DTI. Outsiders, both in government and the industry, tended to see the relationship between the DDG and DGT as akin to that between a Permanent Secretary (civil service departmental head, in UK central-government parlance) and a minister – with the Permanent Secretary – the 'Sir Humphrey' figure in the famous *Yes Minister* sitcom – concerned with administrative detail, policy management and the day-to-day running of the organization and the Minister concerned with policy.

Oftel insiders tended to reject this minister-Permanent Secretary analogy for the DGT-DDG relationship.[8] In the functioning of Oftel as an organization, there was no formal policy-administration distinction between the work of DDG and DGT, even though it was the latter who had the direct statutory responsibility for policy decision. The DGT was intimately concerned with the details of management and the daily processes of Oftel, as well as policy-making. In common with Permanent Secretaries (not ministers), the DGT and not the DDG was the Accounting Officer for Oftel and therefore carried personal responsibility for its spending relative to the Treasury and Parliament. Moreover, given his management background, Cruickshank chose to function as a decidedly hands-on manager and spent a great deal of time on organizational matters within Oftel, in contrast to the style of his predecessor (noted in Chapter Two).

If the beguiling idea of a policy-administration dichotomy fails to describe the respective roles of DDG and DGT, the DDG may be better seen as a fixer, broker or bridge between the different bureaucratic worlds that needed to be synchronized if Oftel was to function successfully, and particularly Oftel and its regulatory partner, the DTI. The DDG was the person who stood at the intersection of several encapsulated structures between which communication was problematic – the DGT and his staff, DTI and Oftel, career civil servants and 'outsiders' within Oftel. Like all interstitial figures of that kind (Bailey 1969: 167–76), the DGT exercised a role that was both powerful and ambiguous relative to the DGT.

The DGT explained the selection and position of the DGT thus:

> The Deputy Directors are seen as 'minders' and are very carefully selected for this role. [The current DDG] has been here seven[9] years and has held two jobs here, which is one reason why I

> selected her. I had a long debate with myself about it, about the role of the Deputy, the relationships with Branch Heads etc . . . But it was as a result of my NHS [National Health Service] experience that I chose to [appoint her]. [She] gives us a capacity to influence Whitehall because, essentially, influence is about information.

According to the DDG herself, 'Don knew he could do the accounting and financial stuff but he recognized that he needed someone good at Whitehall networking'.

The DDG's good connections in Whitehall were valued both in Oftel and the DTI. As noted in the previous section, there was a regular and (more or less) open exchange of views between Don Cruickshank, senior officials and ministers in the DTI since 'Don isn't status conscious . . . not rank conscious, though he definitely cares about being involved in regulation policy. . . .' but at certain times the DDG was used as an intermediary, filter or sounding board for difficult issues instead of direct approaches to the DGT. According to one senior DTI official '[having] a good civil servant as number two to the Regulator is quite sensible', because:

> If I don't want to hit Don with something [unexpected or likely to be unpopular] then I will talk to [the DDG] first. This is very much the usual pattern in the civil service. . . . Some would say that it is cowardice [to use the DDG as a filter] but it is actually just part of good handling . . . He will take something from his deputy, whom he trusts, that he wouldn't take from me.

Hence, while for outside observers of telecoms regulation the rest of Oftel was invisible and attention focused only on the DGT in his deliberately-contrived absolutist persona, insiders had a different view of the organizational space. They pointed to the key role of the DDG as a mediator or interpreter, negotiating the blurred boundaries of Oftel's regulatory independence noted in the last section, defining acceptable norms of behaviour and possessing influence over the DGT, who was often seen to be impatient of delicate sensibilities on the part of other people. Partly this DDG role was shaped by the personal character traits and talents of the incumbent. But it also seems to have been a functional imperative, because of of the DDG's position as a respected fast-steam civil servant with the right contacts and a shared background with those in other parts of the government machine. As she put it:

> I have the experience and training because I have had a number of jobs where economics, politics and practicality come together quite fast. . . . I've been employed by DTI for a long time so I know a lot of people and to some degree that makes things easier, but in this job contacts have to be made with other bodies such as DCMS [Department of Culture, Media and Sport].

Hence, to pursue the baroque-age analogy once more, the DDG functioned as a mixture of chancellor and key diplomat, drawing on a network of confidential personal relations beyond the immediate confines of the office and into the wider world of Whitehall. There were binding personal ties between the DDG and her fellow senior civil servants that were based on parity, reciprocity and common experience. 'All the [Oftel Branch] Heads are ex-DTI. It's a bit incestuous really, all ex-colleagues' said one DTI respondent, cheerfully[10], noting that one such Branch Head had worked with him on electricity privatization, that the DDG was ex-DTI and that even the DDG's husband used to work with him in the DTI. Indeed, several key Oftel staff had been recruited directly through their connections with the DDG. Even so, the DDG considered the specifics of personal contacts to be less significant in her role than her insider's knowledge of what, where and how to get things done in Whitehall; where to unblock decisions, how to motivate ministers, how to time issues.

The DDG's chancellor role was heightened by the organizational characteristics of Oftel as both an immigrant and emigrant culture, as described in Chapter Three. Given the mix of Oftel's staff from different backgrounds, including many from the private sector little accustomed to the elaborate rituals of clearance and consultation in the traditional government machine, the DDG had the role of educating the immigrants into the mainstream culture of Whitehall's ways of doing business. As she put it:

> I spend surprisingly little time [dealing directly with DTI] but an awful lot of my time telling people [in Oftel] that something will have to be cleared with [the] DTI just to stop [DTI people] being taken by surprise. . . . I mean, it is one thing for them not to like something we do, and quite another for it to come at them out of the blue. And this isn't a one-way thing.

Like anyone living in two 'worlds' – Oftel and Whitehall – the DDG had to tread a delicate path to maintain the trust of both sides. To function effectively as Oftel's chief intelligence officer (with access to crucial informal information passing through the network of senior grade civil servants and anticipating, circumventing or reinforcing formal information channels) she had to appear as an honest broker to her counterparts in other parts of government. That meant disseminating information outwards along the same paths to maintain communication and build influence through reciprocity (along the lines classically described by Heclo and Wildavsky (1974) in their account of the use of information in the upper reaches of Whitehall). Yet she had to maintain that role without being seen as a double agent by the DGT, who (as she put it) saw loyalty to Whitehall 'as a betrayal of trust'.

No account of the supposedly absolutist role of the DGT could be complete without an understanding of the finely nuanced role of Oftel's DDG as go-between, influential adviser and fixer. If Don Cruickshank was no Jim Hacker (the egregious anti-hero of the *Yes Minister* sitcom) and the DDG no Sir Humphrey, there were still crucial information channels to the DTI and across Whitehall that the DDG could more readily access than the DGT, and numerous occasions in which the DDG functioned as an important filter between the DGT and the other players in organizational and policy discussion.

The monarch and the court: the DGT and Oftel

While an outside perspective on absolute monarchy sees only the royal personage, an inside perspective may stress the importance of the wider royal apparatus – not just the topmost figures of chancellor, chamberlain or ambassador – in shaping events. Oftel as an organization perhaps had some features of what the management guru Henry Mintzberg (1983) calls a 'simple structure' in terms of its planning and co-ordination systems, with limited vertical and horizontal decentralization. But even in a fairly small organization like Oftel, with its 150-odd people arranged in the various branches and project groups described in Chapter Three, the DGT could not be everywhere. He had no choice but to delegate much of what Oftel did in his name, only stepping in to some issues when he judged an intervention to be needed or where a policy fiasco was developing, as in the telephone numbering case discussed in Chapter Seven.

Don Cruickshank himself, as a highly reflective figure steeped in ideas of business strategy and the lore and language of management consultancy, was well aware of the potential of an organizational apparatus to influence the attitudes of its head and shape policy execution. And he developed ways of dealing with and countering such organizational influence that would have been entirely familiar to baroque-age monarchs.

For example, he made his barons and advisers function as a royal court, obliged endlessly to meet and argue in his presence. During these meetings, Cruickshank (deploying a tactic many monarchs have used in dealing with courtiers and counsellors) often deliberately took an abrasive line, putting his staff on the spot, sharply challenging ideas and provoking arguments in a way many Oftel staff used to more genteel styles of management described as confrontational and intimidating. He fostered a creed ('the best possible deal for the consumer. . . .' discussed earlier) that everyone in Oftel ritually intoned as a sort of loyalty oath, but which, as has already been noted, was so ambiguous in its interpretation (what was best possible, which customers counted for most, what weighting was to be placed on price relative to other desiderata?) that it left him enormous scope in its interpretation.[11]

In addition, Cruickshank made the courtiers compete for uncertain royal favour, since he was seen within Oftel as inclined to listen to some people more than others, dependent on his personal opinion of the individual in question, regardless of orthodox civil service hierarchy and the polite forms of civil service culture. And he deliberately strove to be unpredictable to his staff. Where he saw Oftel decision-making becoming too comfortable and rational (as in the price control review, discussed further in Chapter Seven), he often chose to add a little 'chaos' to the process – in that case, by deciding that Oftel's decision on the value of x should depart from what could be justified with the formal models developed by BT and Oftel. Similarly, he could add chaos by drifting in and out of decision processes that were being managed by more junior staff, reopening issues that were close to conclusion if he did not like the provisional results. For instance, one former member of Oftel commented on the discomfort that Cruickshank elicited in staff by keeping them uncertain about his exact objectives and expectations:

> A lot of the work is staff running after the DG's ideas – which he might then discard later, or this work is done for Don to confirm a suspicion, to test a hypothesis that is not actually expressed. He likes to play games with us and he doesn't tell us his strategy. I don't mind this, but it would still be nice to be able to present the full range of choices right at the beginning.

Cruickshank recognized Oftel as having some influence in shaping his judgements, but considered it to be a relatively minor one – and indeed frequently strove to react against what he perceived as Oftel (or worse, civil service) orthodoxy. He compared the effectiveness of the office to that of advertising – only 25 per cent effective in influencing his opinion, but it was impossible to identify which 25 per cent. Most of his ideas and judgements, he claimed, came from past experience, observation and external contacts, not from Oftel.

On the face of it, this personal testimony seems to portray the monarch as largely independent of the court (redolent of Frederick the Great in intellectual isolation at his Potsdam retreat of *Sans Souci*). Looked at closely, it is more ambiguous. Even if Cruickshank's quantitative assessment is correct, the degree of Oftel influence it implies does depend precisely on which 25 per cent of the DGT's decisions Oftel shaped. Moreover, Cruickshank's assessment may well understate the degree both of his interdependence with Oftel and of the influence of Oftel as an organization in shaping overall regulatory policy, in at least three ways.

First, as noted earlier, much of what went on in Oftel was of necessity outside his direct sphere of knowledge and intervention,[12] such as the classic regulatory role of complaint handling, so even if Oftel influenced only a minority of the DGT's own decisions, those decisions were themselves only a minority of the total regulatory decisions made by Oftel.

Second, if Oftel had not existed, Cruickshank would have been obliged to invent it, since (as noted earlier) much of his management style consisted of intervening unpredictably in ongoing processes – putting grit in the technocratic-bureaucratic machine at key points. That style of intervention – 'collibration' in control-theory accounts of bureaucratic functioning (Dunsire 1996) – depends for its effectiveness by definition on the pre-existence of a bureaucracy programmed to operate in a relatively determinate way. Moreover, even on the frequent occasions when the DGT sought to adopt a bolder or different version of the policy line suggested by his minions and advisers, he could not and did not issue his edicts *ex cathedra*, but was obliged himself to work through Oftel's meetings culture (discussed earlier in Chapter Three) to argue his point, in order to carry Oftel with him. As with Richard Neustadt's (1961) famous account of US Presidential power, Cruickshank's power depended on his power to persuade, to make his highly cerebral organization see things his way. The 'court style' of high-level decision-making within Oftel that the DGT fostered, closeting himself with the organization's top barons in lengthy and discursive dialogue, was as much of a constraint on him as it was on them. Cruickshank himself saw these meetings as providing an important sanity check on the ideas and proposals being debated. And though he sought sanity checks in other quarters too, it would be strange indeed if traffic of influence exerted in the Oftel meetings went only in one direction, from the DGT to the Oftel barons, and not vice-versa.

Moreover (in a way that would also have been very familiar to the courtiers and counsellors of the baroque-age) the views from the Oftel machine against which the DGT reacted consisted to a large extent of what members of the organization thought the DGT would want to hear from them. Staff were constantly trying to second-guess his views, opinions and responses in a way that he may not have fully recognized. For example, one Policy Advisor declared: '[My branch head] does that all the time. He makes his decisions by guessing what Don or [the DDG] would do about a situation – if they ever knew about it'.

In handling matters perceived as low-level or routine, the DGT almost invariably received opinion and analysis that had been honed through successive pre-meetings, branch or project group meetings and extra-meeting conversations according to one overriding consideration – the assumed views of the DGT – before the one-page document reached him or a meeting with him took place. This anticipated-reaction behaviour by Oftel staff indicates the familiar 'hall of mirrors' effect that surrounds many forceful personalities in leading positions within organizations, and the difficulty they face in eliciting any opinions other than those assumed to be their own. So, paradoxically, the 'Oftel view' which the DGT perceived himself as frequently challenging often consisted of what Oftel believed to be his own approach. That meant that a substantial proportion of the 75 per cent or so of Oftel influence over his ideas that the DGT saw himself as rejecting consisted of what the organization believed to be his own 'line' or approach. This complex mirroring process meant that Cruickstank was to some extent debating with himself through Oftel as much as rejecting an organizational view that was in sharp contrast to his own.

Hence, even on Cruickshank's own testimony, the 'Oftel *c'est moi*' equation missed at least a quarter of what he chose to do himself – let alone what Oftel did in making decisions the DGT had no contact with. Despite the powerful effect of a strong personality, the DGT did not act alone in reaching high level decisions. Even though it was not formally a commission, Oftel had strongly collegiate characteristics and several senior staff were closely involved in most major policy decisions. Oftel sometimes functioned as a restraining force on the DGT, who had to justify his own view and lead by persuasion. Though Cruickshank was not a career civil servant and chose as his managerial trademark a style of working against the grain and 'leavening the civil service culture' (see Chapter Three), he could by no means dispense with that culture altogether and policy-making over this period involved significant interdependence between the DGT, the DDG and the rest of Oftel, not a one-man show.

CONCLUSION

The metaphor of baroque-age absolutism captures some features of the DGT's position in the period of our study. Ironically, in view of the earnest debate about the need to bring what are claimed to be overweening regulatory monarchs in check, the features of the DGT's role that baroque-age metaphor best illuminates are the major constraints on absolutism both in formal authority and organizational practice. Beyond the carefully (perhaps unwisely) contrived Sun King image of absolutism lay a reality in which legal authority was not monopolized by any one figure and in which decision-making reflected as much a process of long drawn out wrangling in overlapping committees as of unrationalized royal whims.

Beyond that, the beguiling *roi soleil* metaphor obscures as much as it illuminates. The limited independence the DGT actually possessed under the Telecommunications Act framework described in Chapter Two amounted to the ability to develop and express a view – the 'power to persuade' in Harry Truman's classic phrase (Neustadt 1961). In the complex relationship between Oftel and the DTI, the DGT was a pivotal figure and had the power to advise ministers, but they set policy. Cruickshank recognized that he was more constrained than the letter of the Telecommunications Act might suggest because in Whitehall the most effective way to work was through forging consensus. In his own office, the DGT could posit bold solutions and impart radical ideas but such interventions also required consensual support from his management team. Without the active support of his staff, achieved by long policy debates, the DGT would have been a talking head without an effective body. Hence while Don Cruickshank as DGT undoubtedly left his stamp on the telecoms regulatory regime during his period of office, he was by no means the only significant player.

5 Oftel in space: interdependence and accountability

> If you persist to the threshold of old age . . . you will be a powerful person yourself, with an accretion of peculiarities which other people will have to study in order to square you.
>
> Francis Cornford, *Microcosmographica Academica* (1908) p2.

In the last chapter we described both the internal and external limits to the autonomy of the individual director-general, while in this chapter we focus on Oftel's wider relationships as a regulatory agency. The creation of Oftel caused and continued to cause considerable anxiety among commentators and policy actors concerned at the significant delegation of authority to a non-ministerial government department (Graham 1995: 5). For some Oftel, and the other regulatory offices established in its wake, had too much discretion (Veljanovski 1993b: 25), for others the new agencies did not have sufficient independence (Graham 1995: 53). Some saw risks that the agencies would be captured by those they were supposed to regulate (Veljanovski 1987: 177; Foster 1992: Chapter 11; cf. Prosser 1999: 204).

This study throws fresh light on such concerns. What we observed was that far from being an all-powerful regulator with uncontrolled discretion, Oftel as a regulatory agency was highly constrained in each of its main spheres of activity by relations of interdependence with other actors in the regulatory space. This characterization of interdependence was a product not only of the formal structure of the regime in which significant regulatory power was given to actors other than Oftel, but of the other capacities possessed by actors who shared the regulatory space deriving from experience, possession of information, and ability to bestow legitimacy on the regulator's activities. Central to an understanding of these relationships is the history of a regime, sketched out in Chapter Two, in which Oftel was to be a new player creating a *menage à trois* with two longer established and powerful players, BT and the Department of Trade and Industry.

We look at the telecoms regime in a regulatory space perspective going beyond the activities of Oftel and the DGT to other public and private actors in the telecoms regulatory world. Viewing Oftel as an interdependent regulatory agency puts a different complexion on the accountability debate. The interdependent relations within the regulatory space can be seen as involving elements of extended accountability, acting as constraints on Oftel to explain and justify its actions and decisions; and the constellation of actors within the regulatory space was not just a bipolar world. Rather there was a range of other actors creating a system of balancing tensions that operated as an equivalent on a larger scale of the clash of conflicting pressures within Oftel as discussed in the last two chapters (cf. Prosser 1999: 204). The formal accountability mechanisms described in the final section of this chapter formed a relatively small part of a demanding and extended accountability regime which was the product of interdependence.

THE TELECOMMUNICATIONS REGULATORY SPACE

Numerous studies of regulation in different countries and policy domains have challenged the image of regulators as all-powerful, with effective power to command and control their regulatory subjects. Even in the USA where federal regulatory agencies such as the Federal Communications Commission combined legislative, executive and judicial functions (and have sometimes been referred to as 'governments in miniature' (Prosser 1997: 268; Schultz and Doern 1998)), detailed studies have observed the dependence of such agencies on others for achieving their objectives (Nader and Nader 1985). Broader analytical models of public policy have highlighted the importance of policy networks, and the role of a variety of stakeholders within a policy world or community, though this approach is not without its critics (Dowding 1995) and is open to the same sort of objections as the general pluralist perspective to which it is recognizably related.

For regulation this community approach has come to be termed a regulatory space perspective (developing from an original focus on organizational or policy space: Hancher and Moran 1989; Shearing

1993; Wilks and Doern 1998; Prosser 1999). From this perspective a regulatory agency appears as just one actor among others in a policy arena. Capacities, and thus power, within the space are likely to be unevenly divided among major and minor players (Hancher and Moran 1989: 277). As in the pluralist approach in political science, possession of formal authority, from legislation or contracts for example, is only one determinant of power in regulatory space. Informal authority may be possessed by some, deriving from information experience, culture or some form of legitimacy (Braithwaite 1997: 312–13). The relative power of the actors within the space is likely to change over time, in response to changes in policy (including the legal framework), economics, technology and culture. Critics of pluralist approaches, of course, will expect to find underlying hegemony beneath the interaction of multiple public and private players. It must be stressed that regulatory space is not an objective reality. No one has ever seen a regulatory space, and visions of the space are likely to vary according to position and cultural disposition.

The archaeology of the UK telecoms regulatory regime, set out in Chapter Two, reveals marked changes since the introduction of the telephone in 1880. Viewed in regulatory space terms the process of nationalization up to 1911 represented a reduction in the number of separate actors within the space, such that for seventy years it was dominated by a government department, and latterly a government department and a public corporation, plus a small number of key telecoms equipment suppliers, often claimed to constitute a ring or cartel.

In Chapter Two we characterized the sixth age of telecommunications regulation, from the establishment of Oftel in 1984, as a *menage à trois* era, with Oftel, BT and the DTI the key players. The DTI's power to issue licences and other responsibilities meant that it remained at the centre of the regulatory space. The same went for BT, as a result of its information, experience and ability to veto Oftel's licence modification procedures.

Outside the *menage à trois* were more peripheral players. One was Mercury Communications Ltd (MCL), established by the government as a minor commercial rival to BT for market share, as discussed in Chapter Two. Mobile phone companies rapidly established themselves as important commercial players during the sixth age of telecoms regulation, but were not at the heart of the regulatory world. The Monopolies and Mergers Commission (MMC) was a brooding presence, because of its formal authority to arbitrate on licence modifications which could not be agreed between BT and Oftel (Figure 5.1). The European Union was barely visible at a time

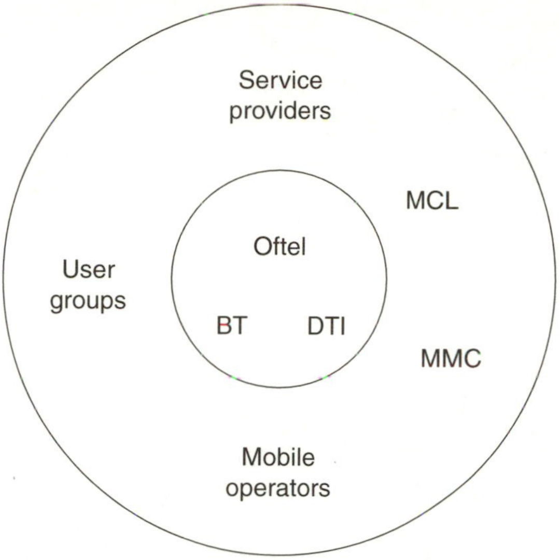

Figure 5.1 The telecommunications space circa 1985

when EU institutions were only just beginning to formulate a telecommunications policy for gradual liberalization, crystallized in a 1987 Green Paper (Scott, C. 1995).

By the seventh age of telecoms regulation, in the mid 1990s, the composition and configuration of the players had altered (see Figure 5.2). As we noted in Chapter Two, the UK Government's decision to promote network competition and end the duopoly for basic telecoms services allowed in many new firms, such as the cable companies which were largely backed by US money and experience, and actively promoted network competition and new technology. As we shall see in Chapter Seven, these new players became important to the regime not just in extension of competition, but also because they could provide information and policy advice to counter BT's previous dominant position in knowledge and expertise. Telecoms user groups could contribute knowledge or influence, and though such groups received active encouragement from Oftel limited resources often kept them on the sidelines.

Subsequently the liberalisation of international licences by the UK Government in 1996 and the 1996 EU Telecommunications Liberalisation Directive (96/19/EC) imposed new demands on Oftel and the telecoms industry, though EU institutions remained on the periphery of the British regulatory space.

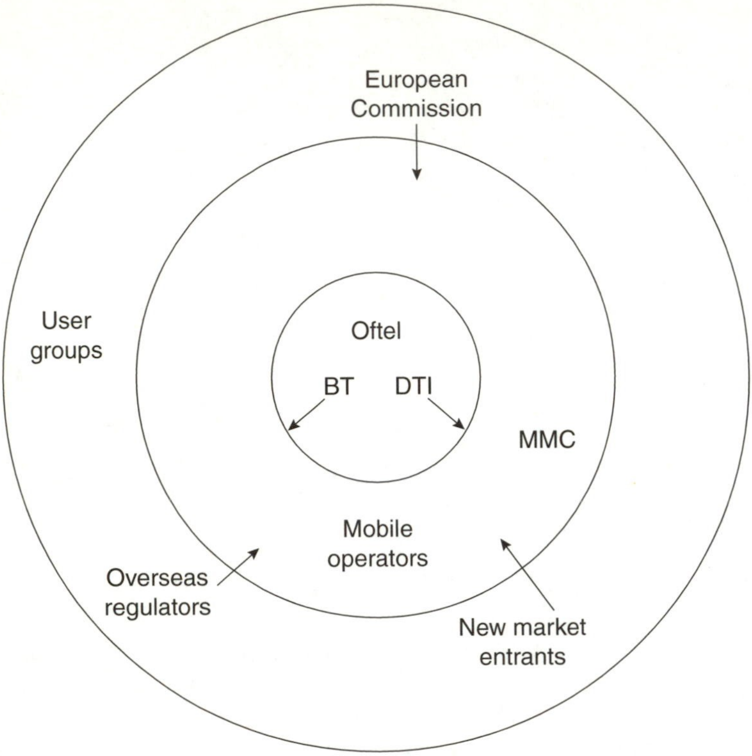

Figure 5.2 The telecommunications space circa 1996

These changes in the structure, capacities, and interests in the policy community in which it was embedded provided both the constraints and opportunities for Oftel to evolve and adapt in the ways described in Chapter Three. The attempts to upgrade itself into a competition authority reflected an urge for survival and also a jockeying for position in the face of the convergence of telecoms, broadcasting and computing technology. A fairly general perception was that sectoral regulators, administering detailed regulatory rules, were unlikely to survive in the brave new digital world (Scott 1998b). Added to that was the effect of globalization and the increasing role of both overseas and international authorities in shaping the regulatory environment. Effective boundaries were moving outwards. But such changes should not be overstated. The character of BT as a single, vertically-integrated former monopoly with a historical and political relationship with the government and

Oftel ensured for BT a continuing central position in the telecoms regulatory space. (*The Economist* 4th April 1998).

AN INTERDEPENDENT REGULATORY AGENCY

As noted in Chapter Two, regulation comprises three main tasks: policy making (or standard setting); monitoring and enforcement; and the application of sanctions. For each of these functions actors other than Oftel controlled key resources. Thus while Oftel was independent in terms of its capacity to reach its own judgements, it was interdependent with others in its capacity to act on those judgements (cf. Melody 1997b). The nature and extent of the dependency which this created changed over the sixth and seventh ages of telecoms regulation for several reasons, including the ending of the duopoly policy, referred to above, which reduced the DTI's control over the market through licensing, and also reduced the extent of BT's monopoly over information relevant both to policy making and enforcement (See Figure 5.2).

Policy making

Oftel's main policy instrument under the 1984 regime was the capacity to modify licence conditions. We noted in Chapter Two (Figure 2.2) some of the structural constraints on Oftel's capacity to modify licence conditions – the need for the consent of licensees or the approval of a modification by a third party, the Monopolies and Mergers Commission and the web of other powers of the DTI. As we shall argue in Chapter Six, the decision style in which issues were processed depended to some degree on how the distribution of formal authority combined with information and attitudes.

Relations with firms

BT's power to influence licence modifications, as noted earlier, gave it a leading role in shaping policy. When the duopoly was ended in 1991–2 BT's licence was amended to make better provision for interconnection – a key requirement of the newly liberalized regime. BT appears to have used its position to negotiate for favourable transitional arrangements (notably the requirement that interconnecting operators pay a contribution towards the loss that BT claimed it made on providing access to the network from its customers' premises

– the so-called Access Deficit Contribution (ADC)) (Oftel Press Release 17/91) and which were sufficiently complex as to make it difficult for Oftel or new entrants to lever open the market. Indeed, the new licence conditions negotiated by BT proved to be largely unworkable. A former senior BT manager, who had been involved in these negotiations, described the ADC regime as

> The first major mistake made by Oftel . . . Oftel allowed BT to pull the wool over its eyes on this, with many difficult consequences.

The same respondent later described it as 'an historic accounting mirage'. It is notable that MCL, the other duopoly operator, had nothing like the same access to Oftel as did BT and DTI officials. MCL became involved in the Duopoly Review very late and, justifiably, felt aggrieved because of it:

> 'We knew who had been in by flicking through the visitors book in Oftel – senior BT people, senior DTI people. . . . The Access Deficit Contribution was sprung on us by Carsberg on the day it was published', according to a former senior MCL manager (See also Vogel 1996: 87).

By the time the post-duopoly changes to the regime were put in place in 1992 other new entrants to the market had become more important for the policy of liberalization than MCL. The ADC regime included a power for the Director General to grant waivers of contributions in order to promote new entrant companies. Various interpretations exist as to why the concession was granted, but having made this commitment, Oftel was then obliged to draft formal criteria for granting such waivers in order to deliver on its promise. One industry figure commented that, nothwithstanding the incorporation of complex formal criteria into BT's licence,[1] it was widely felt within the industry that these measures were not sufficiently robust. DTI staff also had reservations about the new regime negotiated between BT and Oftel, and both the beneficiaries of the waivers and staff in Oftel feared a judicial review instigated by BT. But such a review never took place, perhaps because BT itself did not want the regime examined too closely.

BT's interests and capacities were not the only constraint on Oftel in negotiating new licence conditions after the ending of the duopoly policy. Negotiations over the modification of BT's licence were conducted in haste, in part to permit the Treasury to sell a further tranche of BT shares (see Chapter Two; also Vogel 1996: 87). With hindsight, senior Oftel staff believed that Oftel had been out-manoeuvred through time pressure and deliberately introduced complexity. BT's objectives were aligned with the government's share-sales agenda, and the available staff resources were so much greater in BT than in Oftel that the company could rapidly re-draft conditions under pressure of time and the regulator would then agree to them.

Under Don Cruickshank, however, Oftel became convinced by the arguments of the many new entrants that the ADC regime had to be completely abandoned and the subject of fresh licence modification as the whole interconnection regime was re-negotiated during 1994–5. It was not the only post 1992 condition which proved unworkable. The licence condition introduced in 1992 requiring BT to allow customers departing to new providers to take their numbers with them (known as number portability) permitted BT to charge such punitive rates that no interconnecting operator could take advantage of it. Even after the DGT had directed BT to grant number portability to a cable company, Videotron, in 1994 it was not possible for the parties to reach acceptable commercial terms under the provisions in the licence condition (MMC 1995: 3). Number portability, a key requirement for market entry, thus only became a realistic possibility after a further licence modification procedure.[2]

Thus, with a new DGT and the support of new players in the market, Oftel began to extricate itself from the quagmire which it had itself helped to construct. In wider discussions about interconnection costs and accounting separation, new entrant firms were actively encouraged by Oftel to participate in policy debate in order to counterweight BT and to do so through co-operation as an industry group. Indeed, members of the Cable Communications Association (CCA) were meeting weekly as a group during our study to share views and information on regulatory policy. According to one of the committee members the committee covered:

> the waterfront of regulation, on the premise that it is what Oftel, DTI and others want. The Committee provides a single cable voice. It helps to speak with a single voice and weeds out the wilder ideas, provides a more responsible voice. We [the respondent's company] work through CCA as far as possible but it is not intended to stop individual companies speaking.[3]

Though the bilateral structure of licence modifications excluded the other Public Telecommunications Operators (PTOs), by consultation with other players Oftel could gain intelligence, probe the issues and negotiate with BT armed and shielded by the industry consensus.

One senior regulatory manager in a small firm described a range of contacts with Oftel including a summit with the DGT two or three times a year, monthly meetings between the other licenced operators (OLOs) and the DDG, and much more regular contact with lower level staff a few times each week. According to one regulatory manager:

> The OLO group is one of new entrants and Oftel. BT is excluded, though they have access through Cellnet and we are aware of this. BT and Oftel are in a bilateral relationship . . . The policy of greater openness, of asking questions of BT in public is very useful in putting the views of BT on the public record but basically nothing new is revealed, no surprises, because people like me are paid to know what is going on.

Though OLOs were treated as a constituent group, the view of one senior OLO manager was that this treatment masked the existence of an inner circle of key people whose views were highly valued. This small group consisted of regulatory managers who had had long experience in telecoms and were known and trusted by others in Oftel and BT. For instance, industry workshops were first held in 1993 to deal with Interconnection and Accounting Separation (ICAS), but Oftel used smaller working groups to develop detailed issues and referred to these hand-picked working groups as the 'magic circle'. For Oftel these people were at the centre of the regulatory space and able to be influential at an early stage in the formation of policy although their existence was not recognized by those outside the inner circle.

Relations with the DTI

We have discussed relations between Oftel and the DTI in Chapters Three and Four. Though the DTI's role in telecoms regulation was partly hidden (Hansard Society 1996: 63; Doern 1998: 31; Wilks 1998: 139), the DTI was a central player in the sixth and seventh ages of telecoms regulation (Wilks 1998: 140). Its interest was demonstrated by high frequency of contact between the DTI and Oftel at all levels (not just with the DGT, as discussed in the last chapter). One senior DTI civil servant said he was in contact with Oftel several times a day. The DTI typically commented on draft Oftel documents on substantive issues and vice versa when it was of specific interest to Oftel. 'For example, the recent interconnect document is OK on policy but we think it is very badly written.' Any failure to keep the DTI informed would produce a letter of protest. Another senior DTI official commented:

> We try for early covers of the [Oftel] Consultation Documents, but we don't get them. Again a cultural difference between the traditional Civil Service and Oftel: In the Civil Service it is a capital offence NOT to show a document at an early enough stage but we get a 30 or 40 page document from Oftel with only 24 hours notice and this is because we can't see it until Don has seen it and he only sees it at the end . . . It is annoying, dangerous, but better an active regulator than one in stupor.

Reflecting on the changes in Oftel discussed in Chapter Three, a DTI official suggested that the need to keep Oftel under control on policy-making had increased in its third life-stage because 'there are more people in Oftel from outside the Civil Service who just don't have consultation bred in their bones as we do'. (ie consultation with the DTI not public consultation). The same respondent described the exchange of papers and views as 'a triangulation of ideas'. It is not surprising that the DTI and Oftel might have taken different views on issues. The two departments had different interests and orientations. Most obviously, the DTI also dealt with sponsorship of the telecoms industry and UK telecoms companies world wide while Oftel was concerned solely with regulation.

> This makes sense actually, because it is their responsibility, part of their job, to think about the effect on UK firms and on the UK market. It is OK because it [is] what they should be doing . . . You can have conflicts but the regulators should consider the industry. (Senior DTI official).

The policy episodes discussed later in this book suggest the DTI tended to be cautious about exercising its substantial back-stop power over Oftel. Only when the stakes were very high did the DTI intervene, and not always consistently (see Chapter Nine).

Relations with the users

As noted in Chapter Three, consumer and other user groups were actively encouraged by Oftel to participate in policy debates (Doern and Wilks 1998: 15). Indeed, one senior manager in an OLO thought that consumer groups were 'over-influential in some areas, considering how poorly they argue' and this view was widely shared within the industry. BT engaged in lobbying of the publicly-funded National Consumer Council (NCC), the private Consumers Association (CA) and the local voluntary Telecommunications Advisory Committees ((TACs), established under the Telecommunications Acts 1984 as successors to the local consultative groups for postal and telecommunications services), were considered within Oftel to have been totally captured by BT. During an internal meeting about consumer representation one Senior Policy Advisor commented that 'One TAC even referred to Mercury as "the enemy" '. Oftel was not the central node for all regulatory activity. Notably, the regulator was by-passed in discussions between the CA and BT about disconnection policy.

A specific example of consumer influence was in the development of Universal Service policy. This issue was politically sensitive because it cut across the contradictory economic and social objectives of regulation. Oftel thought it had a simple solution: abandon any ideas of complex costing and setting up a universal service fund and simply make BT provide all services to everyone, including uneconomic customers. This proposal was based on a calculation that the advantages of reputation and ubiquity more than compensated for the financial costs to BT.

> [The Minister] said he would support Oftel if we had the consumer bodies on board. It was hard work with the consumer bodies, but they agreed – if it would support the OLOs. [The Minister] was delighted . . .

since the benefit of universal access was achieved at no political risk to himself or the Government, according to a senior Oftel official.

Though the shift towards more open decision-making in the seventh age of telecoms regulation should have fostered greater consumer participation, the two major groups, the NCC and the CA, lacked the resources to attempt a complete overview of regulatory issues in the sector. Within Oftel there was often frustration at the delay by consumer bodies in responding to consultation documents[4] and the selective approach such bodies adopted over which documents to respond to.[5] The NCC, for example, had not involved itself in the policy debate on numbering because the NCC saw its chief focus as pricing, access and standards of service. As a result of overload the CA had to withdraw from participation in drawing up Comparative

Performance Indicators for the industry. It was Oftel, not the CA, which demonstrated that residential customers had benefited from a reduction in bills of only RPI–2.7% in a period of six years when the overall price cap on BT shifted from RPI–4.5% to RPI–6.25% (1991) to RPI–7.5% (1993), a finding that shaped the 1996 Price Control Review (discussed in Chapter Seven).

Relations with other parts of government

Oftel's environment was affected in uncertain ways by the conduct of other parts of government, including the MMC and other utilities regulators. Given the MMC's potential role in telecoms regulation discussed earlier, Oftel, like other utility regulators, consulted with the MMC over licence modification timetables. Thus the 1992 and 1996 Price Control Reviews (PCRs) were run in such a way that there was a period of more than six months for general consultation plus a further year, if needed, for an MMC reference, with the licence modification to be in place 20 months after the process started. Though the threat of an MMC reference was constantly present, both over licence modification and anti-competitive conduct, very few references had been made by Oftel. Chapter Nine shows how Oftel used the threat of an MMC referral to bolster its bargaining position, but did not actually carry out its threat.

One reason why Oftel wanted to avoid MMC references was the MMC's very closed processes. On the only major MMC reference on a telecoms licence modification (number portability) in 1995 (MMC 1995) Oftel and BT each gave evidence and BT's evidence was not made available to Oftel. A senior Oftel person commented:

> A process where anyone is in a position to win an argument through use of information is very weak. One might question the degree of openness but it is necessary to destroy sole access to information as a basis for power.

Part of Oftel's response to the MMC problem was to work actively with other regulators on definition of regulatory issues and problem-solving. 'Oftel puts a lot of effort into saying it is not a utilities regulator and faces different issues, but the others are coming along behind very fast', said one senior Oftel official. In fact Oftel engaged in co-operation with other utilities regulatory offices at every level. In 1994 the Economic Advisers of the several Offices of Telecommunications, Water Supply (Ofwat), Gas Supply (Ofgas), the

Civil Aviation Authority and the MMC met to reach agreement on a common basis for cost of capital assessment. They were pooling knowledge and expertise to build common practice and to second-guess the conclusion in the event that price control licence modifications from any of the utility sectors were referred to the MMC. Such co-operation was helpful because price control reviews occurred at different times in the different sectors and the experience of one reference to the MMC in one sector could be fed informally into a later review in another sector. These lower level contacts continued and were subsequently supplemented by monthly meetings between Deputy DGs of the several regulators, and more formal quarterly meetings between DGs. Inevitably there were also periodic informal contacts by telephone. Areas of common interest included powers to publish information, low user customers and problems with judicial review. Over a key licence modification proposal (discussed in Chapter Nine) Oftel deliberately sought support against the DTI from the other regulatory offices, initially through chance low-level contacts, and later through high level meetings. A very senior staff member in one of the other utility regulatory offices described such co-operation over the need to improve the UK competition regime as 'very valuable'.

Obviously there were limits to the 'one for all and all for one' approach of co-operation among utilities regulators. The same respondent thought the quarterly meetings 'don't work. . . . everything is rather on the surface, we don't really discuss issues'. For example, it had not been possible to agree a joint submission to the Government's Regulatory Review in 1997 because of lack of agreement over the key issues. Common themes tended to become obscured by different priorities and policy timing.

Oftel often found the interface between itself and other government organizations to be problematic. Difficulties emerged both because of tensions over turf (for example between Oftel and the Independent Television Commission (ITC)) and because Oftel had developed practices of transparency which were somewhat more open than civil service tradition dictated. One commentator noted:

> The abrasive and effective regulation of Oftel under its dynamic Director, Don Cruickshank, has succeeded in impressing the European Commission with its effectiveness, but offending the television regulator ITC with its tactlessness, notably in Oftel advice to ITC regarding the BDB digital multiplex licence award in June 1997
>
> (Marsden 1997).

The transparency of Oftel's opinions thus had the potential to embarrass other agencies, particularly when Oftel held its own line against the views held by other bodies within overlapping jurisdictions. More generally Oftel proved to be a leader in developing more transparent procedures for policy making which were influential in Whitehall and in other government bodies. For example, while the consultation processes were designed to improve the position of the participants in the immediate telecoms policy debate, the new procedures also touched other departments and agencies which were put under pressure to explain why they were less transparent in policy making. As a very senior staff member in another regulatory office commented:

> It's a bit of a pain. A lot of what they put out I can't see the point of – but they regulate a more complex industry . . . Like their consultation document on how to consult: it just wouldn't be appropriate because our industry isn't as complex and they already think we consult too much . . . It becomes too bureaucratic . . . for example their [Annual Management Plan] just isn't appropriate for [us]. [The industry] could have a copy of our plan if they wanted it but no one would dream of ever asking for it. There is a risk that inappropriate procedures will become enshrined in the regime after the review.

A senior DTI official commented: 'DTI processes themselves have become more transparent. For the international facilities liberalization we published documents in the pre-period: spring, summer and autumn, and then a formal period of consultation'. This, he acknowledged, was based on the Oftel's example and he saw it 'as a means to improve the quality of regulatory policy making'.

The European and international dimension

When we began our study in 1994 there was little evidence that European and international affairs and policy were of interest to Oftel, however BT was already well-represented in Brussels where it was regarded as one of the most effective lobbyists of the Commission. As Oftel came to realize that EC policy had the potential to affect the UK regime it increasingly sought to cultivate good relationships with Commission officials involved in the development of EC telecommunications policy. A senior Commission official in DG IV (Competition) said:

> Oftel keep us informed of issues, send published documents, etc. [of which] we have a full set and we use them and keep them as reference documents . . . We regard Oftel as the most sophisticated of the [National Regulatory Authorities (NRAs)] and they are very helpful to us.

Generally the Commission sought to develop close working relationships with NRAs, but secured co-operation with an implicit threat of intervention. A Commission official in DG XIII (Telecommunications) commented:

> [W]e publish guidance for Member States – cost accounting for interconnections, etc. We have bilateral meetings with the NRAs, 6 monthly high-level meetings with [Commission Directors General]. There are also lower level meetings with officials to get commission ideas across. We watch things very closely . . . The NRAs want to do their job and we try to help them with best practice, guidelines, etc.

Though the UK had generally been ahead of EC telecommunications policy in liberalizing the UK telecommunications market, some cracks were beginning to appear by the mid 1990s. It became clear that the UK mode of liberalization and particular detailed choices were difficult to reconcile with Community thinking. The UK regulatory policy which promoted network competition (alongside competition in services) was regarded by Commission officials as more *dirigiste* than EC policy. Thus a particular UK decision to reject a policy of equal access for long distance operators was problematic for the Commission (as well as for the US Federal Communications Commission – see below).

The Commission-Oftel contact was equally felt to be very important as each side sought to influence the policy direction of the other. For Oftel, good contact with the Commission over policy making was not entirely straightforward. The Foreign Office (through the UK Permanent Representation (UKREP) in Brussels) and the DTI (in the Council of Ministers) took the lead for the UK in EC policy fora. Oftel had a duty to 'advise' but this duty increasingly meant full participation. Personal Whitehall contacts proved significant again, as the Oftel staff member dealing day-to-day with EC policy had worked previously with his opposite number dealing with telecommunications in UKREP:

> I'm now routinely copied in for all their documents and I'm on the phone to him frequently. If you don't have personal links then it is difficult. I got off to a really bad start with the other guy.

This personal link made the anomalous position of Oftel, as a non-ministerial department with a profound interest in EU policy (as discussed in the last chapter), somewhat easier to accommodate.

As we noted in the last chapter, international contacts between Oftel and other regulators were a source of some anxiety to the DTI. A senior DTI official said: 'We can't hold back Don if he wants to meet [the Chairman of the FCC] . . . but we need rules . . . as getting mixed messages is fairly disastrous when playing a game of poker like that'.

Part of the pressure on Oftel to assume a more international presence was that other NRAs, often newly organized in a newly liberalized market, were keen to learn from the experience gained in the UK telecommunications industry. Oftel had a constant stream of visitors and more requests than it had resources to accommodate for training and meetings. These requests had to be evaluated according to tight criteria of economic importance to the UK and emerging markets. Many of the NRAs assumed Oftel was the sole authority and did not see or comprehend the role of the DTI as the other telecommunications regulator.

Monitoring and enforcement

As we noted in Chapter Two, Oftel faced a less crowded policy space over monitoring and enforcing licence conditions than it did over policy making; but as we saw earlier a combination of information, experience and high quality staff gave BT informal authority over the interpretation of licence conditions to the extent that it had traditionally sustained the senior role in interpreting its own licence conditions. The result was that the powers formally available to Oftel were not used. For example, the potentially powerful Condition 17 in BT's licence, prohibiting undue preference and discrimination by BT in favour of its own business or the business of others, was for many years believed by Oftel to have little effect in preventing anti-competitive conduct by BT. This position changed only once new firms moved into the regulatory space and created pressure for new interpretations of the conditions (discussed in more detail in Chapter Nine).

In principle the European Commission could have taken on a direct enforcement role in the UK telecoms sector, to the extent that anti-competitive activities of telecoms firms affected inter-state trade within the EU. However, this potential was not realized during the period of the study. The Commission took care not to tread on the toes of NRAs like Oftel. When British PTOs complained to the Commission about alleged breaches of EC competition law the Commission declared itself unlikely to intervene and use its own powers to enforce EC rules directly if the matter was also under the domestic regulator's jurisdiction. In that sense subsidiarity governed the relationship, constraining the use of powers formally available to the Commission. 'The preference is for the NRA to deal with an issue unless we feel they can't do so' according to a senior Commission official (see also Coates 1999).

Where the Commission was engaged in reviewing mergers between telecoms companies, such as BT-MCI and Cable and Wireless Communication, the common view was that the merger should be permitted only if certain conditions were applied to the merged entity. A senior Commission official (DG IV) commented:

> Under competition law these [conditions] are part of DG IV's powers, but these may, in practice, be very similar to the regulatory aims of OFT and Oftel so we always ask OFT and Oftel 'who is going to impose these conditions?' . . . We [then] avoid saying them in different words, we avoid multiple conditions . . . The Commission has a duty, if necessary, to ensure that NRAs comply with Community law, eg that NRAs do not approve behaviour which is contrary to Community competition law.

Oftel had become increasingly involved in issues concerning, for example, the ability of UK PTOs to secure access to EC markets and to be treated fairly, by early 1997, it had not really worked out the ground rules for this sort of work, and in particular how relations of shared competence between NRAs were to be decided. As more problems were brought to Oftel's door an internal brainstorming meeting was organized. A general view expressed was that industry problems relating to the EC must be drawn to the attention of a competent authority, both within the other Member States and in the UK if it was not within the competence of Oftel or DTI. This doctrine would increasingly involve Oftel in communication with other NRAs. The meeting considered there would be risks associated in challenging the views of a NRA in Europe or, indeed, in Oftel itself being challenged by another NRA (as it was by the FCC, see below). In general the Oftel culture of informality, discussed in Chapter Three, was to be preferred in managing such relations. One director commented:

> Doing things on an informal level gets them done more quickly but only a limited number of people should be able to make [a phone call from Oftel to another NRA], there should be boxes to be ticked, you can't do it will-nilly.

This meeting demonstrated that the character of the regulatory space was changing rapidly. The ordinary policy branches were beginning to recognize that they were operating in an increasingly European system of regulation. Subsequently a series of internal lunch-time seminars on how the individual EU Directives on telecommunications would influence the UK regime was organized.

Application of sanctions

The sanctions available to a regulator like Oftel to secure compliance consist of formal and informal measures which can be threatened or applied. As shown in Chapter Two, Oftel was hamstrung over formal sanctions and could only seek orders from the High Court, subsequent breach of which might result in a financial penalty or damages to a third party affected by a continuing breach. No formal sanction of this type had ever been deployed by Oftel up to the time of writing. The dependence of Oftel on the courts for the application of formal sanctions is typical of UK regulatory regimes (and in marked contrast with the independent capacity of many federal US regulators and the European Commission [in its competition jurisidiction]). This dependence seems to be part of the reason why sanctions were never applied, allied with cultural preferences for informality which are discussed further in Chapter Nine.

The main informal sanction possessed by Oftel was shaming through publication. While publication was not deployed systematically, it was used occasionally. For instance, Oftel successfully launched a shaming campaign against BT in 1987, publishing monthly statistics for public payphone reliability after a marked decline in service standards (Scott 1993b). In fact, given that Oftel could use publicity as an informal sanction without recourse to any other organization, it is surprising that publicity did not have a higher status in the regulatory armoury.

ACCOUNTABILITY AND INTERDEPENDENCE

The existence of interdependence within a policy or regulatory space has long been recognized as having implications for accountability relationships (see Hague, MacKenzie and Barker 1975). Accountability is a multi-faceted concept (Day and Klein 1987: Chapter 1) and we do not seek to offer a new synthesis here. Rather we suggest how our account of relations within the regulatory space might support arguments that the main accountability of a regulator like Oftel may be to significant others in its policy community rather than in formal reporting requirements. This involves considering both the formal and extended accountability mechanisms applied not only to Oftel, but also to the other actors – ministers, regulators, firms – who wield power (Wilks 1998: 140). So, Oftel's practical obligation to answer for its decisions and behaviour to the various actors wielding power within its policy community may be more of a constraint on its activity than the formal mechanisms of accountability in holding the regulator within the boundaries of reasonable regulation. Such a claim – a variant on the well-known Bagehot (1963: 61) distinction between efficient and dignified power – is supported by the observation that perceptions that Oftel was making a decent job of regulation in a substantive sense were more important to Oftel's top brass than conceptions of formal legitimacy (based, for example on perceptions as to whether the regulator uses appropriate processes (cf. Ogus 1994: 110)). The balance between these two types of legitimacy generated by such a distinction is actively, constantly negotiated to conform to cultural values, preferences and norms and to fit the current telecommunications environment.

We stress the importance of substantive reputation rather than formal reporting requirements, even though Oftel was much more likely to find itself subject to the constraints of formal accountability in the seventh age of telecoms regulation than in the sixth. Formal mechanisms for Oftel's actions to be examined *post hoc* through the presentation of annual reports and accounts were often argued to be weak (see Graham 1995). In the sixth age the chief formal accountability requirements were the submission of an annual report to the minister, the obligation to answer to Parliamentary select committees and the standard financial and audit controls imposed on any government department, underpinned by the obligation to account, if necessary, to the Public Accounts Committee (PAC).

Formal accountability

Nothwithstanding the existence of various formal accountability mechanisms in the sixth age of telecoms regulation, their potential was only really developed in the seventh age. National Audit Office Value for Money investigations into aspects of Oftel's work (NAO 1993, 1996, 1998) seemed to hold little terror for the organization: Oftel staff did not appear to respect the NAO's methodology and analysis. The most challenging part of the scrutiny was thought to be the subsequent public hearing before the PAC (and equally hearings before other Parliamentary Committees such as the Trade and Industry Select Committee). The DGT had practice sessions with other regulators and one regulator, in turn, admitted to a practice session with 'tame journalists'. But in general select committees were only capable of picking up the most appalling blunders, whether presentational or substantive.[6]

The courts also became more involved in the scrutiny of Oftel's activities in the seventh age, as liberalization challenged the consensual arrangements of the *menage à trois* era and tended to put regulatory relationships on a more formal footing (Scott 1998a). Though the attentions of the courts to Oftel's work were far from systematic[7] – litigation was a device invoked sporadically by licensees for commercial advantage – the juridical turn in regulatory relations did have pronounced effects. As noted in Chapter Three, the legal branch, which had not been influential in Oftel's early days, took on a more important role in ensuring that Oftel's decision-making could be demonstrated to be lawful, reasonable and fair (in the terms of a potential judicial review action). Key players in several firms thought the threat of litigation over an Oftel decision by a major player such as BT might have to be counterbalanced by equivalent threats from smaller operators – to attempt to neutralize the litigation risk for the regulator. Facing litigation Oftel itself took a robust approach to the defence of its position. In the first major legal challenge to Oftel, an action brought by MCL in 1994/5 to challenge the DGT's interpretation of the interconnection obligations in BT's licence, one Oftel Branch Head indicated that top Oftel staff privately encouraged special efforts to be made to 'stuff Mercury' in the court and so 'demonstrate that Oftel will not be thrown off course by litigation'. The DGT publicly indicated at an industry workshop in 1994 that in the event of MCL succeeding on the substantive issue, which was ultimately abandoned by MCL, he might find it necessary to reverse the decision by licence modification.[8]

Court decisions were invariably read across the several utility regulatory regimes. After a Court of Appeal decision which quashed a decision of the Director General of Electricity Supply (Scott 1997), Don Cruickshank commented to us that he felt he and Oftel were '. . . as accountable as any one else under the rules of the land. A few more court cases – not us though! – and it will be clear'.

Litigation bolstered formal legitimacy in other ways. On being questioned by the Trade and Industry Select Committee about his implementation of the Fair Trading licence condition (discussed in Chapters Eight and Nine), the DGT, fresh from a Divisional Court victory over BT, was able to swat the question. When put to the DGT that he now would have powers 'to become prosecutor, judge and jury' he replied:

> The people who matter, the judges, have denied all of that, so it is not a matter of what I think or what the *Daily Telegraph* thinks, it is a matter of what the courts of the land have decided about what the Telecommunications Act means, how I should exercise the discretion and how I should pursue my duties under that Act. That issue is now resolved, and I hope that some of that language that you quote will go away. (Trade and Industry Select Committee 1996: 48).

Extended accountability

Notwithstanding the weak formal accountability mechanisms both this chapter and the last suggest that efficient or extended accountability of Oftel and the DGT was greater than the rhetoric of independence suggested. Oftel's actions were constrained by the capacities of the others within the regulatory space: the regulated companies and the other UK and international regulatory authorities and user groups.

CONCLUSION

This chapter has described the position of Oftel in a heavily populated regulatory space. Oftel shared the centre of the space with BT and the DTI as a result of historical process and the commercial power of the former monopoly. Changes in the market and regulatory regime initially had only modest effects on the relations between these three actors because they remained in a relatively fixed pattern of the legislative framework and cultural values. Movement occurred after the 1991–2 Duopoly Review as Government policy promoted a liberalized licensing regime and network competition. The regulatory space became more dynamic as new entrants moved in. Meanwhile the space came increasingly to be governed by EU Directives and pressures of globalization. Oftel was therefore forced to adapt to new environmental conditions or become extinct.

Oftel's adaptive response – moving into new territory, behaving in new ways – provoked action and reaction amongst the other bodies in the telecoms regulatory world. The process was debated in terms of accountability and independence, in debate about formal powers and substantive legitimacy. The formal mechanisms of accountability for Oftel were comparatively weak and a more powerful influence shaping Oftel's behaviour seems to have been its *de facto* obligation to answer to the other actors within the regulatory space. At first the main interlocutors were the other two members of the *menage à trois* established in 1984, but in the new environment of the seventh age new demands for greater transparency, more formal enforcement of licence conditions and a trend towards general rules not specific conditions arose (discussed further in Chapters Eight and Nine). Oftel was subject to pushes and pulls in a more complex regulatory space comprising substantive checks and balances, but without anybody obviously in overall charge of monitoring and amending them where necessary. The theoretical risk of classic agency capture was reduced by the checks and balances, even if there had been a form of capture in the early years of the regulatory regime. That early capture was more Gramscian hegemony than Stiglerian 'nobbling' in the form of BT's ability to secure licence conditions so complex that only it could interpret them. If that was capture, it was capture of the regime, rather than of Oftel, made possible by the priority given by the Treasury to raising revenue both on privatization and at the end of the duopoly review (as discussed in Chapter Two).

One feature of Oftel's strategy to overcome this form of capture through complexity was a search for allies on particular issues. On some issues the OLOs were important allies and for others the consumer groups and European Community institutions also provided critical support. Co-operation with other regulatory offices, though attempted for its potential in boosting Oftel's own capacities, was felt to be limited. On some issues even BT was an ally rather than an antagonist, for example in arguing for new competition legislation which Oftel would enforce (see Chapter Nine). Much of the ambiguity, fluidity and dynamism of the regulatory space was exemplified in the international sphere where Oftel was forced to ally itself with the DTI, as discussed in the last chapter, because the DTI possessed the formal powers and owned trade policy, even though Oftel staff were often closer to other national and international regulators than the DTI.

Overall, Oftel can be seen as a regulatory agency constrained within a bounded space, but one that was resourceful in using shifting alliances to secure as much as it could from the opportunities within the structure and its lacunae and employing considerable imagination, resourcefulness and energy to re-shape the regulatory environment.

Part IV

Decision-making

6 Regulatory decision styles

> 'Is that a decision?' asked Frank.
> 'Yes, that's final,' I said. 'And now I'm going home.'
> 'Is *that* a decision?' asked Sir Humphrey . . .
>
> Lynn and Jay, *Yes Minister* (1981: 84–5)

REGULATION AS ISSUE-PROCESSING

Telecoms regulation as an issue-machine

Unlike some other government organizations (such as mints, laboratories or munition factories) regulators do not generally produce physical outputs except in the form of documents.[1] They can be thought of as organizations providing services to government, the public at large or specific individuals or organizations in forms such as assurance, security, information, adjustment of the distribution of risk, liability and market power. That 'service' (not that everyone would describe it in those terms) is produced through the medium of decisions. Some of those decisions are juridical or quasi-juridical acts – expressed in rulings, adjudications, determinations, standards, official notices. Some are decisions about decisions, more informal decisions or even decisions not to decide. Abstractly, a regulatory system can be regarded as an issue-machine, a phrase coined by David Braybrooke (1974) to denote a structure in which alternative options are processed in some order of succession and through a range of stations in a series of decision rounds.

As earlier chapters have shown, Oftel was only one of the stations in the UK telecoms regulation issue-machine, albeit an important one. Powers of standard-setting over UK telecoms were shared among several bodies. EU institutions had powers to set framework rules for regulation in the member states. UK Ministers had powers to issue telecoms licences with operating conditions and in some cases to modify licence conditions in order to secure compliance with EU rules. Oftel had general powers to begin licence condition modification processes. Licensees in general – and BT in particular – had formal powers to withhold consent from proposed licence modifications, and substantial informal influence over the shaping of standards. Oftel was the main station in the issue-machine with formal powers over monitoring for compliance with the regulatory regime, because it was entitled to require licensees to provide some types of information. (In practice most evidence of non-compliance with regulatory rules came from industry informers monitoring the regulatory compliance behaviour of their competitors.[2]) When it came to the application of sanctions, Oftel had powers to issue orders and make determinations on disputes, but the courts alone had the power to impose formal sanctions. There was little scope for third parties, competitors or consumers to invoke sanctions in the regulatory regime. In practice such sanctions as Oftel was able to deploy were largely informal, comprising threats, unco-operative behaviour and public shaming through publication of documents.

Within this overall issue-machine, Oftel was continuously engaged in decision-making of a variety of types. Some of its decisions were public front-office decisions that embodied the outcomes of a formal regulatory process, such as licence modifications, the issuing of orders against licensees or determinations of disputes. Such decisions were carried out under statutory procedures, with publication of outcomes. Others were less public or less formal decisions – to issue informal advice to a firm in the hope of modifying its behaviour or to broker a solution to a customer complaint outside the framework of formal rules and powers. A third category was decisions about Oftel's 'internal policies' (Hawkins and Thomas 1989: 6). These were decisions about systems or approaches, how to run the organization or what its priorities should be. Some internal policy decisions were the product of relatively formal consultative processes about how future regulatory decisions were to be taken or what issues should take priority. Others were strictly back-office decisions, invisible from outside, over issues such as how and who to recruit, how to allocate budgetary resources, when to consult ministers or others on particular issues.

Decision styles

Given the variety of decisions being taken within the Oftel issue-machine, it would be surprising if there was any one overall style or approach. But identifying different decision styles is tricky. There is no single generally-accepted typology of such styles, in spite – or more likely because – of a large and diffuse literature on institutional decision-making across the social sciences.[3] Categorizing decisions empirically is difficult because observers and participants differ in what they see. Nevertheless, our observations of regulatory decision-making within Oftel led us to identify at least three different styles which were briefly identified in the first chapter. Labelling these styles is highly problematic, because which name we chose for which style strongly affected the views of participants about which style they felt they should be associated with. So we finally opted for a double-barrelled labelling method that combined words with positive and negative resonances for each type, and labelled them Cartesian-bureaucratic, adhocratic-chaotic and bargaining-diplomatic.

We used Cartesian-bureaucratic to denote a decision process in which an organization functions as a relatively self-contained decision unit and processes issues in a style that approximates to the mechanical rationality of classical bureaucracy, applying well-worked-out internal principles or routines to each new case or problem it encounters to arrive at a determination or solution. Decision processes of this type follow standard operating routines in which objectives or principles are determined in advance, and each case or problem is systematically scanned as it goes through the system.

Some of the decisions taken by Oftel approximated to that style. For example, with most consumer complaints handled by Oftel's Consumer Representation Section (CRS), the issue was handled by a single case officer who had the customer's version of events and, in most cases, a clear idea of the standards to which the licensee was expected to adhere. A telephone call to the licensee could, in most cases, procure their side of the story and the case officer could then process the issue by fitting it into a category and invoking the follow-up action that matched that category. Some higher level policy decisions, such as the telephone numbering case that we discuss in the next chapter, also approximated to a pattern that involved applying pre-set technical principles to a problem to arrive at a determinate solution.

Cartesian-bureaucratic decision-making may be a version of Max Weber's famous vision of bureaucracy (and the judiciary) as pre-programmed slot machines applying categorization principles to cases in order to handle them, or may follow the classic rational-decision procedure in which objectives are worked out in advance, alternative possible ways of reaching the objectives or satisfying the principles are identified for each case or problem, information is collected and brought together about each of the alternatives, and the best or most appropriate solution is adopted (March and Olsen 1989: 27). Machine bureaucracies and even professional bureaucracies, in the organizational classification used by the Canadian management guru Henry Mintzberg (1983) may be expected to deploy such comprehensive rationality approaches to processing information. But all organizations, and most particularly public bureaucracies, are expected to present themselves as rational issue-processing machines (Brunsson 1989), and there is a constant stream of tidy managerial thinking and advice coming off the management presses (of the 'first agree your objectives, then solve your problems' variety). So it is hardly surprising that Oftel's public image was strongly Cartesian-bureaucratic and that in interviews and discussion the first response of most of Oftel's higher-level participants was to represent the decision process in those terms.

However, much of the literature on institutional decision-making stresses the limits of mechanical rationality and the pervasiveness of happenstance and non-linear issue processing. This theme has been strongly established in organization theory since March and Simon's stress on 'bounded rationality' in their 1958 classic, and since then there has been a growing body of writing about fuzzy decision processes (Grint 1997). This stresses the extent to which even – perhaps particularly – the most successful organizations tend to depart from the Cartesian-bureaucratic decision style. For Mintzberg (1983: 263), adhocratic decision styles involve ever-changing structures of participation, lack of certain knowledge of problems and methods and strategy that is 'not so much formulated consciously by individuals as formed implicitly by the decisions they take', and they are associated with many of the leading business organizations of the late twentieth century, in the worlds of high-technology and art, fashion or style. Cohen, March and Olsen's (1972) well-known garbage can model is a more formal (and earlier) account of what Mintzberg calls adhocracy. It draws attention to a form of organizational decision-making in which elements come together like the items that appear in a garbage can or computer recycle bin, in a semi-random way, in a decision-making style which encompasses unclear objectives, uncertain technology or means-ends relationships and a fluid pattern of participation. The organizational sociologist Charles Perrow (1984) has applied the model to a famous analysis of the limits of high-reliability strategies in organizations, and the public policy analyst John Kingdon (1984) has applied it to produce an equally well-known account of the unpredictable interaction of different elements in the policy process, stressing the role of policy entrepreneurs in coupling problems, proposals and political forces at the points where policy 'windows' open. Oftel had many features of an adhocracy in Mintzberg's terms, or of an entrepreneurial bureaucracy (in the phrase used by Corwin (1983) to denote public organizations that recruit bright and aggressive staff, encourage innovation and value expertise more highly than seniority). It was perhaps not surprising that we identified a strain of decision-making within the organization that we labelled as adhocratic-chaotic.

Sometimes adhocracy just happened, but on other occasions it was deliberately injected into the Oftel decision-making process, particularly through Don Cruickshank's style of management as DGT, discussed in Chapter Four. For instance, the Price Control Review of BT that concluded in 1996, discussed further in Chapter Seven, could have been conducted in a stereotypical Cartesian-bureaucratic style. After all, previous price control reviews had established a pattern. There was a well-established procedure, experienced staff, broad consensus on relevant information and clear objective outputs. In the light of the disappointing effect of past Price Reviews to pull BT's rate of return on capital down to the target range, Don Cruickshank chose to inject a little chaos into the PCR process. He set aside the established conventions by insisting that the parameters of the technocratic economic models be set at the extreme of desired outputs, rather than the median more generally expected and preferred within the civil service tradition. He introduced uncertainty into the process by floating in and out of decision-making in an unpredictable fashion, or by allowing his staff to reach a conclusion before he reopened the issue and introduced new variables or actors. His staff hated it. Yet the injection of this adhocratic-chaotic overlay into the normal Cartesian-bureaucratic style produced a tighter and more focused price control.

Cartesian-bureaucratic and adhocratic-chaotic decision styles represent opposite ends of a spectrum. Somewhere in between them we observed another style which we labelled bargaining-diplomatic. In this third style what Desmond Keeling (1972) identified as the diplomatic element of management in government is emphasized, in that outcomes that are acceptable to all the participants or stakeholders in a process are sought through negotiation and bargaining. Such a style is commonly observable in institutional decision-making generally (March and Olsen 1989: 24) and in regulatory decision-making more particularly (Hawkins and Thomas 1989: Chapter 1) and links in to a vast literature on negotiation and bargaining within organizations and policy communities. It is less programmed than the Cartesian-bureaucratic style, in that the final outcome depends on what the various participants will accept rather than on the pre-set objectives of any one organization.

We identified at least two forms of this type of decision-making. The first type, the form of informal negotiation commonly observed in socio-legal studies of regulation (Grabosky and Braithwaite 1986; Bardach and Kagan 1982; Hawkins and Thomas 1984), has rarely been explicitly identified in studies of telecommunications or utilities regulation. The second form, formal bargaining, has been more commonly identified for the UK telecommunications sector, at least in terms of the delineation of the structural features of the regulatory regime, if not of the process itself (Graham and Prosser 1991: 213; Armstrong Cowan and Vickers 1994: 360). The first type was a process of continuous interaction and synchronization of attitudes and beliefs among key players within Oftel and the wider policy community more generally which served to negotiate meanings of the parameters of the decision process – such as what was meant by 'the best deal for the consumer', Oftel's corporate mantra at that time – and align preferences. This form of bargaining-diplomacy, commonly found in many regulatory environments, was not expressed in tense and conflict-laden encounters with exchange of angry letters, table-thumping, legalistic nit-picking, strategic walk-outs and all the other familiar ploys associated with formal bargaining behaviour. Indeed, it was often effective precisely because the synchronization of culture and attitudes it embodied emerged through conversation (Black 1998) and was sometimes hardly visible as negotiation (Reichman 1992). We observed this form of bargaining-diplomacy most commonly in the low level interactions of regulator and licensees over such matters as consumer complaints and licence enforcement, discussed further in Chapter Nine.

The other form of bargaining-diplomacy *was* expressed in formal bargaining, with parties known to have different objectives seeking to arrive at a mutually acceptable deal. As noted earlier, Oftel was obliged to engage in such processes with BT over licence modification, given BT's veto power over Oftel proposals and their mutual incentives to arrive at consensual arrangements. Indeed this formal bargaining type of decision-making was most commonly observed in the context of high level interactions between regulator and licensees over licence modifications. A key example is discussed in

Chapter Nine. While the first variant of the bargaining-diplomatic style can approximate to the adhocratic-chaotic style of decision-making, the latter can approximate to the Cartesian-bureaucratic in so far as the strategic actors in the process are clearly identifiable, and the regulator's objectives or desired goal are clear and well worked out (even if concealed like a poker hand for strategic advantage).

For some issues, Don Cruickshank and his senior staff at Oftel chose a bargaining-diplomatic style – perhaps as an overlay to a Cartesian-bureaucratic one. One example was the way they handled the problem of what to do about interconnection charges between BT and other licensed operators (OLOs), an issue of crucial importance to the new post-duopoly competitive market of the seventh age of telecommunications discussed in the second chapter. Instead of *ex cathedra* rulings, Cruickshank and his staff set up a series of industry workshops and several smaller working groups in 1994, with the aim of securing exhaustive and open debate of the issues. This device also created a subtle form of bargaining. While Oftel could insist that it retained the sole right to determine interconnection charges, it also set up a bargaining procedure within the industry by pitting the OLOs against BT and giving itself extra leverage as an arbiter or broker. It can be hard to dissemble in public under the gaze of an informed audience. Moreover, Oftel often went out of its way to encourage consumer advocacy groups to enter the arena of regulatory debate to balance the voice of the various operators. The desire to have such groups engaged in the regulatory conversation caused Oftel to chivvy them along and grant them extensions to deadlines over consultation inputs (a concession not granted to licensees), even though Oftel was frequently frustrated by the variable and erratic output such groups produced.

Table 6.1 Three decision styles summarized

Decision style	*Cartesian-bureaucratic*	*Bargaining-diplomatic*	*Adhocratic-chaotic*
Objectives	Pre-set at the outset	Mix of pre-setting and discovery	'Discovered' through process
Pattern of participating stations	Stable and orderly	Mixed (identifiable key players across organizations)	Unstable and shifting
Processing style	Linear	Mixed (iterative)	Lateral

These three decision styles, summarized in Table 6.1, are not jointly exhaustive: nor are they mutually exclusive in a strict sense. Decision-making can be differentiated in many other dimensions, some of which will be referred to later, but this trio represents the main approaches to issue-processing that we observed within Oftel. Most cases that we observed were hybrid rather than pure types and as decisions went through the regulatory issue-machine the emphasis could switch from one style to another, as the chapters which follow will show.

ACCOUNTING FOR VARIETY IN DECISION STYLES

One of the central puzzles for socio-legal and other studies of regulatory processes is how to account for variety in the decision styles observed (Black 1997: 82). We have no fully determinate explanation, but we can tentatively identify some of the factors that seemed to influence the form that the decision process took. Contingency theories of organization conventionally link differences in organizational forms to variations in size, technology and environment (cf. Lawrence and Lorsch 1967; Pugh and Hickson 1976; Hood and Dunsire 1981), and we can apply a heavily-modified form of such analysis to variations in decision styles within Oftel.

Three proximate elements seemed to be important in switching issues into one decision style or another. They were:

- the processability of an issue (its perceived tractability or familiarity)
- the policy ownership structure (the extent to which decision rights were owned by any one organization with a clear-cut legal or moral mandate)
- the preferences of the key players (the extent to which preferences were known and consensual).

Each of those three elements was in turn shaped by other background factors. Those factors included the demography of the organization and policy community (affecting the memory and experience that produced high processability); industrial development (affecting the way that products fitted with legal and bureaucratic boundary lines and the demography of the policy community); and the political climate, both in the form of the microclimate of the telecoms policy community and the macroclimate of Whitehall,

Westminster and beyond (affecting the extent of general consensus and willingness to accept informal fixes rather than taking every issue down to the wire in a hyper-legalistic style). That there is a substantial element of tautology or redescription in this analysis is undeniable, but such factors at least help us to sort and explain retrospectively some of the decision processes we observed. The way these proximate and background elements seemed to shape the decision process is summarized in Figure 6.1 and briefly discussed below.

Proximate shapers: processability, policy ownership patterns and preference patterns

The processability of an issue relates to the extent to which it is seen to be capable of being decided within a determinate organizational context on the basis of clear-cut and bounded information which is, or can be, available, according to procedures which are understood or can be discovered. A processable issue is one which is seen as fitting into some existing framework of principles, skills and competences. The more processable issues were perceived to be, the more likely they were to be routed down the Cartesian-bureaucratic track.

Processability is not an objective quality, but a product of culture and bureaucratic (or other) upbringing. Confidence about processability was shaped, like everything else in telecoms regulation, by shared beliefs about what skills or information was relevant. It was accepted, for example, that the economic issues associated with a price control could be clearly separated from the social issues related to service quality or from broader political issues like fat cat executive pay in the privatized utilities (cf. Foster 1992). But processability also seemed to be shaped by factors such as the possession of experience and the degree to which a fixed timetable or procedure was programmed into an issue. Some of Oftel's decisions had a built-in timetable, notably the price controls contained in BT's 1984 licence conditions which had a 'sunset clause', meaning that controls lapsed in 1989. Subsequent licence modifications were written such that price controls lapsed in 1993, 1997 and 2001. Oftel staff calculated that should a proposed price control modification not be accepted by BT a whole year would be needed for the Monopolies and Mergers Commission to report on the case and make its recommendations; thus a fixed and fairly tight timetable was imposed on the process (discussed in Chapter Seven). For other issues the timetable was more fluid and had no governing norms, as in the case of a proposal to

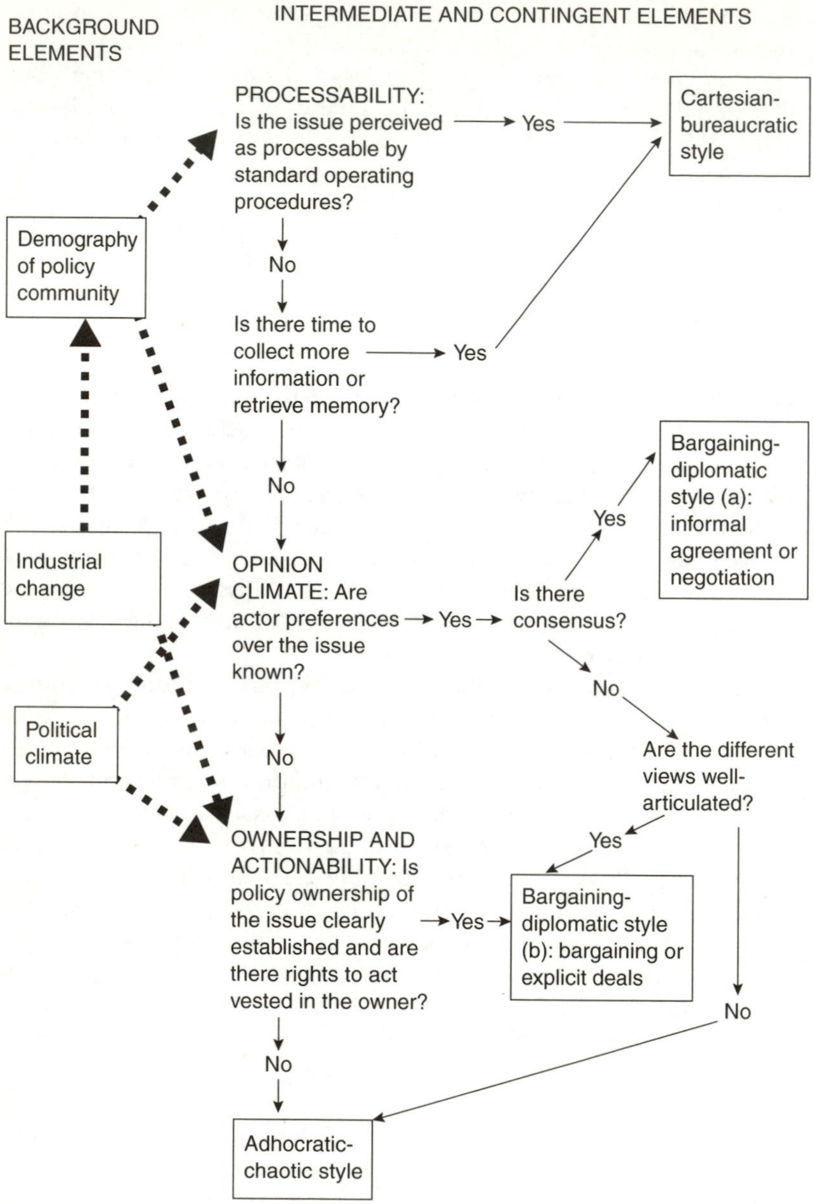

Figure 6.1 Some shapers of decision styles

include a prohibition on anti-competitive conduct as a condition in all operators' licences, with consultation procedures introduced in late 1994 and only concluded in 1997 (and discussed in Chapter Nine). Stretching out decision-making over an extended period reduces processability by encouraging or allowing more issues and actors to enter the process, and tends to switch issue-processing into a more adhocratic-chaotic style. Keeping issues more 'processable' by imposing a tight timetable on consultation processes, as Oftel attempted to do in its 1995 management plan, may overload the decision process and cause more weight to be placed on easily available information, as opposed to information that is difficult to obtain – which in turn may increase the leverage exerted by external well-informed participants such as BT (cf. March and Olsen 1979: 93). Clearly processability can be an ambiguous virtue.

Policy ownership refers to the institutional configuration that surrounds an issue. An issue that was perceived to have a single institutional 'owner' within the government structure, with clear-cut powers to act, was likely to be handled in a different way from one in which there is no obvious owner, or where policy ownership was dispersed among two or more organizations, and where there was no clear-cut legal mandate for action. The more policy ownership of a particular issue was perceived to be vague or dispersed, the less likely was the issue to be processed in a Cartesian-bureaucratic style. Oftel's policy-making over the introduction of the Fair Trading Condition (discussed in Chapters Eight and Nine) and hotel pricing (discussed in Chapter Nine) provide examples of dispersed ownership. The greater involvement of EU institutions in norm-making is likely to exacerbate perceptions of dispersed ownership of policies.

Preference patterns refers to the degree to which policy preferences over an issue, within the formal government structure and the telecoms policy community more generally, are known and are consensual. When preference patterns were unknown or divergent, attempts to ascertain or shape them through a bargaining-diplomatic style were more likely to take place.

In many Oftel decisions there seemed to be a broad consensus among participants as to what the desirable outcomes were. Very often, participants signed up to general objectives even if some of them were not so happy with the final outcome. Under such conditions the regulator could see decision-making as Cartesian-bureaucratic – reaching the best technical solution to a discrete problem through the application of agreed principles – and ignoring the continuous process of negotiation (the softer form of bargaining-diplomatic issue-processing) that built a basic consensus about key cultural terms and appropriate behaviour. However, for other issues consensus was less complete, both within and outside Oftel. Where the lack of consensus remained unarticulated, the probability of adhocratic-chaotic decision-making increased, since participants might ostensibly be seeking the same end but actually pursuing different agendas with a different understanding of objectives or key terms. Where lack of consensus came into the open – for example where Oftel was moving down a Cartesian-bureaucratic decision track and BT or the DTI chose to use the power they possessed within the regulatory space to influence the outcome, the decision process shifted into the more formal, bargaining form of the bargaining-diplomatic style.

For instance, BT often chose to adopt a bargaining style towards Oftel. Instead of allowing themselves to be locked in at an early stage in consultations, BT staff frequently chose to reserve their positions until the BT board had come to a view. That tactic meant that much BT input into regulatory decision-making came close to the end of the process, pushing it towards the formal type of bargaining rather than consensual negotiation. BT was also able to influence licence modification decisions by virtue of its central position in the process (while Oftel had the responsibility of drafting the licence modification, it was BT that actually had to implement it). While BT saw its shared responsibility over licence modifications as a legitimate basis for bargaining, the Oftel view from the other side of the table was rather different. According to one Branch Head:

> In the past BT have been able to play on the lack of lawyers in Oftel to get licence amendments drafted in the ways that suit them . . . Licence modifications have to be mutually agreed and BT always has a stronger negotiating position because they have the legal fire-power to very rapidly draft new terms.[4]

Background elements: demography of organizations and policy community, industrial development, political climate

Each of the three proximate shapers of decision style discussed in the last sub-section can be linked to other background elements. Potentially, the number of possible candidates is infinite, but three important ones seemed to be policy community demography, industrial development and political climate.

Organizational demography particularly shaped processability and preference patterns. We have already noted in Chapter Three that Oftel was both an immigrant and an emigrant society. This characteristic shaped the way it processed information in the issue-machine. A perennial information-handling problem in such an organization – particularly characteristic of entrepreneurial bureaucracies according to Corwin (1983) – is how to share experience across sub-units and over time. In principle, highly developed record keeping and retrieval mechanisms – part of the stereotype of an orthodox bureaucracy though only limitedly developed in Oftel at the time of our study – might have allowed such information sharing to take place. In practice it seemed to be the demography – what individuals happened to be where – rather than the paper or electronic information systems that determined who had access to what. Many issues processed by Oftel were recurrent (the price control review was repeated every four years) or they shifted from one part of the office to another (as in the case of hotel phone charges which we will discuss in Chapter Nine). But given the limitations on institutional memory, it was difficult for people who had not participated in the previous round of issue-processing to understand the basis on which previous decisions had been taken. During the bilateral working meetings in the Price Control Review the personal knowledge held by certain 'wise old men' was heavily drawn upon by both sides and even directed the discussion. Some limited research was done on original drafts and in old files but these written sources, sparse as they were within Oftel, could not always explain the reason why a case was included or why some things were left out.[5] At one working meeting a BT staff member joked, 'I wonder what we will be doing in 2001 when the next [price control] comes up?' The civil servants present all knew they certainly would not be working in Oftel '. . . and we all feel very smug about it. But it does mean an experienced BT will be facing an inexperienced team from Oftel'.

Nor was it just people that were mobile within Oftel. In an effort to maintain coherence and synergy within the branches of the organization, whole sections – generally dealing with specialist topics like numbering administration or international relations – were liable to be moved to another branch as the focus of their work shifted. Even physical office space was fluid in Oftel. As numbers of senior grade staff increased new office accommodation had constantly to be found within the limited area of two floors, confounding the unwritten conventions that civil servants above a certain level are entitled to have their own office. It was not unusual for the whole configuration of the office to alter over a weekend, with partition walls added and new rooms created, so that the space was quite different on the following Monday morning from what it had been on the previous Friday evening. The impact such changes had on decision-making was hard to determine, but since next door neighbours and people sharing an office tended to be used as sources of information and opinion, they perhaps added an additional randomizing element to the decision-making process.

Industrial development was closely related to organizational demography and the telecoms community culture. In particular, the liberalization of the UK telecoms market following the 1991–2 Duopoly Review and heralding the seventh age of telecoms regulation discussed in Chapter Two unleashed a pack of new companies, in many cases using novel technology or offering new services. This development – brought about by the actions of Oftel and the DTI – had the effect of destabilizing the telecoms regulatory space in terms of culture and knowledge base. In the changed environment, the experience and information that had been used for the sixth age of telecoms regulation was of less relevance. There were many new sources of information from which data had to be gathered to gain a comprehensive picture of the industry. The increasing number of actors in the field changed the regulatory agenda from a firm-specific process to an industry competition focus, meaning that all the actors in the process were moving into unfamiliar territory. Such novel conditions often pushed the decision process towards the adhocratic-chaotic style by their effects on processability as well as on organizational demography and consensus. In such circumstances, firms tended to lack the time, resources or interest for participation in abstract discussions of general principles or future problems. Political interests tended to focus on short-term issues and that was reflected in the preoccupations of the DTI and other government departments. The result was conditions in which the sort of information relevant to a decision might not be immediately apparent, the details of who to consult might be uncertain and the response of other actors unpredictable – features often associated with the adhocratic-chaotic style.

Closely related to industrial development was the political climate within which the issue-machine worked. At one level was the macro-political climate of Whitehall and Westminster, as it related to matters such as trade politics, the standing and preoccupations of particular ministers as they came and went or prevailing attitudes towards the privatized utilities. As explained in Chapter Two, it was a change in the climate at that level with the sale of the final tranche of BT stock in 1993 that helped to give Oftel under Cruickshank the opportunity to spread its wings more widely over issues of telecoms competition. Another change of climate, towards greater scepticism about the value of the supposedly monarchical style of individual utility regulators (discussed in Chapter Four) came with the change of government from Conservative to Labour in 1997. Aside from such major weather windows in the political climate, the DGT and DDG stressed to us the importance of having highly sensitive antennae within the Whitehall village over issues of policy timing.

At another level was the political microclimate of the telecoms policy community – arguably a synonym for culture. Culture, as we have noted earlier, shaped the meanings of rules, what counted as information, what was appropriate behaviour in what circumstances. It was perhaps most effective in shaping behaviour when it was invisible, as reflected in the comment of a former Oftel staff member: 'One of the questions we never ask in here is why? Why are we doing it in this way? By the time you have reached the level to ask, it is time to move on.'

Culture shaped not only the operations of Oftel but also the wider telecoms policy community. We have already commented on the willingness of most actors within that world to use and indeed to prefer a consensual negotiation version of the bargaining-diplomatic style of decision-making over telecoms regulation during the period of our study. This shared attitude arguably derived from the fifth and sixth ages of telecoms regulation discussed in Chapter Two. In particular, the influence possessed by BT in detailed definition of its licence conditions (discussed in Chapter Nine) was a product of history, of relative status within the regulatory space and a preference for informality in enforcement which prevented Oftel from testing the meaning of BT's licence conditions in a legal arena. Only when new players emerged within the regulatory space was this cultural consensus contested and new meanings placed upon the licence conditions, although up to the time of writing the new consensus also remained substantially untested by the courts (as discussed in Chapter 4).

The contingency paths sketched out in the algorithm in Figure 6.1 are tentative, and the information base which would be needed to turn that algorithm into a predictive model (as opposed to a retrodictive heuristic) is substantial. Whether it is even a causal scheme in a strict sense is debatable; but the algorithm does sum up some of the key elements which seemed to direct the decision style within the telecoms issue-processing machine in one direction or another. The next three chapters flesh it out by discussion of decision episodes within each of the main styles identified above.

ASSESSING DECISION STYLES

Self-image and observed image

As noted earlier, Oftel's self-image, as propagated by its senior staff, laid heavy stress on a Cartesian-bureaucratic style of decision-making. Such a style, with its apparent overtones of controlled rationality, seemed to be the type considered most appropriate to a public regulator, in conformity with the stereotype of orderly and highly programmed issue-processing expected of such organizations. The notion that Oftel might engage in bargaining or negotiation over its regulatory mission appeared to smack of *laesa majestas*. It was strongly at odds with the theology of bureaucratic independence and arms length dealing as the preferred operating style. Moreover the idea that there might be elements of chaos in the decision-making process was likewise firmly rejected by many of Oftel's senior staff as sharply at odds with the organization's self-image of peculiar and well-honed rationality.[6]

This self-image was a key part of Oftel's wider identity as a cerebral mission-driven organization free from any taint of regulatory capture; but while self-image is undoubtedly important, 'to see oursels as ithers see us' (as the poet has it) may offer a rather different perspective. The style that an outsider may observe can differ from what actors claim to be doing (or to have done). Moreover, Oftel's self-image over decision style was, as was noted at the outset, labile in that the way that participants characterized their decision-making depended more on the words we used to label different styles than on the substance of the distinctions we were trying to draw. For example, there was a notable disjunction between the orthodox self-image of peculiar rationality on the part of the Oftel top brass and an automatic tendency to reject what were seen as alien academic models of decision-making – models that were claimed to be over-neat to capture the irreducibly complex dimensionality of real life. In fact, the pattern of decision-making the figures at the top often described – dynamic, non-linear, with an ever-changing cast of characters, unexpected roadblocks or boosters and a complex politico-economic environment – closely approximated to the adhocratic-chaotic style. We could perhaps draw an analogy with the way superstitious fishermen use roundabout ways of describing a phenomenon whose name itself may not be mentioned at sea without the risk of dire consequences, such as 'clever feet' for rabbits. (The presence of chaos in decision-making was more readily acknowledged by those further down the bureaucratic food chain.) Oftel senior staff sometimes acknowledged the existence of bargaining as well, but typically with the qualification that such bargaining was not 'real bargaining' but a highly controlled process, in which the regulator tended deliberately to overstate initial demands or proposals with a clear view of what the eventual outcome would be.

One best decision style or horses for courses?

The Oftel self-image we encountered (as discussed earlier) implied that one decision style – the Cartesian-bureaucratic one – was generally more appropriate than the others, and that any departure from a Cartesian-bureaucratic style was to be avoided. Our own assessment differs sharply from this implied view.

The Cartesian-bureaucratic style certainly protects decision-takers from the legitimacy problems associated with entrepreneurial activity by appointed officials, since it casts them as 'engineers' rather than 'entrepreneurs' (Diver 1982), and hence is often considered to be the most appropriate decision style for a regulator appointed to pursue a legislative mandate. Our observations led us to conclude that Oftel worked in Cartesian-bureaucratic style less universally than the self-image implied – and often for very good reasons. Undoubtedly the Cartesian-bureaucratic style sometimes worked well, especially in matters of high-grade routine where parameters were known. But the Achilles' heel of that approach is its capacity to produce dramatic error as a result of faulty assumptions that can be taken for granted as part of some technocratic consensus (cf. Hood 1998: 28). As in the famous Sherlock Holmes story *The Speckled Band* (when a deadly snake is substituted for a bell-pull, with fatal consequences), something that seems to be part of the policy furniture can be surprisingly destructive if not carefully examined. Where participants in the decision process had deceived themselves or been deceived into believing that they had garnered all the relevant information and there was an effective consensus over key assumptions that merited closer examination, the Cartesian-bureaucratic style could lead to errors just as embarrassing (if not more so) than the adhocratic-chaotic style. In the next chapter we examine cases of the Cartesian-bureaucratic style of decision making, producing both positive and negative outcomes.

The bargaining-diplomatic style of decision-making, despite the reluctance of Oftel's senior staff (though not their counterparts in the DTI) to acknowledge that they ever operated in that way, was inevitable for the processing of some issues because of the legal framework of the 1984 Act, as described in Chapters Two and Four. The rules for consensual licence modifications tied the regulator into a bilateral relationship with the regulatee to the exclusion of other interested bodies. Moreover, the bargaining-diplomatic style in the softer of the two senses discussed earlier may invest decisions with a legitimacy among the stakeholders that cannot be produced so easily through an *ex cathedra* style of regulatory decision-making or when any single actor dominates the process. Underpinned by what seemed to be a common cultural preference among many of the players for consensus and co-operation, consultation and negotiation seemed to enhance the legitimacy of regulatory decisions within the wider policy community. The bargaining-diplomatic style that we observed often functioned in a relatively informal way and produced flexibility and accommodation (though in principle there is nothing about a bargaining-diplomatic style that inherently leads to such an outcome: such a style could be highly formal and tense), and seemed to contribute to policy learning in so far as the wider telecoms community sometimes became more willing to accept the regulator's role and approach through a process of consultation and discussion. That is not to say that the bargaining-diplomatic style was any more error-proof than was the Cartesian-bureaucratic style, and in Chapter Eight we look at cases of bargaining-diplomatic decision-making that produced both positive and negative outcomes.

As noted earlier, the adhocratic-chaotic style did not fit with the self-image or *amour-propre* of Oftel's top brass. For those who believe in orthodox business-school clichés about tight mission statements and orderly issue-processing it may seem like the antithesis of effective organization or an admission of managerial failure. Certainly such a decision style sometimes produced eccentric or unfortunate policy outcomes, as we will show in later chapters. But so did the Cartesian-bureaucratic and bargaining-diplomatic styles; and adhocratic-chaotic decision-making, as authors like Mintzberg (1983) have noted, can also be a highly creative process. Within the context of a rapidly expanding regulatory space, it may have been the most effective way – or simply the only way – to deal with novel issues within the broadest policy community. Adhocratic-chaotic decision-making could contribute to policy learning by identifying issues and information needs in a way that might have been more difficult in a linear processing style. It may also have worked against exposing the regulator to capture by making the pressure-points and key decision nodes more difficult to identify than in a Cartesian-bureaucratic style (cf. Rose-Ackerman 1978).

In short, contrary to the (reflex) Oftel self-image of Cartesian-bureaucratic decision-making as the only and best way of processing telecoms regulation issues, no one out of the three styles that we observed seemed to be an all-purpose approach guaranteed to produce good – or bad – results in all circumstances. A 'four legs good, two legs bad' approach seemed to be less appropriate than a more contingent judgement. Each decision style seemed to be capable of producing both positive and negative results, as subsequent chapters will demonstrate from our case-study material, and the system could be plastic, switching from one decision style to another as problems and debates went through the telecoms issue-machine. One particular pattern that we noted was for issues that initially went through an adhocratic-chaotic decision style to pass through a bargaining-diplomatic style involving wide participation before moving into a Cartesian-bureaucratic style. Far from involving a lapse in some ideal standard of bureaucratic rationality or intelligence, such transitions could be seen as combining a discovery system for issues and information with a consensus-building system on outcomes and procedures, and hence providing key elements of learning that would probably not have been achievable within a pure Cartesian-bureaucratic decision style. If there was no 'one best way' to make telecoms regulation decisions, moving successively through different decision styles was capable of producing a result that no one of those styles could have achieved on its own.

7 Price controls and numbering administration: Cartesian-bureaucratic issue-processing episodes

> Political input into. . . . decisions can have unpredictable results so the regulator or an independent authority is the best bet
>
> (Oftel numbering technocrat, advising visiting South African telecoms regulators, 12 May 1997)

The trio of decision-making styles discussed in the last chapter represents some of the different ways in which the issue machine handled telecoms regulation. As we noted in that chapter, many issues involved hybrid rather than pure forms, and most of the policy cases we observed switched from one dominant style to another as circumstances changed. So rather than recounting complete policy cases we focus instead on policy *episodes* – part of some larger policy story – that appeared to be dominated by one of the three main processing styles.

Accordingly, in this and the next two chapters, we give an account of episodes in six policy stories, with three pairs, each of which was dominated by one of the trio of decision styles. By giving a pair of episodes for each style, we aim to bring out some of the different ways in which those styles could play out. In particular the pair of episodes considered in each chapter is intended to show – as we argued in the last chapter – that each of those decision styles could be associated with both positive and negative policy outcomes.

This chapter looks at two policy episodes that seemed to be handled mainly in the Cartesian-bureaucratic style outlined in the last chapter. It will be recalled from that discussion that this style is the one that approximates most closely to the classic Weberian or mechanical-rationality form of issue-processing, with objectives or desiderata developed first and then applied to problems or cases by a relatively fixed and ordered process through systematic scanning.

The characters involved are a relatively known and bounded group with defined roles and arrayed in a fairly clear hierarchy.

Two policy episodes are discussed in this chapter. One is a nearly-complete set of scenes from the review of the regulatory regime governing BT's prices (a form of licence modification procedure) in 1995–6. The other is the early part of Oftel's approach to handling telephone numbering after it acquired the responsibility for numbering from BT in 1993 to ensure that numbering did not disadvantage other licensed operators against BT. Both episodes have elements of paradox for those who believe in the universal applicability of the Cartesian-bureaucratic decision style. The PCR episodes are a story broadly considered by telecoms regulation-watchers as having a positive result, but that result came about in large part by adding an adhocratic-chaotic element on to the Cartesian-bureaucratic style. The numbering episodes could be told as a story of 'policy fiasco' (Bovens and t'Hart 1996), at least in terms of the management of the regulator's public image, and that outcome could be attributed to a process where the Cartesian-bureaucratic issue-processing was founded on flawed assumptions about public and industry attitudes and misplaced trust in the competence of the previous numbering authority.

'BT DOUBTS OFTEL PRICE CALCULATIONS'[1]: SCENES FROM THE 1995–6 PRICE CONTROL REVIEW

Background

Reviewing and modifying controls over BT's prices was central to the regulatory regime for the sixth age of telecoms described in Chapter Two. The Littlechild Report (1983) had recommended that on privatization, BT's ability to raise prices should be limited to a figure equivalent to the Retail Price Index increase minus a figure (x) for efficiency gains, expressed in the form RPI – x. To give BT incentives to improve efficiency, the original RPI – x price control was to last for four or five years. After that, Oftel would need to initiate licence modification procedures if it wanted to maintain existing price controls or introduce new ones. Oftel carried out such procedures in 1988, 1992 and 1996, in each case modifying BT's licence by consent, to apply a new control. The changes are summarized in Table 7.1.

Table 7.1 Changes in price cap over BT 1984–97[2]

Year	*Value of price cap*	*Percentage of BT turnover under price control*
1984–89	RPI–3.00	48
1989–91	RPI–4.50	54
1991–93	RPI–6.25	69
1993–97	RPI–7.50	71

Source: Burns (1994: 78)

Having decided that competition was not sufficiently developed to be able to dispense with the price control in BT's licence altogether, Oftel had to decide two basic issues concerning a new price control to be applied to BT from 1997. First, to how much of BT's services should price control apply?[3] Second, what number should *x* be? Broadly, Oftel aimed for price controls to act as a substitute for competition, preventing BT from making excessive profits on services for which it faced little or no competition[4] but still allowing BT and its fledgling competitors to cover their costs and make a reasonable profit.

When Oftel embarked on its third price control review in 1995, many of the conditions for a Cartesian-bureaucratic style of issue-processing, as discussed in the last chapter, seemed to apply. Oftel had acquired substantial experience of handling PCRs in two previous decision rounds. Obligatory regulatory accounting imposed on BT as part of the regime to promote interconnection made price control easier, to the point that (according to one long-standing member of Oftel) 'We obtained the information for our start-up model largely from their published accounts'. Such conditions meant the issue could be considered relatively processable in spite of the classic information-asymmetry problem (Armstrong *et al.* 1994: 26–8; Lapsley and Kilpatrick 1997: 28–34) Oftel faced in dealing with a giant utility corporation that could be presumed to know more about its costs and revenues than an outside regulator. The issue was also considered to be relatively technical, with a central role for Oftel's econocrats (in its Economic Branch) in setting a new value for *x* in the RPI–*x* formula. The underlying policy mandate of the regulator – to restrain market dominance and promote competition – was also fairly stable and well understood. Even so, elements of the other two decision styles figured in the process, as will be shown later.

Timetable and organization

The timetable of the PCR is summarized in Table 7.2. The organization of the overall project was somewhat fluid, changing as new issues (for example the FTC discussed in Chapters Eight and Nine) were attached, and as new processes (for example public hearings and advisory panels) developed. Accordingly Figure 7.1 shows a simplified snapshot of the way the main packages within the project were organized, together with selected sub-packages. As Figure 7.1 shows, the PCR was conducted by a large project team within Oftel, with a firm time-scale – the review needed to be completed within seven months with a new control to be introduced in August 1997. What Oftel had to do in setting a new value for x was to make a plausible and informed prediction about BT's commercial performance and that of the UK telecoms industry more generally, over a four year period. The value of x was central to the whole telecoms industry, because most other licensed operators were competing with BT on price alone, so the x factor on BT's prices affected all the other companies.

As Figure 7.1 shows, the PCR project was sub-divided in classic bureaucratic fashion into work packages assigned to named individuals, with people in different branches working on their allocated

Table 7.2 Chronology of Price Control Review (PCR)

December 1995	– Publication of first consultative document *Pricing of Telecommunications Services from 1997*
January 1996	– Industry workshops
March 1996	– Publication of second consultative document on PCR
April–May 1996	– Series of public meetings held by Oftel on PCR in London, Glasgow, Cardiff, Belfast and Birmingham
June 1996	– Publication of final statement on PCR and FTC and statutory consultation
July 1996	– Oftel submitted final proposals on PCR and FTC to BT
August 1996	– BT accepted proposals, with some changes to FTC (discussed in Chapter Nine) and so second statutory consultation necessary
October 1996	– BT's licence modified to incorporate new price control from August 1997 and FTC

Source: Oftel Annual Reports

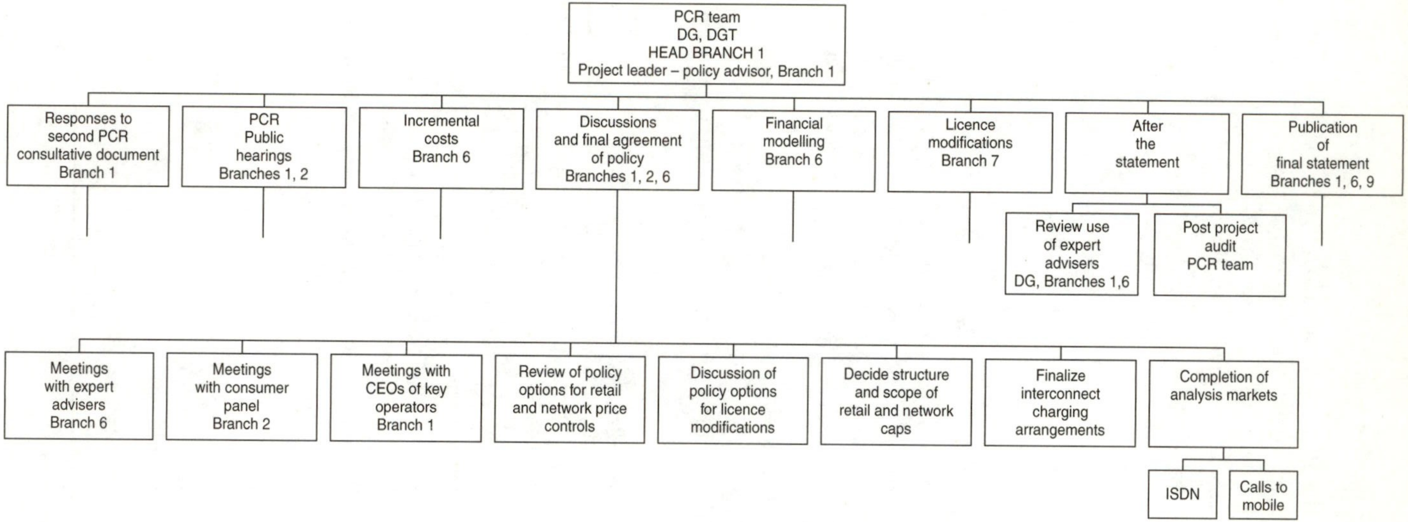

Figure 7.1 Simplified model of Oftel organization of PCR project – snapshot at March 1996*

* The diagram shows eight main work packages on the PCR. The smaller work packages for two of the eight main packages are shown. Two further work packages – the FTC (see Chapters Eight and Nine) and Effects on service providers – were also linked to the PCR. In total there were 47 smaller packages nested within the ten main work packages. (Oftel's branch structure is set out in Figure 3.1 in Chapter 3).

Source: Oftel Internal Documents

tasks. Given that Oftel drew a (rather fine) distinction between work packages and projects, the PCR became a bundle of small projects nested in the larger one. Most of the analytic work plus definition of issues, drafting and modelling, was done at Policy Advisor (Grade 7) level, with input from lower grades and guidance from the branch heads or project leader. In common with general Oftel practice, the price control licence modification package was seen as a policy matter and therefore handled separately from the technical issues of economic modelling or the development of new accountancy techniques.

But Oftel's PCR organization included elements of integration as well as specialization. The project as a whole was co-ordinated by regular team meetings held at increasingly frequent intervals until they became daily, even twice daily immediately before the publication of the final documents. Major PCR project meetings were always chaired by the DGT himself, took precedence over other Oftel meetings, and were re-scheduled if the DGT could not attend in person for any reason.

This degree of hands-on involvement by the DGT was not typical of general Oftel practice. Don Cruickshank and some other key people seemed to have the PCR project linkage clear in their heads and effectively formed the core team for the project. This team included the Branch Heads most closely involved and some Policy Advisors who attended most PCR meetings and/or had personal experience of previous PCRs. Outside the core team, several other Oftel staff worked on more than one package within the PCR project and were therefore in a position to take a view of the policy as a whole. Other members of the larger PCR project team were merely drawn into it briefly before moving out again to resume their other interests. Thus PCR engaged staff within Oftel to various degrees, with most Oftel staff having no contact or knowledge of the PCR, a small number engaged on it for almost the whole of the time, and others involved with it to only a small extent within a busy work schedule.

Most of the work on the PCR within Oftel was done through discussion at a personal level, by phone, e-mail or by 'going to see your pet specialist and talking face to face'. In the process information and opinion moved around small networks of people with equal or near equal status. Policy tended to emerge in the form of conversations or e-mail within *ad hoc* groups. Occasionally small informal meetings were called on some specific topic or problem between three or four people with recognized skills and knowledge, when 'you want all your colleagues to genuinely express opinion, or when you want them all – dare I say it? dreadful Whitehall jargon – to sing from the same hymn-sheet'. The aim of these meetings was to consider an issue carefully from different angles and disciplinary bases, since 'the worst thing is when you run off on your own on something and then find that someone wanders in and says 'Do you realise this is fatally flawed?''. The scope for such meetings was somewhat limited during the PCR process because of pressures to produce documents according to publicly announced deadlines. But to the extent that they took place, such meetings had elements of the bargaining-diplomatic style as well as the Cartesian-bureaucratic one, because they also involved consensus building, developing common understanding though exchange of information and attitudes. Such practice was seen as '. . . a kind of joint sign-off on many things, it's informal and it isn't political'.

Policy first emerged in a written form as background papers, draft chapters of the consultation document or draft licence modifications. These papers were circulated within the project team for comment and often went through several drafts. Following the normal way of doing business within Oftel, the author of a draft approaching its final form would meet with senior team members to obtain their comment and agreement. Such meetings would assess the quality of the arguments, the rationality or sanity of the proposed policy, and its probable effect relative to other parts of the PCR, and the 'signing-off' was semi-official before the document moved on to the DGT for his agreement. As time pressures increased during the PCR process and authors of policy documents became more confident in their analyses, a draft might go immediately to wider consultation in the big PCR meeting or, particularly the draft licence modifications, to a working meeting with BT. At this level much of the debate was about specific words or phrases, issues of language and interpretation rather than the substance of policy – which had been chewed over many times before at a lower level. Approval of policy was implicit through lack of comment. When an issue needed a speedy resolution and could not be sorted out immediately by the team leader it would be taken directly to the DGT.[5]

Another feature of Oftel's organization for the PCR, as shown in Table 7.2 and Figure 7.1, was the use of specialist advisory panels and public hearings. Both of these devices developed from Oftel's earlier work on interconnection. A 'Panel of Experts' (with expertise mainly defined as economics) originally set up to advise on interconnection was asked to move on to the PCR issue, and an advisory panel of consumers was set up as well, reflecting Don Cruickshank's view that the recognized consumer organizations were 'moribund' and largely ineffective in presenting the consumers case in telecoms. How much influence these panels had on the final price control regime is debatable: opinions differed within Oftel. But they seem to have served two purposes. One was improving the quality of policy input, both directly in the form of '. . . a genuine intellectual input, good minds, backgrounds, good experience' and indirectly as a 'hair shirt' requiring Oftel to submit to the discipline of explaining and justifying its thinking to outsiders. The other was to mobilize a constituency of reputable experts behind Oftel's policy stance as a potential defence against any challenge: 'They are also expert witnesses to defend our policies, in court cases or at the MMC'.

Bargaining diplomatic overlays

These characteristics of the PCR decision process broadly fit with the account of the Cartesian-bureaucratic style described in the last chapter. But in the case of the PCR that style was mixed – perhaps augmented – by elements of the adhocratic-chaotic and bargaining-diplomatic styles overlaid on top of the Cartesian-bureaucratic process.

The bargaining-diplomatic element came mainly in the strategies Oftel developed to handle the information-asymmetry problem posed by the fact that BT had more data about its production functions and revenue structure than any outside body. In principle for the regulator to obtain the data needed for a fully-informed price control regime requires full disclosure from all the relevant actors and particularly from the dominant telecoms utility. This condition was not fully met in the PCR process, meaning a bargaining-diplomatic decision style emerged to some extent over the securing of information.

BT's response to information requests by Oftel over the PCR was generally slow and limited, and this is not untypical of relations between Of-type regulators and their regulatees (Lapsley and Kilpatrick 1997: 52–4). For example, over economic modelling, BT was seen by some Oftel staff as deliberately choosing to 'keep *stumm*' in the expectation that Oftel had poor modelling capacity and that it would make mistakes in BT's favour. Oftel's notes on the PCR 'Wash-up' (17 June 1996) observed:

> . . . as always, BT had been dilatory in producing information, and unhelpful in identifying sources of information. Performance

> on retail information had been better than on network information ... Delay in providing information resulted in pressure at the end of the timetable.

Delay tends to be a standard first-order response by big organizations to pressures for information disclosure. Opinions within Oftel were divided as to how far BT's 'dilatoriness' was a product of deliberate strategy as against inertia, creaky administration and limited knowledge within the company itself. Some Oftel people were aware of tensions within BT, with internal fragmentation within the corporation ('No-one is allowed to have a model of the whole business, no one individual [or group] is trusted to do it') meaning the information Oftel wanted was not readily available within BT. One Oftel staff member suggested:

> Our hardest task is making obvious the difference between inefficiency or inadequate staff, no information or processing capacity and just swinging the lead. They don't want to give anything away as they are certain it will only be used against them.

Another opinion was that 'BT staff do know what is happening but they don't want to rock the boat: it's not career enhancing. But you also have the rottweilers who just enjoy being obtuse and objectionable'. Don Cruickshank himself saw BT's approach in terms of strategy or culture rather than simple lethargy or incompetence:

> BT is ... a guardian-type culture: what they have they hold ... Basically, the less the information and the greater the delay the better the outcome is for them and they know this. They know that I am constrained by my obligations under the Act, by due process and potential judicial review *et cetera* and they know that the less information a DG has, the more likely that DG is to be conservative. BT see the price control as a straight transfer of money from BT to the consumers so they push against any imposed deadline. It is very rational ...

BT's Regulatory Affairs Department (RAD) staff, not unnaturally, presented the relationship in rather different terms. They considered Oftel's demands for information to be unreasonable, often amounting to 'fishing expeditions' ('Oftel feel there is a kind of vat of information into which [they] may dip a cup and if they don't like it, then they dip for another cup'). They argued:

> Both sides have different views of what is reasonable, for example in economic or financial information . . . but if there is no need for that information within the company then it won't be there [and BT has to] employ people, train them and that all takes time . . .

When asked if BT tried to explain to Oftel that information requested was hard or expensive to obtain, or not used for management purposes the response was:

> No, we've given up. It is like water off a duck's back. We try to put a case together, to explain why it is not there, how long it takes. . . . RAD press for compliance [within BT]. There may be judgement on the part of the person providing information . . . but there is not much gamesmanship.

Faced with a slow and minimal information flow from BT – stemming from some mixture of strategy and lethargy – Oftel could have invoked the formal information gathering powers the DGT possessed, both under the operating licences granted under the 1984 Telecoms Act and under the Act itself. All the licences contained a more or less standard condition obliging the licensee to provide the DGT with 'such information as he may request to carry out the functions given to him under Parts II and III of the Act'. But invoking the legal procedures for enforcing a requisition for information was potentially cumbersome and generally avoided. As Oftel's Competition Casework Procedure document (Annex 2, 'Information Gathering, April 1997) put it:

> In making such requests . . . you should bear in mind that the licence condition requires the Director to ensure that 'no undue burden is imposed on the licensee in procuring and furnishing such information . . .'. Although refusal to supply information would be a breach of the licence, there are no immediate practical penalties for failure to comply . . . The Director could enforce a request made under the licence condition by making an order under Section 16 of the Act. If the licensee failed to comply . . . the Director could seek a court order to enforce, and failure to comply with that court order would mean that the licensee would be in contempt of court. That procedure is difficult to use and therefore in contentious cases the power to obtain information under Section 53 of the Act provides a more effective power, where it can be used . . .

Moreover, the formal information gathering powers were only usable under specific conditions, involved obligations of confidentiality and were restricted to authorized individuals and specified types of information. Within a seven month PCR timetable and doubts as to whether BT in fact had comprehensive business models and forecasts of the kind Oftel needed for the PCR, any attempt on Oftel's part to go through the formal information requisition procedure would have been most unlikely to produce the information it wanted within the necessary time frame. So the legal powers served more as a threat than a weapon that could easily be deployed in practice.

Faced with these conditions, Oftel did not invoke its formal information gathering powers against BT for the PCR (it did on one occasion prepare a 'Condition 52' letter formally requisitioning information from BT, but the letter was never sent). Its preference was for informality, linked on occasion with rottweiler responses to rottweiler tactics by BT. For example, a senior BT manager wrote to the DGT seven months after the DGT's letter setting out the timetable for the PCR process saying that BT would not be providing any further data until it was satisfied that the transparency of the review procedure proposed by Oftel would not prejudice the commercial confidentiality of its data and forecasts (Letter from BT Regulatory Affairs Department to Oftel 7 November 1995). Don Cruickshank's response was an uncompromising letter to BT's CEO describing BT's position as 'totally unacceptable', refusing to give any assurances that would fetter his statutory discretion, threatening to invoke his legal powers of information requisition and to make public his reason for doing so (Letter from DGT to BT CEO 17 November 1995).

However, just as important as occasional exchanges of angry letters and threats over information supply was Oftel's way of 'working round' the information-deficit problem (described in an 'inside account' by Wigglesworth 1997). With changing relations within the telecoms regulatory community, and in particular the growing importance of new entrants to the market in the seventh age of telecoms regulation, Oftel became less dependent on BT for securing and testing the reliability of information than it had been in previous price reviews. Indeed, it could be argued that simple information asymmetry was a declining problem for Oftel. When one company proved obstructive another source could provide the required information or an adequate substitute. In contrast to previous PCRs, in the 1995–6 PCR Oftel had material from sources other than BT – notably the Other Licensed Operators (OLOs) who were playing a different game with information, one of co-operation with Oftel to secure market advantage over BT. Moreover, with increasing experience, more skilled staff and more published data produced by the telecoms regulation regime, Oftel's intelligence both about specific regulatees and the wider UK telecommunications industry was building up. Consequently Oftel was becoming a provider of information about the industry as well as a seeker after it. Increasingly regulator and regulatees were using the same base data and debate turned on matters of interpretation.

Part of the way Oftel worked round information asymmetry with BT was through the industry workshops and public hearings it ran as part of the PCR process. These devices were part of a general Oftel strategy of transparency in issue-processing, going beyond the formal consultation requirements stipulated by the 1984 Telecoms Act (Oftel 1995a: 4–5; Oftel 1995b: 14; Oftel 1997b). They were a marked feature of the way Oftel handled the PCR, as indicated in Tables 7.1 and 7.2. Five public meetings under independent chairmanship were held in different UK cities in the second stage of consultation over the PCR, with opening statements about price control from Oftel, BT, local cable companies and consumer advocates followed by questions from the floor. Most of these meetings were dominated by producer interests, with the voice of the residential user weak and subdued. There were mixed views within Oftel as to their value (except as 'a PR exercise' and to some degree an exercise in triangulating the responses of different players) and Oftel's technocrats found it hard to evaluate or use the highly subjective and diffuse information they produced (Oftel Notes on PCR Wash-Up 17 June 1996). However, such meetings and more particularly industry workshops created a framework within which Oftel could secure the support of OLOs in challenging and testing information supplied by BT and providing alternative information about matters such as costs and revenues, projections of future market share and, in some cases, experience in other countries.

Through industry workshops, private meetings and correspondence, the OLOs provided a substantial part of the information on which the new PCR calculations were based, though they sometimes needed a good deal of prodding from Oftel. For instance, one company wrote:

> Over the past 2 weeks we have handed over to and discussed with [Oftel], detailed nominal and discounted cashflow models of our business, which include financial data and algorithms on

> incremental costs and revenues, common costs and financing costs and provisioning. These models deliver outputs showing the impacts on revenues and cash flow of different values of 'X' for BT's retail and network price controls and they supplement information provided in February and March of this year covering areas such as our pricing strategy post 1997 and our options for growing our business. We believe that all of the information provided should be of great value to you in reaching your final decision (Letter to DGT 21 May 1996).

The DGT saw the consultation process as giving OLOs strong incentives to co-operate in providing information: 'Information given [by OLOs] means tighter [price] controls but more information also means that they are able to convince me better so they are in a bit of a bind . . .' In general OLOs welcomed the industry workshops, though BT understandably seems to have had more reservations about them (Fax from BT to Oftel Evaluating the PCR Process 27 September 1996; Letter from Cable Company Representatives to Oftel on Evaluation of PCR Process 17 September 1996) and one OLO representative in an interview thought that Oftel's demands for information on the PCR were:

> Fine for us. They don't need to know much . . . Most of my time is giving Oftel the information that I think they should have and haven't asked for. . . . The biggest problem in Oftel is that they simply don't know how BT and commerce works.

Adhocratic-chaotic overlays

The adhocratic-chaotic overlay on the Cartesian-bureaucratic processing of the PCR stemmed in part from the problems Oftel as an adhocracy or entrepreneurial bureaucracy experienced in exchanging information among its ever-changing cast of bureaucratic immigrants and emigrants and in retaining information over time. But it also consisted, as mentioned in the last chapter, in unexpected interventions by the DGT. Such an intervention eventually shaped the price control into a form different – and bolder – from that which Oftel's technocrats would have produced on their own. Towards the end of the PCR process, Cruickshank proposed a dramatic shift in the parameters for price control. As a result of his own experience, observation and a 'gut feeling', he believed BT could achieve far greater efficiency gains than had previously been allowed for.[7] This belief led him to re-examine the historical pattern of past PCR forecasts against actual outcomes one weekend, comparing BT performance over time rather than comparing it with US telecoms companies as a supposed efficiency yardstick. He found BT consistently and easily beat its own public predictions and those of the regulator. So he reasoned in front of the core PCR team, 'A game player would suggest [BT] haven't been honest, so can I suggest we crack on another two points?' [to the *x* figure for potential efficiency gains.] 'The only reason I don't say 10 per cent is because I'm too embarrassed.' It was this last-minute hunch about BT's strategic behaviour and the quality of the information base that the technocrats were working with that informed Oftel's final decision to impose a price control of RPI–4.5. Coupled with a narrow basket of BT services, amounting to about a quarter of BT's revenues, RPI–4.5 was a tighter price cap than might have been expected or justified by the analysis carried out by the Oftel technocrats – creating risks for Oftel if BT had chosen to contest the new price cap through an MMC referral. Like other cases of last-minute major alterations to an emerging design, this application of an inspired hunch did not fit the Cartesian-bureaucratic decision style and indeed constituted a reaction against that approach. But it could be argued that the ordered consultation and technocratic models produced by Oftel's professional economists were a necessary precursor to Cruickshank's final intervention.

Overall

As the preceding account has indicated, the PCR was by no means an unalloyed case of the Cartesian-bureaucratic decision style. There was a core process of information-gathering and modelling conducted by technocrats according to relatively established procedures with fairly well understood objectives. In principle, the information-gathering element of the process might have been dominated by a bargaining-diplomatic style with high-level wrangling between Oftel and BT about disclosure, but the combination of new regulatory accounting and the advent of OLOs as substantial players within the regulatory space allowed Oftel to work round BT's strategic/lethargic delays in providing PCR-relevant information. Moreover, as shown above, in the endgame the DGT's intervention pushed the outcome off the technocratic-bureaucratic tracks that the PCR was following as it went through the issue-machine.

'IT'S 1 TO EXPLAIN'[8]: SCENES FROM TELEPHONE NUMBERING ADMINISTRATION 1993–7

Background

According to Don Cruickshank, '[Telephone] Numbering isn't an inconvenience for us: it is something someone in government had to do and we were asked to do it,' or, in a rather less temperate mood, 'I inherited forty years of crap and so I've done my bit!' The 'forty years of crap' to which Cruickshank delicately referred began with a UK National Numbering Plan designed by the GPO in the third age of telecoms regulation in the 1950s, when the country was divided into 638 approximately equal areas each of which was allocated an individual geographic area code. Piecemeal changes to numbering were introduced as demand grew and new technology like STD introduced and the main responsibility for running telephone numbering continued to be held by BT on privatization in 1984.

However, that task was transferred by a licence modification from BT to Oftel ten years later (after the 1991–2 Duopoly Review) because of a perceived risk that BT would use control over numbering to stifle its potential competitors (BT Licence Condition 34B). Indeed, the commercial significance of telephone numbering changed substantially between the fifth and seventh age of telecoms regulation. What under a monopoly operator had simply been a set of routing instructions for the single provider became telephonic addresses of commercial significance in the sixth and seventh age of telecoms regulation, and 'fair and equitable access' to numbering became a central competition issue in the telecoms market (see Oftel 1993: 6–7). New services such as freephone numbers and personal (non-geographic) numbers were dependent on allocation of new codes and the way numbers were allocated affected supply costs too. Thus control of established numbering patterns potentially gave substantial commercial advantage to the established operator in inhibiting new market entrants.

However, in inheriting the responsibility for telephone numbering in an era when it had a new significance, Oftel did not simply have to allocate numbers in a way that was neutral among different telecoms providers. It also assumed the responsibility at a time when a shortage of telephone numbers was developing as a result of exponential growth in demand for telephone numbers in the 1980s and 1990s.[9]

The numbering problem was lucidly explained to members of the then newly-formed South African Telecommunications Regulatory Authority (SATRA) on a visit to Oftel in mid 1997. An Oftel numbering specialist told them he didn't know the South African situation but if they could tell him how long their local codes were he would explain some of their potential problems. When the visitors explained that South Africa Telekom used long area codes and short personal numbers, the Oftel expert declared, 'Ah, there's your problem'. He explained that a block of three digit numbers would be filled much more quickly than a four, five or seven digit block. Longer customer telephone numbers mean more space is available behind the specific codes that route calls to the switches. Short numbers provide hundreds of spaces in the block, longer ones provide several thousand. He gave an example of ten digits after a zero:

e.g. 0 1234 234567

These digits were then lettered off:

```
0 1 2 3 4   2 3 / 4567
  s A B C   D E
```

The first sABC segment of code identified the location (the geographic code), then at the DE segment the network system could identify the individual operator, thus 23 might be one company, while 24 and 25 might be others. Behind each DE block – the crucial point – there are 10,000 individual customer local numbers. But for various reasons, not all of these numbers could be available. For example, turnover of customers (churn) meant that some personal numbers could not be re-allocated for at least two years. Such numbers are deemed sterile. Add in other technical problems and as many as 50 per cent of numbers are unusable. An operator was considered 'efficient' by Oftel if it had 5,000 active numbers in a block. The key regulatory problem, however, was that short customer numbers permitted a dominant operator to maintain control of the network. By dropping customers' numbers randomly into several different blocks the dominant operator could control available numbering capacity and so hold off potential competitors since it was far easier to allocate and administer entire blocks than scattered individual numbers. As the Oftel expert put it:

> It is in [the monopolist's] interest to spread numbers as wide as possible across the spectrum in order to make entry difficult for competitors. . . . It might be necessary [for the regulator] to change the numbers to allow competition in. BT kept numbering for about ten years and, in hindsight, this was not the best situation.

In addition to preventing numbering from giving an advantage to the dominant former monopolist there was the related problem of how to increase numbering capacity for rapidly growing demand. There were three possible approaches. One was to use a split, dividing an area into concentric rings (as in London after 1990) or slices of a pie (as in New York city) with different codes for the rings or slices. A second was to use an overlay, with two geographic codes for the same location. This approach had the disadvantage of being confusing for users, preventing them from making an educated guess about the correct code for an area. It could also disadvantage later entrants into the telecoms market if such firms could not use familiar codes in their numbers and involved extra costs because the switches have to read more digits to direct the traffic. But it was fairly easy to implement an overlay and old numbers did not need to change. The third solution was to go for numbers with more digits; shorter geographic codes with longer customer numbers, provided spare capacity was available for future growth. The Oftel expert exhorted the SATRA visitors to start planning numbering allocation immediately for long-term growth in demand.[10] This advice conveyed lessons that Oftel had learned the hard way.

Organization and chronology

Numbering was initially seen within Oftel in classic Cartesian-bureaucratic terms as a dry and technical issue, in which policy would be determined by the specialized knowledge of a few experts. In classic bureaucratic fashion, the issue became the responsibility of a specialized sub-division created to handle the problem – the Numbering Administration Unit (NAU) – which formed a relatively self-contained part of Oftel (as part of the Consumer Branch from 1995) and grew in numbers and expertise after 1994. The NAU, small and inexperienced at the outset, was heavily dependent on BT and industry expertise in numbering and worked closely with a pre-existing statutory consultative body largely composed of industry experts (the Telecommunications Numbering and Addressing Body).[11]

Table 7.3 Chronology of numbering administration 1991–7

September 1991	–	Modification of BT's licence to transfer responsibility for numbering administration to Oftel (Condition 34B)
June 1993	–	Publication by Oftel of consultation document *Numbering: Choices for the Future*
January 1994	–	Numbering Administration Unit established in Oftel
March 1994	–	Draft Numbering Conventions published by Oftel
June 1994	–	Issue 1 of Numbering Conventions published and Oftel began processing applications for numbering capacity
October 1994	–	Determination by DGT of the Specified Numbering Scheme. NAU commences publishing monthly Numbering Bulletins
16 April 1995	–	National Code Change Day (phONEday) – all area codes adopted leading digits '01'
June 1995	–	Publication by Oftel of consultation document on the future of telephone numbers with geographic significance (the 01 and 02 ranges)
October 1995	–	Publication by Oftel of statement on numbering following June consultation
April 1996	–	Local publicity for Reading area change code commenced
January 1997	–	Final phase of UK National Numbering Scheme announced by Oftel
April 1997	–	Second Issue of Number Conventions published
August 1997	–	Publication of plans for Corporate Numbering published by Oftel

Source: Oftel Annual Reports

Indeed, recognizing its own limitations, Oftel intended eventually to pass control of numbering administration to an independent self-funded industry body and only intended to run it itself for a limited time. Perhaps because direct rule over numbers by Oftel was seen as a limited-term exercise, Oftel's top brass took relatively little interest in the numbering issue at first. Table 7.3 gives a brief chronology of the key events in numbering policy from 1994 to 1997.

The numbering project that preoccupied NAU when it took over numbering from BT in 1994 was the introduction of a new national

10-digit numbering system to take effect from April 1995 ('phONEday' in the publicity jargon). The change involved adding an 01 prefix for most existing area codes and thereby creating many other numbers in the 02 to 09 ranges. This scheme was one of a succession of changes in telephone numbering intended to meet increasing demand for numbers. The London codes had been changed in 1990 from 01 to 071 and 081 (on the split model noted above); the 1995 change involved an 01 prefix for all area codes; and there was to be a later phase in the numbering plan (not discussed or worked out when Oftel assumed control of numbering) when the 02 to 09 ranges came fully into play, as well as the 01 range.

Oftel had been involved in preparations for the national code changes on phONEday well before it assumed direct responsibility for numbering. Like any project requiring change in the behaviour and established habits of almost everyone in a country (new coins, time changes, new units of measure), all the apparatus of mass publicity was employed, and considerable media and political interest could be expected if there were hitches in the changeover. Over 220,000 leaflets were issued, and other publicity devices included a dedicated phone line for information, press conferences and briefings and a new National Code Change Forum which was convened four times to help business firms adapt to the changes. The new telephone codes began to run in parallel with existing codes early in 1994 to ease the changeover, and the formal documents embodying the numbering changes were published in mid 1994.[12]

As well as preparing for a smooth changeover to the new national codes on phONEday, when Oftel took over responsibility for numbering it was engaged in consultation over how to handle the third phase of changes to the national numbering system (when the 02 to 09 codes came fully into play). Since the statutory advisory group (the TNAB, referred to earlier) had no clear views about how the 02 to 09 ranges should be used, Oftel produced a consultative document in 1993 (*Numbering: Choices for the Future*) proposing to place a range of both service and geographic area codes behind each leading digit: 01 current geographic fixed public networks, 02 additional geographic numbers, 03 spare for future use, 04 mobile services, and so on. Responses to this consultative document were muted and lukewarm, particularly over the issues of using the 02 range as an additional geographic code (an 'overlay). As one NAU specialist put it, 'No-one came out and said "no", but they were not overwhelmingly enthusiastic'.

The late discovery of the numbers famine

From mid 1994 Oftel's NAU began a further round of consultation over the use and management of the new numbering range, having kept the formal Convention (B4) over the proposal to use the 02 range as an additional geographical overlay in draft form to allow further discussion. A letter sent out by the head of NAU to 'Members of TNAB and others who have expressed an interest in the subject' in July 1994 elicited responses from some twenty companies over the following months, with views about how to use the newly available number ranges and the 02 range in particular.

It was at this point that Oftel suddenly discovered a serious dearth of phone numbers. According to one member of NAU:

> We only got the BT database in June 1994 and it was in such a mess,[13] it took until October to get it into shape. Only then did it become possible to make any predictions about future demand. And we then found that several more cities [than previously recognized] were going to run out of numbers very soon – including Reading in 1998! By that time . . . phONEday was only six months away.

It is not clear how Oftel came to be caught out in this way. Either BT had not been able to detect the scale of the problem because of the poor organization of its records or, knowing that responsibility was going to move to the regulator, it had ceased to take an active interest. Whatever the reason, Oftel got no hint from BT of the impending numbering crisis and had evidently placed its trust in BT's competence in a way that in hindsight was altogether misplaced. But when awareness of the crisis spread, telecoms industry concern soon began to be expressed. The Director General of the Telecommunications Managers Association (TMA) wrote to the DGT on 7 February 1995 (*The Public Availability of Numbering Information*):

> The commercial impact of discovering at the 11th hour that a telecoms strategy cannot be implemented because of an unpredicted, unannounced number famine can be severe. Reading was not one of the five (deprived) cities identified by BT when the National Code Change was planned and there are now rumours circulating about imminent shortages in Southampton, Belfast and Cambridge. TMA has two concerns about this situation; the lack of warning and the implications of a possible early introduction of an S=2 [02] as an overlay network. . . . Not only

> is the situation in Reading unsettling for the customer, it also lends credence to the view that the implementation of an S=2 overlay is about to be announced for NCC day [phONEday].

Although no final decision on using 02 as an additional geographic overlay had then been taken within Oftel (the relevant Numbering Convention Condition B4 being still in draft form pending further consultation), the Head of NAU apparently felt an urgent need to do something about the impending crisis in Reading and the prospect of capacity exhaustion in several other cities. So he drafted what was later called 'a semi-consultative letter to the industry' in February 1995, proposing to deal with the numbers shortage by using 02 immediately as a geographical overlay on several 01 code areas, including Reading and London. Doubts were expressed about this approach when the draft of the letter circulated within Oftel (including worries about the legal status of the letter in fulfilling Oftel's statutory obligation to consult with TNAB over numbering, given likely opposition from the industry, the view that more consultation was needed and a feeling by one senior Oftel manager that 'we must not be bounced into the wrong decision') but the head of NAU still pressed for the adoption of the policy he was proposing:

> The principal objective of the Numbering Administration Unit is to have ample numbering capacity available to enable licensed operators to satisfy their customers requirements. If Oftel is to maintain credibility (by avoiding yet more code changes) and properly discharge its responsibility for administering the UK Numbering Scheme we must take steps to open up s-digit 2. (*Briefing Note to the DG: Use of S-digit 2 Numbers* [14 February 1995]).

However, while Oftel's technocrats were moving towards an 02 geographic code overlay it became apparent that there was considerable industry and public opposition to this solution. Research showed that customers preferred to retain a single, recognizable geographic code even if it meant more inconvenience and change to achieve it. As a result, there was suddenly great uncertainty about what policies phONEday heralded. The industry faced the unexpected imposition of the 02 range at unexpectedly short notice – and it felt consultation had been inadequate. Hostile media interest, scenting 'bureaucratic incompetence' involving further telephone number changes on top of the phONEday upheavals, was readily aroused. The *Financial Times* (6 February 1995) declared:

> Further upheaval is in prospect for UK telephone users under plans to introduce another numbering scheme after all Britain's numbers change on phONEday next month. Under the plans, telephone users will be faced with two sets of codes for the same UK regions. . . . Telecoms operators are complaining that Oftel, the telecommunications regulator, is pushing through the changes without adequate consultation.

The influential BBC Radio 4 *Today* programme (6 March 1995) interviewed Oftel's numbering scheme manager ('in his pyjamas', according to Oftel legend[14]) and then, according to an NAU staff member, 'things blew up'. The DGT appeared on the BBC Newsnight programme later that day, and repeated Oftel's official line that there would be no more telephone number changes in most people's lifetime and committed Oftel to no further number changes until after more consultation.[15]

A member of NAU gave the following account of how the DGT had come to make such a commitment:

> I think he was trying to give reassurance but he was also sold on the idea of an overlay by [the head of the NAU] – and [by the Deputy Director General] actually. Using 02 as an overlay was Oftel's preferred option and [the DGT] thought that is what would happen without really testing the idea. There hadn't been an overwhelmingly negative response from industry about 02 and [the head of the NAU] had great influence.

With continuing negative media comment, and DTI ministers facing questions from MPs about phONEday, the DTI (which normally took little interest in numbering) weighed in with a sharp note to Oftel. The note reminded Oftel that the DTI still had responsibility for general numbering policy and for international numbering (because of its duty to oversee telecoms policy in general), requested that information and drafts of documents be exchanged and that the difficult issues be discussed at Oftel/DTI progress meetings.

PhONEday itself, in April 1995, saw the successful implementation of the 01 prefix for most UK geographic codes, a new international code for the UK and entirely new codes for a few cities. But the day was not deemed a popular success within Oftel because media coverage continued to be hostile. Oftel was seen to have mishandled the public presentation of the changes. Cruickshank's public declaration on TV that the phONEday code changes would be the last number change needed 'in most people's life time' sat uneasily beside the concurrent news that several UK major cities would run out of numbers between 1998 and 2000. Predictably, the DGT's words were quoted back by the media every time another numbering change was announced (as in Reading in 1996).

Nor was it just a matter of inept spin-doctoring by Oftel. In hindsight it was clearly a mistake not to have worked out the third stage of the numbering changes (the policy for the numbers in the 02 to 09 ranges) and agreed it with the industry before phONEday. As it was, the phONEday numbering change took place 'in a policy vacuum' according to one Oftel consultant, because Oftel had no agreed plan for the five cities that were facing imminent telephone number exhaustion. It was that policy vacuum that produced the industry dissatisfaction that in turn sparked the hostile media coverage and Parliamentary questions.

The bad political vibes stirred up by the phONEday numbering episode continued with strong criticism of Oftel's handling of the issue from the House of Commons Trade and Industry Select Committee in 1996:

> Although the Director General implied that the numbers will not need to change again, we note that the recent European Commission Green Paper on Telecoms Numbering Policy may result in further changes to the UK before long. . . . We believe that the most recent proposal, involving 02 codes for London and for some provincial cities, is clumsy and likely to lead to more customer confusion. . . . We are not persuaded by the Director General's arguments about Oftel's improved planning and forecasting methods. . . . We recommend that the Government commission an independent examination, by world class consultants, of the UK's methodology and approach to numbering schemes, and that this review should take account of EC and world numbering requirements (Trade and Industry Select Committee 1996, pp. xvi–xvii sections 35 and 36).[16]

To defend its record against what it saw as a grave misunderstanding by TISC, Oftel sent a further letter to TISC giving an account of the numbering saga from the pre-1995 system to the eventual 01–09 number ranges and explaining the pressures Oftel had faced. As the Branch Head responsible wrote, in a briefing note to the DGT:

> The only explanation that we can give is the truth – that during the period running up to phONEday we were proceeding on the basis of using 02 as an overlay. This was why we did not agree with [a named consultant] and others who raised with us the need for London exhaust to be dealt with at PhONEday (7 February 1997 *Briefing Note to DG from Head Branch 2, TISC – Numbering*).

Whitehall Departments are used to shrugging off critical Select Committee reports and other forms of media/political gunfire, and within government, the DTI apparently believed that there was no case to answer: Oftel had done its job by consulting widely on its proposals and received strong support for them, both from consumers and from the very experts that TISC suggested should be consulted again. But in the wider world Oftel was faced with the difficult task of repairing the damage to its reputation and restoring public, industry and government confidence in its ability to handle numbering administration. It embarked on further consultation on the next set of numbering changes, established a Numbering Advisory Group which was much smaller than TNAB, and had representation from consultants and consumer groups as well as the industry bodies, and canvassed fresh solutions to the outstanding numbering problems, such as using 05 for company numbers.

Overall

In principle, numbering was an issue well suited to a Cartesian-bureaucratic decision style. It was a technical problem in which basic objectives – to increase overall capacity and prevent BT from using the numbering system to hamper competitors – were fairly clear. And in spite of the bad spin Oftel received in 1995 from the media and Parliament, most people we spoke to considered that Oftel in fact did reach appropriate technical solutions to the problems it faced, in the form of a logical and rational numbering plan implemented in 1998.

But there were undoubtedly elements of the adhocratic-chaotic decision style overlaying the Cartesian-bureaucratic one, and in this case (in contrast, perhaps to the PCR case described earlier), the adhocratic-chaotic overlay had some negative consequences, particularly for Oftel's reputation. Oftel was implementing a technical plan inherited from the previous numbering administrator, but lacked all the information it needed to form policy and placed an unjustified trust in the quality of BT's planning and information. Decision-making was protracted while the players changed, and views within the telecoms industry and the public about longer-term change in numbering policy were inchoate and labile. If Oftel's technocrats failed to read signs of the approaching politico-media storm over 'phONEday', Oftel's top brass also failed to realize in time how difficult and political a policy issue numbering administration could become, particularly when carried out in the goldfish bowl accountability context of a government body rather than of a privatized firm.

CONCLUSION

Neither of the two sets of policy episodes discussed here displays a pure Cartesian-bureaucratic decision style, but both contained strong (and growing) Cartesian-bureaucratic characteristics. The PCR was a repeat exercise in gathering information for econocratic modelling according to relatively well understood procedures and the post 1994 numbering administration story involved relatively technical problem-solving in finding new number ranges to augment capacity for the seventh (competitive provision) age of telecoms regulation. In both cases the regulator's specialized knowledge and understanding of the underlying technical issues developed rapidly.

It seems difficult to argue that either of these issues could have been handled effectively except through a process dominated by a Cartesian-bureaucratic style. They called for the classic features of Weberian bureaucracy: specialization and technical knowledge to develop rationalizing solutions. If there was a problem with the numbering case in terms of technical (as opposed to media-political) management, it was that Oftel was not able to be Cartesian-bureaucratic enough, as a result of its initially limited expertise, BT's failure to give any indication of the 'sleepers' hidden in the policy system Oftel inherited in 1994 and Oftel's apparently naive belief that a BT information system devised for the third age of telecoms regulation could be readily adapted for the seventh. The Cartesian-bureaucratic features of Oftel's handling of the PCR could also have been augmented if it had not been for familiar Oftel organizational problems (discussed earlier) of poor institutional memory and weak information exchange across its changing structure.

However, both episodes also indicate some of the weaknesses of relying too heavily on the Cartesian-bureaucratic decision style. In the PCR case, that style was set to produce a perhaps excessively safe and tame price regime, presenting little challenge to BT, until the DGT's last-minute intervention pushed it away from the econocrats' models to a bolder stance underpinned by a strategic hunch rather than the formal information base (but at the same time running the risk of legal or administrative challenge in a worst-case outcome). In the numbering case, the Cartesian-bureaucratic style produced a solution that was defensible and workable as a way out of a yawning crisis, but involved a potentially dangerous underlap between the numbering technocrats and the Oftel top brass with their finely-tuned political antennae when the policy suddenly encountered choppy media-political water producing a PR disaster for Oftel. If the numbering policy, rather than being left to the organization's 'technostructure' (in the language used by Mintzberg (1983)), had been developed by a combination of technostructure and strategic apex in the way that the PCR was through its core project group, that underlap could have been reduced and political intelligence integrated with technical problem-solving at an earlier stage. We leave to the final chapter the more general issue of how far telecoms regulation experience suggests it is possible to combine the strengths of the Cartesian-bureaucratic style with those of the others, without risking a worst-of-all-worlds outcome.

8 Regulating anti-competitive conduct and not regulating hotel phone pricing: adhocratic-chaotic issue-processing episodes

A difficulty for every solution

Attributed to Lord Samuel (1870–1963)

This chapter gives an account of two policy episodes in which issue-processing seemed to be dominated by the adhocratic-bureaucratic decision style. As described in Chapter Six, the adhocratic-bureaucratic decision style is characterized by an unstable and shifting set of stations in the issue-machine; semi-explicit or disputed objectives that are 'discovered' mainly through process rather than established *ex ante*; and a style of issue-processing that is lateral rather than linear, with solutions looking for problems and different elements intermingling in an unpredictable way as the policy saga unfolds.

One of the two policy episodes discussed here is only a small fragment of a larger story, more of which will be told in the next chapter. That is the early part of the 1994–7 Fair Trading Condition episode (the process by which a new licence condition to control anti-competitive behaviour, originally directed at BT, came to be included in operating licences for all UK telecoms operators). This episode – only the opening scene or act in the whole FTC drama – is a classic case of 'a solution looking for a problem', although later the action shifted into a predominantly bargaining-diplomatic style, as will be discussed in the next chapter.

The second episode is the way that allegedly excessive charges for the use of telephones in hotel bedrooms were handled by the telecoms regulatory issue-machine in a decision round in the mid 1990s. The latter case is a classic example of a polycentric issue (cf. Fuller 1978; Yeung 1999: 52) involving a changing cast of actors with different preoccupations and in which the locus of decision kept moving sideways until, finally, all impetus was lost. If the FTC episode indicates some of the policy creativity that an adhocratic-chaotic decision style can achieve (as suggested by Mintzberg (1983) in his account of adhocratic organization), the hotel phone pricing story is a case of largely fruitless expenditure of bureaucratic energy in reinventing the wheel, passing the parcel or going round in circles.

As in the last chapter, neither of these episodes constitutes a pure case of a single decision style, even if the adhocratic-chaotic style seems to have been the predominant one. The Fair Trading Condition story involves a strong element of the bargaining-diplomatic style from the outset, given the way the rules of the game for licence modification encouraged agreed solutions between BT and Oftel, as noted in Chapter Two. But the focus of interest here lies in how the FTC emerged as a perceived solution within Oftel shortly after the advent of a new DGT and was then followed by a search for problems. The mid 1990s hotel phone pricing saga also involves some element of the bargaining-diplomatic style, particularly at the point where predictable conflicts developed between producers who wanted self-regulation and consumer lobbies who wanted legal compulsion. But the bargaining did not become the central feature of the story because instead of policy closure being achieved through the striking of a deal (as happened with the FTC), the action simply moved to another location. The Cartesian-bureaucratic decision style seems to play a minor part at best in both of these episodes.

'A WATCHDOG READY TO LEARN NEW TRICKS'[1]: SOME EARLY SCENES FROM THE FAIR TRADING CONDITION STORY

Background: a solution in search of a problem?

This episode concerns the way that the idea of a new licence condition to control anti-competitive behaviour by all UK telecoms licensees emerged from the policy process in the mid 1990s. What is of interest here is the agenda setting part of this decision process: we deal with the later bargaining and the endgame in the next chapter.

In December 1994 Oftel published a consultation document setting out plans to develop a licence condition for BT's licence which would create a general prohibition on anti-competitive conduct. It declared (Oftel, 1994: 26): 'Oftel believes that it should be possible. . . . to draw up a new general licence condition prohibiting anti-competitive behaviour by a licensee.'

How and why did this idea emerge? The equivalent paragraph of the original draft of the same consultation document, written only a month earlier, makes no reference at all to the idea of a Fair Trading Condition and indeed contains a policy conclusion very different to that suggested in the final draft. The corresponding paragraph of the original draft states:

> Oftel believes that once [customer interfaces] has been resolved [through a specific licence modification] and the proposed new ['general prices'] condition is in place, *there are currently no significant gaps in the scope of the powers within UK competition law* (draft chapter, Oftel consultation document, 14 November 1994 – emphasis added, but square brackets in original).

A search of Oftel's internal files revealed no evidence of any fresh in-depth analysis having been carried out within the organization over the month between the draft and final version of the consultation document to underpin this remarkable shift in policy diagnosis. So it seems hard to attribute the change to a Cartesian-bureaucratic process of the type discussed in the last chapter. Nor was it even clear that there was any immediate policy problem to be resolved, or (to put it differently) that the measure being mooted by Oftel could plausibly be expected to deal with those problems of anti-competitive behaviour that *were* perceived within the telecoms policy community.

The proposal to insert new rules of conduct into BT's licence certainly did not come from Oftel's Branch 4, which was responsible for competition enforcement. In fact, information available to Oftel on the subject was absent, confusing or contradictory, since (curiously) the organization lacked much previous experience in the evaluation of anti-competitive behaviour. Branch 4 staff had not detected a problem and had not argued for a new licence condition in the interval between the draft and final version of the consultation document.

Moreover, BT's operating licence contained a number of conditions that already prohibited specific forms of anti-competitive conduct. In fact, even during more than two years of work to introduce a specific Fair Trading Condition (FTC) not a single example of anti-competitive conduct that would not be caught by the existing rules was discovered, in spite of strenuous attempts to do so. Such an absence of a 'problem' might suggest to the sceptical observer that Oftel's original analysis in the November draft of the 1994 consultation document made more sense than the final version.

Third, the idea of a Fair Tradition Condition did not emerge directly from the telecoms industry. Though there undoubtedly was concern among other telecoms firms about potential anti-competitive behaviour by BT, there was no real prospect that a licence modification would effectively deal with the problems that those firms perceived. What mainly concerned the OLOs, BT's competitors, was the lack of effective enforcement of *existing* licence conditions applying to BT, not gaps in those conditions that needed to be filled. Oftel received numerous complaints from OLOs on this subject. What the OLOs were seeking was more vigorous enforcement combined with the threat of real penalties for breach of licence conditions. For example, a senior Mercury manager published an article in 1995 (Bryan-Brown 1995: 121) arguing that the burden of action should shift 'from action by the regulator to self-enforcement by the regulated firm' (thus eliminating much of the informal dialogue which figured large in Oftel's *modus operandi*), leaving the regulator with the task of wielding the big stick at the point where self-enforcement failed.

In fact no amount of licence modification – by a fair trading condition or anything else – would have directly addressed such concerns. At that time the UK competition law allowed little scope for private enforcement, and much of the emphasis in enforcement lay in discretionary investigation by regulatory bodies with no direct powers to impose fines on firms they found guilty of anti-competitive conduct, in contrast to the powers exercised by the European Commission (see Yeung 1999: 49–54). There is some parallel with Oftel's position over the enforcement of telecoms regulation in that, as noted in Chapter Two, it was heavily circumscribed by enforcement rules preventing speedy action against violators or putting sanctions such as fining ability directly into the hands of the regulator. Any formal enforcement action by Oftel was therefore a cumbersome and long drawn out process, involving the publication of a provisional or final order: no hard penalties were available until a breach of the relevant order enabled Oftel to bring a case to court and the court was satisfied there had been a violation. If a licence modification prohibiting anti-competitive conduct was a policy solution, it certainly did not emerge from (or even plausibly address) the problem the OLOs were chiefly concerned about.

Accounting for the emergence of the FTC idea

If, as argued above, the emergence of a proposal to include a licence condition prohibiting anti-competitive conduct cannot be explained by internal analysis within Oftel, new thinking emerging from Oftel's competition experts in Branch 4, the discovery of obvious gaps in BT's existing licence conditions that permitted anti-competitive conduct, or pressure from BT's competitors, how can this 'solution in search of a problem' pattern (a key feature of garbage can decision processes, according to Cohen, March and Olsen (1972)) be accounted for? Was it simple confusion, or something more?

It seems that at least three interrelated elements combined to produce this outcome. One was the beguiling force of EC competition law as a model for utility regulators to emulate, a model which appears to have played an important part in the thinking of a number of Oftel staff and of the DGT in particular. Don Cruickshank wished to appear as ferocious to telecoms licensees as the European Commission had seemed to him during his career in business. As he put it, in characteristically incisive style: '[I]f the UK competition authorities called on a Friday afternoon, the matter could wait until Monday. However, if the European Commission turned up, the weekend golf was called off'.

In fact, the corporate behaviour Cruickshank observed probably derived as much from the *in terrorem* effects of European Commission's direct ability to impose fines for anti-competitive behaviour (unlike the UK competition authorities, as noted above) as from the substance of the law. Nevertheless, the FTC proposal was justified on the grounds that it would make control over BT more like the framework of EC competition law, involving a move from highly specific to more general rules (cf. Diver 1982). Cruickshank had followed that line of analysis seven months before the December 1994 consultation document, when reporting to DTI Ministers after his first year in office. He had argued that special provisions for the utilities regulators, based on Article 86 of the EC Treaty:

> . . . would paradoxically, lead to much less intrusive and detailed regulation of privatised companies. Only BT's residual sense of public service and deep-seated need for public esteem prevent current competition problems becoming unmanageable. (Letter of April 1994, supplied by DGT).

At the outset, the FTC proposal emulated the EU model only in moving from specific to more generalized rules, not in the enforcement features of that model. Only later (perhaps to link the proposal more closely to OLO concerns) did senior Oftel staff start to suggest that making the rules more general would serve to speed up enforcement. As time went on the Oftel top brass started to argue that it was the number and complexity of the specific anti-competitive conduct conditions built into the licence that worked against tough enforcement by Oftel. (Though a sceptical observer might attribute Oftel's enforcement style less to the specificity of licence conditions than to a mixture of a cultural penchant for dialogue and informality mixed with the procedural obstacle course the organization had to go through to exercise its enforcement powers.) For example, at the first public hearing on the FTC, held in October 1995, Don Cruickshank argued a new licence condition was needed to fill gaps and speed up enforcement.

Closely related to the EU analogy was a developing ambition on the part of senior Oftel staff to reposition the organization within the regulatory space as a competition authority rather than a mere industrial regulator. Such a measure was seen as a way for Oftel to come to terms with the shift from the sixth to the seventh age of telecoms regulation as discussed in Chapter Two (and in the process, no doubt, to move up market in the bureaucratic world). As noted in Chapter Two, Oftel's original formal mission of 1984 was becoming outdated after a decade, as a large number of firms entered the telecoms market and new technology changed the nature of the business. And much of the legal authority needed to shape that developing market was controlled by other bureaucratic actors. In particular, the DTI owned general UK competition policy and an increasing flow of Directives from Brussels established a growing ownership claim over the telecoms policy space for the EC. Changing its stance from a predominant focus on nitty-gritty price control over BT to a broader competition authority remit would enable Oftel to present itself as responding decisively to the advent of the seventh age of telecoms regulation and (given the culturally sacred status of competition in the public language of business and politics at the time) would establish the organization as something other than an old-fashioned utility regulator.

A third (and also closely related) element that may have contributed to the emergence of the FTC as a policy idea is the play of 'symbolic politics' (Edelman 1964). Or – what would amount to the same thing in this case – it could reflect the commonly-observable bureaucratic trait of delivering the readily doable, even if the doable is a solution ill-matched to the underlying problem. (Schaffer and Lamb (1981) call this propensity the 'bureaucratic paradox' or irony). As explained earlier, what the OLOs really wanted to deal with anti-competitive behaviour by BT (tougher enforcement of existing licence conditions) could not feasibly have been delivered by Oftel given the legal and political constraints within which it had to operate. Fixing the underlying enforcement problem perceived by the OLOs would have required fundamentally new legislation from the government and might well have raised more general – and politically very sensitive – issues about the underlying framework of competition law. That route was firmly barred, since the then government had explicitly rejected the idea of introducing a general statutory prohibition on anti-competitive conduct (Oftel, 1994: 26–7). So if Oftel wished to be seen to be doing something in response to OLO concerns about anti-competitive behaviour and to establish its 'competition authority' credentials, licence modification – a procedure on which it had the power to take initiative – was effectively the only route open to it.

The consultation process: looking for the problem, seeking allies

Having come up with a preferred policy solution, probably as a result of some mixture of the elements outlined above, Oftel began to seek a problem for its solution to address. It did so by embarking on a lengthy process of debate, consultation and deliberation that lasted for more than two years – from the publication of the December 1994 consultation paper to the final incorporation of the new condition 18A into BT's licence early in 1997. In common with other utilities regulators, Oftel developed a considerably more elaborate and lengthy procedure for consultation with industry and the public than was required by the statute establishing the regulatory regime.

In that consultation and deliberation process, Oftel needed to do two things to build up support for its FTC proposal. One was to persuade the telecoms regulatory community that there was in fact a problem to which the FTC was the solution. (Rather than, as was suggested earlier, a confusion of two analytically distinct issues, namely: whether there were adequate substantive rules in BT's licence which prohibited anti-competitive conduct, and whether Oftel had adequate and effective procedural powers to require BT to comply with those substantive rules.) As noted earlier, the OLOs had not been involved in the initial definition of the FTC proposal (in spite of the fact that they were likely to know most about actual or potential anti-competitive conduct by BT) and their involvement in the deliberation over the process was limited and late.[2] However, through the consultation process Oftel did succeed in obtaining the support of most of the OLOs.

To smooth the path of the FTC proposal, Oftel also needed to use the consultation process to obtain critical support from other key actors. It needed to obtain BT's agreement if it was to achieve a consensual licence modification according to the procedure summarized in Chapter Two, rather than having to refer the issue to the MMC as an outside arbitrator. And it needed to allay the bureaucratic jealousy that the DTI was likely to display at the prospect of another organization – and a junior partner at that, as several senior DTI staff seem to have seen Oftel – trampling on its general competition policy turf. So both BT and the DTI needed to be won round to the idea of the FTC.

How that result was eventually achieved will be discussed in the next chapter; but it is worth noting here that it was very unusual for the DTI to participate at all in deliberations over licence modification proposals, either in telecoms or in any of the other utility domains. That the DTI was an active participant in the FTC policy process seems to have stemmed from two related factors. One was a basic issue of bureaucratic turf. The DTI saw itself as 'owning' competition policy and perceived Oftel as trespassing on that territory through its FTC proposals. Second, some senior DTI staff were concerned that Oftel's FTC proposal might be inconsistent with general government policy. When shown drafts of the December 1994 consultation document, one DTI interpretation was that Oftel was seeking to take on powers to control anti-competitive conduct in a form which the Secretary of State for Trade and Industry had already explicitly rejected. A senior DTI official warned Oftel that the 'Secretary of State would need to be persuaded of the value of a general anti-competitive behaviour licence condition, if he was not to refer the proposed amendment to the MMC . . .' and suggested demoting the idea of a new licence condition to the level of speculation rather than a firm proposal.[3] But the DTI seems to have been seen within Oftel as playing its cards in a rather unpredictable way during the FTC process. Part of the explanation of that inscrutability may be that there seem to have been divisions within the DTI itself over the issue, notably between its Competition Policy Division (CP) and its Communications and Information Industries Division (CII). According to one respondent the CII 'had to fight an internal battle in favour of the [new licence condition] because many people here could see further trouble down the track'.

Indeed, the long drawn out policy process over the FTC meant that a wide range of actors could participate in the debate – including BT and its competitor firms, the DTI, the European Commission and user groups. Not only did many actors drift in and out, but the FTC policy process was also the focus for discussion of a range of loosely connected issues extending beyond the anti-competitive conduct of BT. The DTI introduced discussion of other mechanisms for making Oftel's enforcement of anti-competitive conduct rules more effective. Competitors to BT sought not only to give Oftel enhanced powers, but also to gain enforcement powers for themselves as third parties to pursue BT for damages. BT itself introduced the principle that any new anti-competitive conduct rules should be applied to all PTOs and not just to BT's licence.

In principle such features could easily have led to the same sort of crabwise policy movement that resulted in our second episode on hotel phone pricing (to be discussed below), with a directionless process culminating in stalemate or exhaustion. In fact, as we shall see in the next chapter, the FTC process shifted into a mode dominated by the bargaining-diplomatic decision style. As the process went on, Oftel chose to link the proposed new licence condition with its proposals to deregulate BT's retail prices and introduce a price cap on BT's wholesale prices (part of the 1995–6 PCR discussed in the last chapter). Such a deal was calculated to appeal to BT, since it offered substantially reduced regulatory price control over much of BT's business, and it produced eventual policy closure in the form of a licence modification agreed between BT and Oftel without the necessity of a referral to the MMC.

Overall

Our account suggests the FTC was a supply-driven rather than demand-driven policy proposal. One key element shaping that proposal seems to have been a new DGT (and some other Oftel staff) whose previous career had impressed him with the structure of EU competition policy as a model or metaphor for a more effective approach to utility regulation. Interacting with that impulse was an 'entrepreneurial bureaucracy' (Corwin 1983) seeking to reposition itself within its policy space in a way that called for an upgraded policy role and corresponding decline in the nitty-gritty of detailed control over BT. It seems difficult to make sense of the radical shift in policy stance between the consultative document that initiated the FTC policy process in December 1994 and the draft as it stood a month earlier except by reference to such factors. It was a moment when actors were changing, objectives were in flux and means-ends relationships were not clear.

What emerged from this process was a creative policy proposal that ultimately led to a major shift in Oftel's regulatory stance, with a sharp reduction in the scope of detailed price control over the dominant provider accompanied by more general conditions governing behaviour in the telecoms market. Not only did this change support Oftel's repositioning of itself as a competition authority, it also served to enhance the regulator's capacities and credibility in licence enforcement generally, notwithstanding the fact that the licence condition eventually agreed was less than wholly useful (to be discussed in the next chapter). It could be considered a species of policy entrepreneurship involving a vision of how Oftel could adapt to the seventh age of telecoms regulation that went ahead of current industry demand or the preoccupations of the competition experts in the bureaucracy and the information they were working on. This episode therefore shows some of the ways that the adhocratic-chaotic decision style – involving lateral processing, multiple overlapping players and pervasive polyvalence involving ambiguous policy technology – can bring innovation into the policy process.

EPISODES FROM 'THE GREAT HOTEL PHONE SCANDAL'[4]

Background

In this second case of adhocratic-chaotic issue-processing, the initial problem was a perception that hotels charged rates far above ordinary residential or business prices (measured against BT's tariffs) for calls made from hotel bedrooms. How much of a 'problem' such behaviour was, is debatable. Complaints to Oftel about the issue from the public ran at about one or two a month (Internal Oftel Memo, 2 December 1994 *Payphones – Information to be Displayed*), hardly indicating that it was a burning popular issue. And though hotels might be viewed as local monopoly suppliers of telephone facilities able to use their position to exploit their customers, any such monopoly was far from complete and was certainly being rapidly eroded by mobile phones and charge cards.[5] But in some cases the mark-ups were clearly exorbitant, producing adverse comment and complaints to Oftel. From a consumer protection viewpoint, the problem might be seen as one of unfairness: there was a limit to what hotel customers could reasonably be expected to contribute towards the infrastructure of handsets, networks and telephone switchboards.

However, hotel phones did not count as public payphones and thus could not be regulated by Oftel in the same way. Public payphones (those with open access, for example in the street) were subject to regulation through the RPI–*x* price control described in the last chapter. But payphones in an area to which public access could be controlled – for example in a pub, sports hall or hotel – were deemed private payphones and no price control applied to them at all. (Such phones were covered by a class licence, the Telecoms Service Licence (TSL) or the Self-Provision Licence (SPL)). The 1984 Telecoms Act did not control retail prices of services and indeed specifically precluded the DGT from exercising such powers; thus hoteliers could legally charge anything they wished for the telephone service they provided.

The only power the DGT had over the use of payphones was through licence conditions. The TSL class licence required a display of information about tariffs (Condition 9) and the Oftel Technical Requirement (OTR: 002 1991) which set approval standards for payphones also required tariff information to be displayed on or near the phone (Section 7). Failure to display such information was held to alter the equipment and, since the altered equipment did not meet the technical approval requirements, it became illegal, in principle allowing Oftel to take enforcement action. But the vast majority of payphones failed to display any information at all and Oftel did not perceive itself as adequately resourced for 'hard' policing of those conditions. (When Oftel received complaints about failure to display charges, the organization's standard operating routine was to write to the phone owner explaining the legal requirements and such letters usually resulted in apologies and promises of future compliance.) The Technical Requirement (OTR: 002 1991) only covered pre-paid payphones, where a coin, card or token had to be inserted before the call went through. It did not apply to the post-paid type (where payment was demanded after the call had been made) which was typical of hotel bedroom phones. It seems that post-paid phones were simply forgotten when Oftel had drawn up the relevant technical standards in 1990–91 to replace an earlier 1988 standard.

That omission is curious, given that Oftel had received a steady trickle of consumer complaints about hotel phone charges over many years, and the issue also produced periodic media interest to which Oftel seems to have felt obliged to respond. A case in point was an

1993 article headed 'Outrage at Hotel Calls Surcharge' in *The Times* (3 October 1993), which declared:

> Business and leisure travellers are becoming increasingly concerned about the high mark-up estimated at 700% or more charged by some hotels for using hotel telephones. They are also angry at moves by some hotels to block toll-free calls made to telephone chargecard companies such as AT&T or BT, a tactic often used by frequent business travellers to avoid paying hotel telephone surcharges. Many hotels have now agreed to allow such toll-free calls but make a charge, on average about £1.50, every time the number is called . . .

The hotel phone charge policy minuet

Indeed, it was critical media coverage of this type that provoked Oftel in 1994 to a renewed search for a policy in a domain within which it had no firm mandate, no clear ownership of the policy issue or well-understood policy technology for addressing it. There were at least four other chaotic features on top of those characteristics of adhocratic-chaotic decision-making. First, as with the FTC case, a wide range of actors drifted in and out of the process. Although the hotel phone charge issue was apparently a minor one (and in a developing age of mobile phones, arguably a backward-looking one as well), it drew many participants into policy deliberations. Those participants included not only consumer and hotelier groups, but also the DTI, which had general responsibility for consumer protection policy, and local authority Trading Standards Departments which enforce consumer protection laws.

Second, the issue cut across the activity of different functional divisions of Oftel, exposing the tendencies for weak horizontal information exchange within the organization (as discussed in Chapter Three), which meant that the various branches often did not know what the others were doing. In this case, just as staff in Oftel's Branch 2 initiated one set of actions to increase Oftel's leverage over hotel phones, staff in Branch 5 were moving in the opposite direction, busily removing the non-technical, consumer protection aspects of the TSL class licence in accordance with EU policy. Third, Oftel's powers in this domain were uncertain, and legal opinion about what those powers actually were changed once the licence conditions had been closely scrutinized. Finally, the issue exposed the weaknesses in Oftel's institutional memory that were discussed in Chapter Three.

It emerged that Oftel had in fact attempted to tackle the problem in a previous round of decisions only four years earlier, but – contrary to Weberian bureaucratic stereotype – all memory of this policy episode had been lost within the organization.[6]

When the issue re-emerged with the publication of *The Times* article in October 1993, a new DGT (Don Cruickshank, appointed five months earlier) asked his staff whether steps could be taken to address the problem to which the article referred. The new DGT (who had been on holiday in France, noted there was a 40 per cent surcharge limit for using phones in French hotels and thought the UK could do better) had the idea that Oftel could campaign for a self-regulatory solution. What he had in mind was some 'informal well publicized "expect a 30 per cent surcharge, no more" rule in hotels'. But the idea was taken no further. Contrary to the absolutist stereotype of the utility regulators discussed in Chapter Five, the DGT was held back from taking further action by his senior staff, no doubt reluctant to involve Oftel in a policy domain where it had neither clear authority nor a clear reason to act.

Oftel's next move in the hotel pricing saga was prompted by another newspaper article in 1994. Under the heading 'How Hotels Ring Up a Rip-Off', *The Observer* (24 April 1994) reported that a major hotel chain was publicizing a plan to charge for hotel phone calls at the price it paid BT for them. Oftel's immediate response to this news was to draft a public letter of congratulations on the good practice of the hotel chain named in the article, to be sent by the DGT with the intention of shaming other hoteliers. But on checking the facts, Oftel staff realized they did not actually know anything about the practices of other hotel chains. So the letter was never sent. Nevertheless, Oftel staff continued to look for a way of tackling the hotel phone charges issue because of the DGT's continuing interest. An internal briefing document (*Hotel Telephone Charges, Memo 23 August 1994)* laid out the options:

> The two avenues of regulation that Oftel has explored are the Telecommunications Services Licence (TSL), which covers those providing telecommunication service to others, and the possibility – currently dormant due to lack of resource – of drawing up a Payphone Code of Practice . . .

But the memo noted that both of these options only concerned measures to oblige information about costs and charges to be provided to consumers to make their choices better-informed:

'Controlling price levels is perhaps more problematical, and it is not immediately clear whether this is a regulatory issue within Oftel's remit or whether it is a desirable policy to pursue'.

In fact, Oftel's initial legal advice to the DGT was that he had no powers of legal compulsion because the wording of OTR: 002 failed to include post-paid phones (as noted earlier). The DGT was advised that he might establish a task force to act as a 'catalyst, bringing interested parties together to seek to resolve the problem' (*Memo 30 August 1994*). This advice pointed in the direction of establishing a voluntary Code of Best Practice concerning the provision of pricing information to users of hotel room phones.

Accordingly, a Hotel Telephone Charges Task Force was established in September 1994 to initiate change in a policy domain where the DGT was believed to lack any formal powers. It was set up using the Secretariat of the Statutory Advisory Committees (ACTs) based in Branch 2, because the ACTs were 'a good independent medium that [Oftel] can support (with time, money etc.) on this issue'. The Chair of the Business Advisory Committee on Telecommunications (BACT) was to act as chair of the Task Force. Membership was carefully selected to balance consumer and commercial interests, with representatives from the ACTs, hoteliers, a representative of the English Tourist Board and representatives from both a hotel industry trade association and a consumer advocacy group. Support from the consumer and trade associations was seen by Oftel as a political precondition for any legitimate solution.

As soon as it was set up, the Task Force was presented with Oftel's favoured solution, a voluntary code of practice for hoteliers. But though the Task Force was intended to report to the DGT by the Spring of 1995, it was only able to meet three times and not with great regularity, owing to the other commitments of its members. It considered three areas for action, suggested by its secretariat: how to inform customers about charges for hotel telephones; how to set charges for telephone services involving direct cost to hotels; and what arrangements should be adopted for other telephone services and equipment (like mobile phones and charge cards) which did not involve any direct cost to hotels. At its first meeting the Task Force agreed on two main courses of action. The CA would lead on a campaign of public education to convey the message that hotels were entitled to recover the costs of providing telephone services. Second, action would be taken to persuade hotels to display charges where customers would see them. The trade association would draft a code of practice and voluntary compliance would be included in the hotel grading systems used by the Tourist Boards. After this meeting the secretary of the Task Force told the Oftel Press Office (*Memo 20 December 1994*) that Oftel's stance on hotel pricing had changed and it was now taking a much more robust line than before. 'At this point everything was hunky dory . . .' The problem was clearly defined and responsibilities allocated.

Soon, however, there was an unexpected development. An internal memo (*Memo, 2 December 1994 'Payphones – Information to be Displayed'*), which derived from a review of public payphones being carried out by Oftel's Branch 5 and Branch 2, noted that the Oftel standard OTR: 002 1991 for payphones (which it described as 'an unhappy marriage of technical and consumer standards') was due to be withdrawn the following year to be replaced by National Technical Regulations (NTRs) linked to an EC Directive (91/363). NTRs would not generally contain any consumer requirements but in anticipation of the change a condition (Condition 9 [Display of Tariff Information]) had been included in the Telecommunications Service Licence requiring tariff (or other information) to be displayed as specified by the DGT. Condition 9 was 'applicable to telephones by which a person may, on payment of a charge however levied, initiate and make a call over one or more PSTNs' and the memo noted that the condition would apply to telephones in hotel bedrooms as well as open access payphones. It went on to discuss issues of enforcement, noting that Oftel did not engage in proactive enforcement of the existing payphone tariff display requirement, and instead confined itself to following up complaints from the general public (running at one or two a month) and occasional local purges by trading standards officers. It concluded cryptically that 'We need to adopt a balanced attitude to enforcement'.

It is said that the actual way this information passed across Oftel's subdivisions was through a conversation between the author of this memo and the secretary of the Hotel Task Force over a cigarette in the smoking room (noted in Chapter Three). The smoking room was the only communal, neutral space in the office and so was the best place to hear gossip and news. From a close examination of the licence regulating payphones the author had found a section on tariff display that he thought might cover all payphones of any type. He thought the Hotel Task Force might be interested after learning of its work in Consumer News, an in-house news sheet put out regularly by Branch 2. But what he had to say about the powers of the DGT under the TSL licences could have been readily discovered by reading Oftel's own Explanatory Guide to

Self-Provision Licences (SPL) and the Telecommunication Services Licence (TSL).[7]

Accordingly, a few days later the DGT was told that he might after all have the legal power to require display of tariffs within hotel rooms. The members of the Task Force were also informed of the newly discovered powers in a letter (9 January 1995) and asked to consider if they wished to pursue a formal regulatory route involving the exercise of those powers. But by the time the Task Force met for a second time in March 1995 Oftel had already decided to continue with the proposal for a voluntary code of practice, to be secured with the support of the Task Force. Perhaps predictably, the option of exercising legal power versus self-regulation split the Task Force between consumer and commercial interests. Indeed, at one point the representative of the Consumers Association suggested the CA might not be able to continue on the Task Force unless the DGT was prepared to use his powers to protect consumers. It required delicate negotiation, and a promise to use the threat of compulsion, albeit 'sensitively',[8] to keep the voluntary scheme afloat within the Task Force. Only three requirements relating to tariff display for hotel phones were proposed compared with the ten requirements for other payphones. The DGT broadly supported this approach, preferring to see if a voluntary scheme would work before turning to regulation based on powers of compulsion as a last resort.

An article on the Hotel Charging Task Force in an issue of *Oftel News* (March 1995) led to more information being volunteered to the secretary about related problems. As a result, Oftel discovered that hospital payphones were seen as presenting a problem similar to hotel ones, but (in the nature of the case) with an even more captive market. The secretary to the Task Force was contacted by Oftel staff in other branches who were dealing with related issues like blocking or charging for Freephone numbers, attempts to block mobile phone use, and even a major fraud involving phone cards at an airport hotel. Most importantly, the issue of hotel charging became linked to a payphone review going on in the Technical Branch.

In fact, the existence of multiple and overlapping regulators with a stake in the hotel payphone issue caused substantial turbulence in the policy process. Local Trading Standards Officers (TSOs), who had powers to prosecute for the provision of misleading information under general pricing legislation, were concerned about prices and tariff information for payphones generally.[9] In March 1995 their co-ordinating group, the Local Authorities Co-ordinating Body on Trading Standards (LACOTS), published a report, *Counting the Cost,* which showed that most private payphones did not display tariff information and even if displayed it was usually incorrect. This report attracted widespread publicity and caused renewed concern to the DGT about Oftel being seen to be failing to act within a domain where it might have been expected to take the initiative and be the main focus of expertise. While publicly welcoming the LACOTS report, the DGT stated that enforcement of the technical requirement by Oftel was not the best way to improve standards, since Oftel patently lacked the resources for extensive local enforcement.

So the issue moved sideways again, with a member of Oftel's Technical Branch writing to the DTI in May 1995 proposing that enforcement powers of TSOs be extended to include tariff information provided with private payphones. The DTI finally responded seven months later by suggesting an Order under section 4 of the Prices Act 1974 (as amended by the Price Commission Act 1977) to require provision of charging information with private payphones, which could be enforced by TSOs. The stately pace of correspondence continued, with a reply two months later from the head of Oftel's Branch 2 urging the DTI to extend the proposed Order to both pre-payment and remote payment phones to cover hotel room phones (*Letter of 14 February 1996*). But the proposed Order was the sort of solution that only brings fresh difficulties. Such a measure would necessarily add to local authorities' enforcement costs, possibly requiring central government to provide more funds to them and hence raising the politically sensitive issue of local authority finance. The proposed measure also ran counter to the spirit of deregulation espoused by the then government and its creation would unavoidably draw other government departments, such as the Department of Health, the DOE and its counterparts in Scotland and Wales, into the policy process.

By the time of the Task Force's third meeting in September 1995, its work had been overtaken by the DTI proposals to issue an Order involving legally enforceable tariff disclosure requirements on all operators of private payphones. Even if the voluntary route were to continue to be pursued, any code of practice would also need to be applied to NHS establishments, adding to the complexities of drafting. However, by this time the hotel industry members of the Task Force had become preoccupied with another technical problem. BT had proposed to phase out the metered pulses which hotels used to log call charge information, a change which would make hotel telephone logging systems obsolete. The problem was summarized in an internal memo to Branch 6 (*Possible Unfair Cross-Subsidy Issue 12 September 1995*):

> BT explained that, since it no longer had a need for the pulses for its own charging purposes, it would cease to generate them. The hoteliers asked what pricing would be necessary to secure retention of the service to them. BT would not quantify, but simply said 'too much'. The hoteliers suggested that they as customers should be the judges of how much they were prepared to pay, but BT was unmoved. However, it is not entirely true that BT has no further internal need for meter pulsing. It will remain the charging basis for all calls made from public call boxes. Therefore the company must continue to generate the pulses and could, presumably, still make them available to customers. How would Oftel's accounting separation and cross-subsidy rules impact? Would it be allowable – or, indeed, preferred – for the bulk of pulse generation cost to be met by the payphone account and charges to external users set to recover only the incremental costs of delivering the service to them? I would be grateful for your thoughts on this point.

At this point the hotel room phone price issue moved sideways yet again, in the direction of issues of interconnection and account separation. Thereafter the Task Force seems to have been paralysed by the uncertainties surrounding the issue, and no clear proposals emerged.

Overall

The hotel phone charging issue shows a recurring cultural propensity for informal solutions within Oftel and a disinclination to be involved in extensive enforcement activity over powers of legal compulsion, even to the point of being prepared to argue for additional funding for other organizations to do the job. But – more to the point here – it brings out the potential downside of an adhocratic-chaotic decision style. Policy ownership of and authority over the issue was diffused and uncertain, cutting across central and local government, Oftel and the DTI and different branches within Oftel. Since much of the work done in Oftel was personalized and compartmentalized, knowledge about other activities within the organization was precarious and often seemed to consist of serendipitous discoveries through limited informal information networks (as in the smoking room episode noted earlier) rather than firmly-established 'knowledge of the files' in Weberian bureaucratic style. Policy setting and enforcement powers were divided among three different bureaucratic spheres. Information was fragmented and confused, to the extent that even Oftel's legal experts did not readily grasp the regulator's own formal powers. Institutional memory of a previous decision round within the issue-machine in 1991 that had dealt with exactly the same issues and considered both voluntary measures and legal compulsion, had apparently been lost.[10] And the issue kept moving sideways in the rarified policy and organizational space; what began as a discrete issue of consumer protection became successively or simultaneously interlinked with issues of technical regulation, interconnection, billing information, local enforcement, deregulation policy, EC directives, competition and cross-subsidy. Hotel telephone charging was finally totally subsumed into the broader issues of private payphones, also under review. So in spite of all the energy and time devoted to the issue, no distinct policy output emerged in this case.

CONCLUSION

Adhocratic-chaotic issue-processing produced a bold new policy proposal in the shape of the FTC while Oftel spun its wheels going nowhere in the hotel phone pricing saga. We might conclude that the adhocratic-chaotic decision style can lead to both productive and unproductive policy outcomes. The most obvious difference between the two cases is that the hotel pricing issue never moved out of the adhocratic-chaotic decision style, while (as we shall see in the next chapter) the FTC case eventually resulted in policy closure because it moved into a predominantly bargaining-diplomatic style, through a linkage between the new licence condition and the new price regime discussed in the last chapter. Without that development, the FTC could easily have resulted in a (lack of) visible result similar to that of the hotel pricing case. Indeed, novel issues in the telecoms policy community over the period of our study often seemed to have been handled in predominantly adhocratic-chaotic style at the outset, with a later transfer of emphasis to the Cartesian-bureaucratic or bargaining-diplomatic style.

Why the hotel phone pricing case failed to make such a transition is not clear. As we have seen, it seems to have been a victim of Oftel's organizational demography as an emigrant and immigrant society (as discussed in Chapter Three). Staff changes, together with underlaps in the communication system in a 'bureaucracy of strangers' (cf. Heclo 1977: particularly if the strangers were non-smokers) meant that recollection of the previous decision round was wiped from the organization's memory banks and even that understanding of the regulator's current powers was weak and confused. But even once the point had been passed when those issues had been cleared up within Oftel, the issue failed to gel bureaucratically, perhaps because just at the point where a bargaining-diplomatic phase might have been reached (bargaining in the shadow of the law with the hoteliers, in the light of the DGT's rediscovered powers over all payphones), technological change in the form of the pulse-metering issue produced a completely new problem for the hoteliers.

Finally, one feature that links both of these cases is the way Oftel tended to handle regulatory enforcement. As we saw earlier, what really concerned the OLOs about BT licence conditions was what they perceived as roadblocks to effective enforcement, in the form of restrictions on third-party enforcement actions and an enforcement process which relied on the discretionary behaviour of a bureaucracy that seemed to be predisposed to accommodative solutions rather than wielding a big stick over Oftel (and which in any case had no direct sanctions in its own hands over licence enforcement). In the hotel pricing case, when it turned out that Oftel did after all have the legal powers to require display of tariff information by hoteliers, the reflex response was to seek to pass the responsibility to local Trading Standards Officers and to negotiate a voluntary agreement, rather than to exercise the powers it did have except as a last resort. A tendency to avoid confrontational policing tactics over enforcement might be considered a regulatory analogue to the 'patrol abandonment' so often observed in studies of police organization (cf. Hood 1998: 31–4), and it has been linked by some with a UK and more general European style of regulatory enforcement, in contrast with more formalistic US styles (Vogel 1986). Or it might be related to the patterns of negotiation the regulator pursued within the regulatory space. It is to negotiation and bargaining that we turn in the policy episodes considered in the next chapter.

9 Complaint handling, licence enforcement and anti-competitive conduct II: bargaining-diplomatic issue-processing episodes

There it was. My offer of a deal. Out in the open . . .

Lynn and Jay, *Yes Minister* (1981: 121)

This chapter explores policy episodes that appear to have been dominated by the bargaining-diplomatic decision style discussed in Chapter Six. It will be recalled that the bargaining-diplomatic style was seen as coming somewhere between the linear and lateral processing features of the Cartesian-bureaucratic and adhocratic-chaotic decision styles. In this decision style, outcomes depend on what the various parties to the process will accept rather than on the objectives of any one organization (as in the Cartesian-bureaucratic style) but the stations involved in issue-processing tend to be more identifiable and stable than in the adhocratic-chaotic style. As we noted in Chapter Six, the bargaining-diplomatic style appears to consist of at least two variants, namely a continuous process of cultural adjustment and definition of meaning through mutual interaction in the regulatory space, and periodic explicit bargaining, often conducted by high-level actors.

The latter type of bargaining was particularly encouraged by the rules of the game governing modifications to BT's operating licence, as noted in Chapter Two. BT was entitled under the 1984 Telecoms Act to reject licence modifications proposed by Oftel and thereby to force the issue to go for consideration by the MMC. These rules gave BT and Oftel strong incentives to come to terms, in order to avoid the uncertainties associated with arbitration by a third party outside the charmed circle of the telecoms world. But the rules also gave each party a holdout threat (to take the issue to MMC) that they could use to bring pressure on the other side. These conditions set the stage for strategic bargaining between Oftel and BT over what became Condition 18A in BT's licence. The underlying game structure had elements of the famous 'chicken' game of brinkmanship, with each side aiming to persuade the other that they would not be the first to blink or budge (cf. Scharpf 1994). It also had elements of the well-known Prisoner's Dilemma game, in that the benefits to both sides were greater if they were able to co-operate than if one side dug its heels in (see Melville 1994).[1] In the end BT won substantial concessions from Oftel during the policy process and used the threat of an MMC reference and a judicial review action to secure such concessions.

As in the last two chapters, two different policy episodes are examined. The first is the middle game and endgame that developed over the Fair Trading Condition case, the opening stages of which were explored in the last chapter. The bargaining about the legal details of the new regime established the relative power of the players to define what counted as competition and compliance, and resulted in the eventual creation of a licence condition which would be difficult if not impossible to use. The second decision-making specimen considered in this chapter is more a mini-case than an episode, and concerns the way Oftel went about handling complaints from consumers and telecoms firms. For both types of complaint the decision process was dominated by negotiation and bargaining with minor Cartesian-bureaucratic elements, and the process of responding to complaints involved both of the variants of the bargaining-diplomatic decision style identified in Chapter Six. It was, for instance, part of a larger process of mutual accommodation and negotiation within the telecoms community about the meaning of such culturally-defined terms as 'effective competition' or 'good service'. But at the same time the consumer complaint handling part of Oftel involved its own distinct organizational culture, semi-detached from the rest of the organization and not effectively used as part of its general intelligence capacity.

'OFTEL REVIEW GIVES WITH ONE HAND AND TAKES WITH THE OTHER'[2]: EPISODES FROM THE FTC MIDDLE GAME AND ENDGAME

Opening shots and general bargaining strategies

The last chapter described how Oftel came to float a proposal for a new condition prohibiting anti-competitive behaviour to be introduced into BT's operating licence in 1994. As has already been noted, to secure such a change in licence conditions, Oftel needed either to secure BT's agreement or refer the proposed modification to the MMC. The stage was therefore set for an extended process of bilateral bargaining, the chronology of which is briefly set out in Table 9.1.

Knowing its consent was needed to avoid the uncertainties of an MMC referral, BT's opening move was publicly to oppose the proposed FTC. It did not oppose general rules on anti-competitive conduct in principle. Instead it objected to Oftel having the legal power to determine what counted as anti-competitive conduct with no right of appeal. This move put BT into a relatively strong position to bargain over the details of the proposed new licence condition, because any such formal right of appeal could only have been created by legislation, which the DTI was unlikely to be willing to provide.

Table 9.1 Chronology of events – Fair Trading Condition policy process

December 1994	–	Publication by Oftel of *A Framework for Effective Competition* consultation document
July 1995	–	Publication by Oftel of *Effective Competititon: Framework for Action* policy statement
November 1995	–	Oftel held its first public hearing on proposals to deal more effectively with anti-competetive conduct
December 1995	–	Publication by Oftel of Proposed Fair Trading Condition (FTC) licence modification
June 1996	–	Publication by Oftel of final proposals for FTC linked to new price control
July 1996	–	Submission by Oftel to BT of final proposals for FTC and new price control
August 1996	–	BT accepts proposed licence modifications to introduce FTC and new price control
October 1996	–	BT Licence Modified to incorporate FTC and new price control
December 1996	–	Lawfulness of Oftel's modification of BT's licence to incorporate FTC upheld in judicial review action brought by BT
January 1997	–	FTC takes effect on BT
December 1997	–	Fair Trading Condition Advisory Committee holds that Oftel has failed to apply FTC correctly in first case in which condition is used against BT

Source: Oftel Annual Reports

Oftel, seeking to secure BT's agreement to the FTC without the necessity of an MMC reference, responded to BT's opposition to the FTC proposal in several ways. As described in the last chapter, it engaged in extensive processes of consultation, far beyond what was strictly required by the 1984 Telecoms Act, in an attempt to bolster its legitimacy and obtain support for the measure it was proposing from the OLOs. Moreover, it bargained extensively with BT over the details of the proposed licence condition throughout the decision process. The DGT claimed that Oftel did not engage in true bargaining over the FTC, and that any changes made during the consultation process were either trivial or did not amount to substantial concessions to BT. But this view was not widely shared within Oftel and seems hard to square with Oftel's observed behaviour or with the eventual outcome of the FTC. Moreover, notwithstanding his frequent protestations, Cruickshank himself had occasion to let the mask slip, as at the Oftel 'Awayday' when he was trying to explain to his staff how relations were conducted between Oftel and BT: 'Not that a regulator ever negotiates of course – we do everything in public, transparently – but, in reality, we are engaged in negotiation . . .'.

Oftel's broad bargaining tactics consisted of two general strands. One was to present BT with a credible threat of an MMC reference (just as BT aimed to use the same tactic against Oftel). In the background was the possibility that the DGT might propose to the MMC (or advise the Secretary of State to propose) that BT be broken up, along the lines of the 1984 break-up of AT&T in the US (Oftel, 1995d: 38).[3] Since the MMC had recommended as recently as 1993 that British Gas should be broken up, separating retail from wholesale operations (MMC 1993a; 1993b), such a risk had to be taken seriously by BT. (But the credibility of Oftel's threat was somewhat diluted by the fact that in the British Gas case the Secretary of State had failed to follow the MMC's recommendation.)

The other general bargaining tactic used by Oftel was a process of linkage – making BT's acceptance of a licence condition controlling anti-competitive conduct contingent on Oftel's agreement to deregulate other parts of BT's business. Oftel dangled the offer of removing various existing detailed conditions from BT's licence (and in particular of greatly reducing the scope of controls over BT's prices) as a *quid pro quo* for BT's acceptance of the FTC. Thus a linkage was established between the proposed FTC and the Price Control Review that was described in Chapter Seven.

The linkage of those two policy elements was first made in a speech by the DGT to a *Financial Times* conference late in 1995.

How far the linkage was rooted in a fundamental analysis on Oftel's part and how far it was a casual link adopted tactically for bargaining purposes, is debatable. In practice Oftel seems to have handled the two issues through parallel processing by different groups of people. Oftel's backroom staff appear to have done little or no detailed analysis on the linkage between the PCR and the FTC. During internal preparations for the subsequent judicial review, a Branch Head later said, 'I don't remember any analysis, it was all rather hand-waving stuff . . .' (e-mail on Oftel file). In fact, it seems unlikely that the outcome of the PCR, described in Chapter Seven, was in any substantial way affected by the putative link with the FTC. Nevertheless, Oftel's public stance was to stress the rational policy basis for the linkage. In a statement of June 1996, Oftel indicated that the very substantial reduction in the scope of the price control on BT (from more than 64% of revenue to about 26%) following the PCR would only be possible if the regulator '. . . also has powers to deal effectively with anti-competitive behaviour. Oftel therefore regards its Fair Trading proposals and the price control as part of a single package'. (Oftel, 1996: 11).

Thus Oftel was using a classic linkage tactic in bargaining, by presenting BT with the option of accepting or rejecting the PCR and the FTC as a single package. The carrot was deregulation of prices and the stick was the possibility of re-evaluation of this PCR policy should the FTC proposal fall.

Bargaining over this linkage was partly conducted in public. When it published its 'final' draft of the FTC for statutory consultation in June 1996, Oftel also published a letter from the DGT to the BT Board. The letter explained why Oftel considered the PCR and FTC to be indivisible proposals and why BT's rejection of one would be taken as a rejection of both. The argument was that the risk of narrowing the scope of price control gave BT the possibility of targeting particular groups of consumers for predatory pricing tactics (to the detriment of the effective competition that the DGT was statutorily required to maintain). So the claim was that the PCR needed to be balanced by powers available to Oftel 'to deal with such behaviour quickly' (Oftel Press Release, 42/96).

The suggestion that Oftel's rationale for the FTC-PCR linkage amounted to little more than 'hand-waving stuff' is supported by the fact that the DGT only mentioned one specific instance of additional risks of anti-competitive behaviour created by the reduction in the scope of price controls in his letter. And even that instance was not very convincing, since the predatory pricing behaviour to which the DGT referred in his letter was in fact already covered by existing conditions in BT's licence which prohibited undue discrimination or undue preference to particular classes of customer.[4] Indeed, it could be argued that the major deregulation accompanying the proposal was not the reduction in the scope of the price control associated with PCR. Rather it seems to have lain in the removal of detailed rules and conditions from BT's licence which were either already redundant or rendered redundant by the new Condition 18A. In fact, when Oftel sought Counsel's opinion (i.e. they consulted a barrister) on BT's prospects of winning a judicial review action over Oftel's FTC proposal, Counsel felt Oftel's inability to provide a reasoned justification for linking the PCR and the FTC was its weakest point (Counsel's opinion, 25 July 1996). (Fortunately for Oftel, BT did not choose to probe this linkage in the subsequent judicial review, even though it had questioned the linkage earlier in the policy process ([letter of 1 April 1996].)

The middle game

BT countered Oftel's tactics in several ways. First, it drew on its considerable capacity to evaluate Oftel's drafts and propose alternative measures – the familiar negotiating tactic of matching proposal with counter-proposal. BT pressed arguments it had made in many previous consultations with Oftel and also raised new issues. For example, it pressed for the FTC to be incorporated into all licences and not just that of BT (a proposal that chimed with Oftel's own thinking, as indicated in a letter to BT [2 November 1995]). Early in the process BT proposed an independent Hearing Officer, a senior figure removed from day-to-day operational tasks within Oftel, to handle complaints under the new licence condition. This proposal for a regulator built into a regulatory office was modelled on the Hearing Office within DG IV of the European Commission (OJ 1994 L 330/67, 21 December 1994) and was intended to stop Oftel acting as 'prosecutor, judge and jury' in competition cases. It was part of a broader attempt by BT to Europeanize the FTC, rendering it as close as possible to the EC competition regime with an advisory panel and powers to grant exemption. This in turn could be seen as a new twist on a long-established bargaining strategy by BT over licence conditions, namely to make enforcement procedure so complex as to be unworkable in practice.

Second, BT made use of other resources such as the media and its own shareholders. During the early part of 1996 BT shareholders were encouraged to attend several Oftel public hearings about new licence conditions. Substantial numbers of BT shareholders wrote both to the newspapers and to Oftel. But the use of press cuttings by BT in an attempt to show that the media supported its case does not seem to have been effective in influencing the DGT, who protested to BT's CEO about BT's use of selective quotations from reports and editorials and commented: 'This is the sort of thing that stokes the adversarial, personalized coverage of issues between us, and which I hope you would want to discontinue'*(Letter from Oftel to BT*, 20 February 1996).

Third, BT frequently supplied Oftel with various Counsels opinions on the DGT's legal powers to introduce the proposed Condition. This tactic hinted at an expensive and tiresome judicial review action if Oftel persisted with the FTC. And, as we shall see shortly, BT's eventual response to Oftel's linkage of the FTC with the price control took the form of a tactic Oftel had not anticipated. That is, it chose to agree the package of licence modification changes but then immediately sought a judicial review of Oftel's *vires* over the FTC issue alone. But BT's early threat of judicial review was a strategy designed to keep pressure on the regulator throughout the bargaining process. Even though BT eventually lost the judicial review action (and did not appeal it), it succeeded in obtaining a wide range of concessions. One senior BT lawyer saw the litigation as focusing the mind of Oftel and believed the threat of judicial review over the whole process led Oftel to limit its own discretion over enforcing the new licence condition.

Oftel in turn responded to BT's threat of judicial review by sending BT's Directors a summary of the Counsel's opinion it had received on the DGT's *vires* to implement the FTC (Oftel Press Release 42/96, Annex D), which contradicted the advice received by BT. BT had received advice that the specific Telecommunications Act 1984 regime was secondary to the general competition law regime under the Fair Trading Act 1973 and Competition Act 1980, and that any licence modification by the DGT which encroached on the general competition law would be *ultra vires*. Oftel paraded with a flourish the contrary legal advice it had received (Oftel Press Release 42/96, Annex D, para. 5).

The DTI weighed into the policy process in mid 1996, apparently prompted by effective lobbying by BT and, possibly, by BT's threat of judicial review action against Oftel. Oftel and BT had earlier jointly lobbied the DTI to secure new competition legislation, which would have satisfied BT's desire for a formal appeal mechanism against Oftel's decisions. At the time DTI refused this request but later appeared to waver about its earlier decision, thereby increasing uncertainty and driving a wedge between Oftel and BT. A newspaper report that the Secretary of State planned to introduce secondary legislation prohibiting anti-competitive conduct by PTOs, offering a right of appeal and possible appeal to the Secretary of State (*The Independent*, 2 July 1996) was used by BT as an argument for further delay in licence modification discussions. Oftel had not been informed about the DTI's apparent change of heart over its earlier decision, and the DGT protested to the Minister about a proposal on which he had not been consulted being canvassed in a press report. When the Minister subsequently met with BT and promised to implement secondary legislation rapidly, the DGT wrote again to the Secretary of State, refusing both his and BT's requests to delay modifying BT's licence. The DGT claimed that the DTI's proposed Statutory Instrument (which would make Oftel the competent UK authority for enforcement of Articles 85 and 86 of the EC Treaty) was 'highly deficient' as it would catch only conduct affecting inter-state trade. The DTI's intervention was a 'matter of regret' to Oftel as it hindered the regulator reaching an agreement with BT, possibly encouraging BT to seek an MMC reference (Letter of 18 July 1996).

The endgame: bargaining over details and the judicial review

As Table 9.1 shows, a draft of the proposed FTC was published in December 1995 (Oftel, 1995e), consultations over the draft took place during the first three months of 1996 and Oftel geared up for a final drafting session at the end of March 1996. Within Oftel there were two parallel teams at work, one on the PCR discussed in Chapter Seven and one on the FTC. The FTC timetable slipped a little owing to the DTI's involvement, as noted earlier, but the statutory public consultation over the draft FTC in June 1996 did not, in Oftel's view, raise any new issues and all consultees were in favour of the licence modification except BT. So from that point onwards it fell to Oftel and BT, virtually in closed session, to negotiate the final terms of the Condition. The rest of the industry was excluded from detailed participation by the mechanism of licence modification in the 1984 Telecommunications Act.

Indeed, for BT the key bargaining period began only after the public consultation over the 'final' draft of the FTC ended in the summer of 1996. New amendments agreed included, for example, a requirement that Oftel publish its office procedures for enforcement of the FTC; that the DGT was to give reasoned decisions for orders as well as determinations, and give reasons for departing from its Guidelines or decisions of the European Court of Justice; and that the FTC was to give a right to BT to require a reference to an Advisory Panel. The Advisory Panel was to be a statutory committee (under s54(3), TA 1984), comprising persons of such expertise and independence that they would not be compromised simply by having been appointed by the DGT. Its main role would be to advise on generic issues, but it would also advise on specific issues, and in the event of a final order for enforcement of licence conditions being made, BT could require the Panel to be consulted – inserting yet another step into the licence enforcement obstacle course described in Chapter Two. Oftel would in turn have to give reasons for any failure to follow the Panel's advice. To retain bargaining power BT indicated that because there was still no right of appeal in the proposed arrangements the BT Board was unlikely to consent to the licence modification under s12, TA 1984 (*Letter of 10 July 1996*). The extent of the concessions made at this point casts doubt on the DGT's claim, noted earlier, that no real negotiation took place over the FTC, except over trivial details. Oftel may have feared the MMC more than it admitted, or may have seen itself as vulnerable to an alliance between BT and the DTI.

Shortly before the final draft of the FTC, the DGT wrote to the BT board of directors explicitly setting out the bargain. Cruickshank told the BT Board they would benefit from the FTC because:

> – You will have a less intrusive regulatory regime.
> – Your managers will have more certainty . . .
> – Crucially, you will be able to operate more like managers in a competitive market, less like administrators of regulatory decisions.
> – You and the UK market, seen from abroad, will be more competitive and easier to 'sell' when that is required to advance your business overseas.
>
> (Oftel Press Release 42/96, Annex C, 4).

The latter point suggested that more explicit controls on anti-competitive conduct in the UK could improve BT's opportunities for reciprocal access to other markets by giving US and EU competition authorities less reason to express worries about the vertical integration of the BT operation. Indeed, The DGT made a controversial speech in the USA early in 1997 with the aim of convincing the US authorities that the UK market was both genuinely open and effectively regulated.

The final draft of the FTC was sent to BT on 18 July 1996, with the requirement that BT respond by 2 August. Numerous letters were exchanged in the cliff-edge wrangling between Oftel and BT in the subsequent fortnight. Oftel provided explanations and legal opinions that it was acting within its powers (*Letter from Oftel to BT*, 19 July 1996). BT argued the opposite (*Letter from BT to Oftel* 27 July 1996),[5] and sought delays pending the legislation promised by the DTI, as discussed above. Six days before the deadline for BT's response, there was a high-level meeting between the DGT and DDG and BT's Chief Executive and Company Secretary which went over the same sort of ground. In the face of BT's legal and other objections to the FTC, the DGT refused to delay its introduction. He tried to put extra pressure on BT by indicating that he had the draft of a reference to the MMC in front of him and that the reference would extend beyond the FTC to broader issues over BT's conduct.[6] The DGT was also invited to address the BT Board on 31 July prior to its final meeting on 2 August.

In the last few days of the countdown to the 2 August deadline, Oftel made yet another visit to Counsel to secure advice on revisions of the FTC and on a draft reference to the MMC. Four days before the deadline, on 29 July, BT hit Oftel with a draft notice of application for judicial review and 48 pages of affidavits, and indicated that BT might seek an expedited judicial review before an MMC reference. The next day the DGT wrote again to the BT Board setting out the concessions Oftel had agreed to and outlining the commercial advantages of the FTC and the risks for BT in rejecting it. Cruickshank's aim was to appeal directly to the BT Directors, possibly splitting the BT Board between the company officers and the other Directors.[7]

As noted earlier, BT's eventual tactics were not anticipated by Oftel. When Oftel's deadline expired, BT chose to agree the package of changes under s12 of the Telecommunications Act 1984, thus permitting the licence modifications to go ahead (*Letter from BT to Oftel*, 2 August 1996), but reserved its right to challenge the lawfulness of the measures. Then BT immediately sought a judicial review of Oftel's *vires* over the FTC alone. One Oftel employee saw this tactic as an ingenious way for BT to separate the PCR from the FTC and challenge the FTC on its own. Such a separation could not have been achieved through an MMC reference. But ironically that strategy led BT away from what (according to legal advice) was the weakest point in Oftel's legal armour – its inability to provide a reasoned justification for its claim that there was an indissoluble link between the PCR and the FTC.

After BT's agreement to the licence modification, Oftel embarked on a further round of statutory consultation with the telecoms industry. It did so because the changes made between the original consultation in June and BT's final agreement had been so extensive (another development that casts doubt on the DGT's claim that no real bargaining took place over FTC). During these consultations, a representative of the Cable Communications Association objected to a number of the changes, but such adverse comments seem to have had no bearing on the final form of the FTC. The bargain between Oftel and BT had been struck, and only minor drafting changes were made before the FTC was incorporated into BT's licence by consent on 1 October 1996.

Matters then proceeded to the final stage in the game in July 1996 – BT's application for judicial review of Oftel's *vires* for introducing the FTC. The DGT had refused to sign a 'side letter' prepared by BT agreeing not to oppose judicial review proceedings on any technical ground.[8] But Oftel did not use such technical grounds to oppose the proceedings (even though it might have been possible to argue that, since BT had not gone to the MMC, it ought not to be entitled to bring a judicial review application). Different accounts of this tactic were offered by Oftel staff. Several junior Oftel staff and BT legal staff believed there was an informal understanding that Oftel would not seek to stop the judicial review proceedings from going ahead. An alternative view within Oftel was that it made more sense to proceed directly to judicial review at that stage, since a hearing would clarify Oftel's powers and be likely to involve less cost and delay than a challenge over a particular application of the FTC.

Right up to the eventual courtroom drama, fairly intense and high-level contact between BT and Oftel continued to take place. The DGT was briefed for a telephone conversation with BT's CEO, to suggest that BT was in a no-win situation over its judicial review tactics. The argument was that BT should drop its litigation because the FTC would make the FCC (the US telecommunications authority) more likely to permit BT to operate in the US market without pressing for divestitute *à la* AT&T. The DGT made the same point to BT's Chairman just before trial started. However, BT rejected the DGT's advice, pressed ahead with its judicial action – and lost. The regulator prevailed in the Divisional Court but BT chose not to appeal, and indeed seems to have seen the litigation as worthwhile on the grounds that the judges' *dicta* on the case would further constrain the operation of the new Condition 18A.

Overall

The development and endgame of the FTC saga was a decision process dominated by bargaining and negotiation. As Table 9.1 shows, the FTC proposal underwent many changes during the middle game and endgame, though the significance of those changes (and in particular the importance of the concessions wrung out of Oftel by BT in the endgame) is debatable. And in this case, in contrast to the bargaining-diplomatic overlay for the PCR discussed in Chapter Seven, the bargaining was largely bilateral, apart from the occasional wild card intervention from the DTI and the role of the OLOs as cheerleaders for Oftel.

Unlike the hotel phone pricing saga considered in the last chapter, the FTC resulted in a clear outcome, in the sense that a new condition 18A was incorporated in BT's licence to take effect in January 1997, and a similar condition was incorporated into the licences of all the other PTOs. On the face of it, the new licence condition equipped Oftel to enforce rules against anti-competitive conduct against BT in a more timely and efficient fashion. Whether the reality was quite so positive for Oftel is much more debatable. In the course of countering BT's threats of judicial review and MMC referrals it had agreed to so many concessions that the shiny new weapon in the regulator's arsenal was likely to be difficult if not impossible to use. Indeed, with the ink barely dry on the new condition 18A, a lawyer from Oftel's own Legal Branch advised the Competition Branch (Branch 4) responsible for enforcing the FTC, that the new condition was so encumbered with procedural requirements that other licence conditions, and especially condition 17, should be favoured in enforcement actions wherever possible. The limitations of the new licence condition were demonstrated on the first occasion on which Oftel used it, to order BT to desist from charging for its charge card service at less than cost. The Advisory Committee set up under the new condition considered Oftel's analysis and held that Oftel had been wrong to find BT's conduct in breach of the rule. As a consequence Oftel was unable to move to a final order against BT (Oftel Press Release 95/97, 18 December 1997).

REGULATION AS NEGOTIATION: COMPLAINT-HANDLING EPISODES

In contrast to the high-level bargaining exhibited in the later stages of the FTC saga the style of negotiation and bargaining associated with the way Oftel responded to complaints by firms and consumers about public telecommunications operators was much less dramatic. While responses to both types of complaint involved a decision style that emphasized negotiation and bargaining over appropriate behaviour, complaints from telecoms firms carried far more weight than those coming from the general public (for all the Oftel rhetoric of 'the best possible deal for consumers . . .'). Indeed, within Oftel industry and consumer complaints were treated as completely different species, industry complaints being core to the regulatory agenda and providing a key source of information about licence breaches, and consumer complaints being a low level chore. The handling of consumer complaints was hived off into a separate unit in Oftel that was insulated from the 'policy' work of the rest of the organization.[9] There was, however, nothing inevitable about such a radical distinction between the two forms of complaint: rather it appears to be the product of an office culture in which industry problems were regarded as important while consumer problems were considered trivial.

Handling complaints from telecoms firms

Complaints from within the telecoms industry about the behaviour of PTOs were the source of the vast majority of Oftel's investigations into anti-competitive conduct.[10] During the first ten or more years of its existence Oftel sought co-operative solutions and rarely, if ever, invoked its formal powers to enforce the licence conditions setting out the obligations of PTOs.[11] This pattern of behaviour, observed in many other fields of business regulation in the UK, was noted by the Public Accounts Committee in 1998 (para. 5):

> Of the 217 investigations completed by Oftel between 1995 and 1997, only 17 led to any enforcement action being taken. We recognize that in a number of cases enforcement action was not taken because the parties reached agreement between themselves or the operator stopped the alleged anti-competitive behaviour. Nevertheless, we consider that taking enforcement action at an earlier stage in more investigations would send a clearer

message to the industry that Oftel are committed to tackling anti-competitive behaviour . . .

We observed this pattern of negotiation over industry complaints in several cases. One example was the issue of old-fashioned hard-wired telephones – those without a modern jack and socket. Between 1.6m and 1.8m customers in the UK were estimated still to have such phones in 1997 and for several years the statutory Advisory Committee on Telecommunications for Disabled and Elderly People (DIEL) had been concerned that these old-model phones prevented vulnerable low-income people, like the deaf and elderly, from making use of community telephone services designed to help them. Such services were only available on modern handsets that many of DIEL's constituents could not afford.[12] At first DIEL argued its case on grounds of fairness as a general consumer issue, with little success; but when the case was later reconfigured as a competition issue (inhibiting freedom of access to other operators and thereby limiting consumer choice for customers with hard-wired phones) Oftel took up the cudgels with BT. (During the period of our study, Oftel staff increasingly came to see anti-competitive conduct as the main problem to be addressed over licence enforcement. Thus if a complaint could be shown to raise issues of competition it received a more sympathetic hearing and was more likely to result in clear follow-up action.)[13] BT's response was a grudging agreement to run a special offer to promote conversion to modern sockets at no charge. The offer, however, was 'voluntary', and at no point was BT formally obliged by the regulator to take action.

Another example – this time of a sudden crisis rather than a long-running issue – was a complaint that originated in an irate phone call from a new-entrant PTO to Oftel's Branch 4 late on a Friday afternoon in 1996. The complaint, raising the issue of a potential breach of licence by BT, concerned the operation of the BT Tower in central London. The Tower is the major communications hub for south east England and is also the gateway for most European vision traffic (i.e. TV signals) into the UK. Traditionally the practice was for the various TV companies to telephone the BT Tower and directly book use of the circuits they needed. The introduction of competition into telecoms in the seventh age of telecoms regulation had enabled other network operators, such as the complainant, to lease private circuits in the BT Tower and, in turn, rent the capacity to TV companies as part of their own network service. But the old practice of directly booking circuits in the Tower through BT had continued.

The complaint in this case arose when BT unilaterally and without warning abandoned the informal practice of making bookings for the circuits that BT no longer owned in the BT Tower as well as for the ones it did own. Oftel's Branch 4 (colloquially called the competition branch, the fast-changing branch that handled licence enforcement and fair-trading issues) helped to facilitate a temporary solution involving a reversion to the *status quo*. ('Common sense would prevail for the weekend.' [Oftel *File Note* recording the telephone conversation between the complainant and Branch 4 and between Branch 4 and BT 13 December 1996]) On further investigation it turned out that the source of the problem was the interpretation placed by BT staff on a letter about another interconnection dispute, which had been mistakenly sent by Oftel straight to the BT Tower rather than to BT's Regulatory Affairs Department. That letter had been interpreted to mean that BT could not continue with informal arrangements for accepting switching instructions at BT Tower. Once Oftel stated it had no interest in the issue as a regulator, both sides returned to commercial negotiation.

What is notable about such cases is the extent to which the players in the telecoms industry used Oftel to resolve matters over which they were in dispute, and the characteristic style of informal brokerage with which Oftel approached such issues.[14] Neither BT nor the complainant responded to the crisis by immediately seeking legal opinion, and the complainant did not go to court to obtain an injunction. ('It just didn't occur to them', according to a member of the casework team.) Both the complainant, a new entrant to the industry, and BT, the former monopoly operator, apparently saw Oftel as the first resort and arbitrator, with Oftel's solutions taking precedence over normal commercial contracts. As long as the industry culture accepted rapid regulator-brokered solutions to disputes, such a response to problems was a rational step by the players. After all, in this case, there were no legal costs to the firms involved and a rapid informal solution was achieved because Oftel through its contacts knew exactly who to approach in BT to fix the problem quickly (the head of Branch 4 spoke directly to a senior BT manager). In that sense, Oftel's bargaining-diplomatic approach could be considered to have a certain logic for all the players in the regulatory space.

However, as the seventh age of telecoms regulation wore on, this pattern of informal accommodation in response to industry complaints showed signs of changing. During the sixth age, BT's legal and substantive expertise in the interpretation of its licence conditions served to prevent formal enforcement actions by Oftel in response to complaints from other firms. Such expertise derived in part from the fact that the DTI civil servant who had drafted the original licence conditions then moved to BT on privatization and headed its Government Relations Department. There was also a perception, within both Oftel and BT, that Oftel was totally outgunned by BT in terms of the quality and quantity of legal expertise it commanded for interpretation of licence obligations. For Oftel this was reflected in a set of beliefs that the licence conditions imposed on BT were less extensive in the conduct they covered and therefore less useful than in fact they were and proved to be once Oftel began to use them. This was a case of the much neglected phenomenon of 'self-inflicted capture' (Litz 1995). Given these conditions, it is scarcely suprising that for the first 12 years of Oftel's life no formal enforcement action was taken against BT for breach of a licence condition, and that the stock Oftel response to complaints about BT by telecoms firms took the form of attempts at resolution through informal bilateral accommodation.[15]

That pattern began to change in the 1990s in two ways. First, Oftel encouraged BT to improve its own internal capacity to secure regulatory compliance. With Oftel's encouragement and blessing, BT in 1996 appointed a Compliance Director, a senior BT official located outside the BT management structure and reporting directly to the BT Board Audit Committee, which comprised non-executive directors (*The Guardian* 11 September 1996). Oftel tried to prevent the new appointee from going 'wholly native' within the BT structure (the Compliance Director had a very small direct staff and thus was dependent on BT's Regulatory Affairs Department for interpreting BT's licence obligations) by initiating a practice of regular meetings with senior Oftel staff. It was agreed that the BT Compliance Director would meet with the DGT every two months and meet Oftel's Licence Enforcement Director (Branch 4) every month to review matters, in an attempt to prevent BT from reproducing its traditional approach to licence enforcement.

Second, Oftel moved in the direction of more formal enforcement rather than informal bilateral accommodation, with increasingly frequent resort to formal powers to make enforcement orders, particularly from 1996 onwards. In part this change reflected the attitudes of a new *roi soleil* at Oftel. As noted in Chapters Two and Four, Don Cruickshank had views about how a regulator should act that were at odds with the traditional civil service assumptions and the shared Oftel-DTI-BT culture, going back to the fifth and sixth ages of telecoms regulation, that saw informal brokerage of solutions as the natural way to resolve disputes. Cruickshank's approach gained force because it went with the grain of wider change in the telecoms industry that made the sixth age practices of dispute resolution increasingly problematic. With more players and less cultural homogeneity in the industry, there was growing criticism of Oftel as failing to protect new entrants from anti-competitive conduct by BT and not exercising the formal powers that it possessed to do so. In particular, third-party rights to compensation over breach of licence conditions could only be invoked after formal enforcement proceedings by the DGT (TA 1984 s18(6)). This issue was of little importance in the sixth telecoms age of 1980s duopoly, though MCL certainly bemoaned Oftel's style of informal accommodation and bilateral bargaining with BT during that era. But the issue became increasingly salient in the more competitive market of the 1990s, when Oftel's traditional reflex of bargaining-diplomatic responses to industry complaints started to come under increasing challenge. Paradoxically it was the process of introducing the new licence condition to regulate anti-competitive conduct, described in the first part of this chapter, that enhanced the authority and confidence of Oftel in using existing licence conditions as the basis for formal enforcement action against BT.

Handling consumer complaints

Oftel handled complaints from individual consumers quite differently from the way it dealt with complaints from within the industry. The DGT's obligation under the 1984 Telecoms Act (s.49) to consider all representations made to him was discharged by separating the function of handling consumer complaints from Oftel's other work (unlike the way it handled complaints from firms). The work was assigned to a special unit within the Consumer Branch, the Consumer Representation Section (CRS).

CRS was widely viewed as a Cinderella unit or poor relation within the organization, within a civil service culture where policy work traditionally enjoys higher prestige than front-line dealings with the public. In spite of the organization's oft-repeated official mantra, 'To provide the best possible deal for the consumer in terms of quality, choice and value for money', consumer complaints seem largely to have been considered within Oftel as an irritation, distracting the regulator from the main tasks of industry regulation. (Though CRS was seen by some, in Oftel-speak, as a 'sanity-check', a direct link with the individuals who were ultimately affected by the arcane and complex policy decisions Oftel made.) They do not seem to have been perceived as a key intelligence input for understanding corporate behaviour, assessing how effective the regulatory regime was and as key material for sustaining formal licence enforcement proceedings. The wide-ranging statistical and qualitative data held by CRS was little used as a useful information resource by the policy branches in Oftel, and was largely used as a basis for mechanical and formal annual reports about the volume of caseload and the like.[16]

CRS was thus a world within a world, a coping culture of relatively low-status staff who saw themselves as 'being at the pointed end' of Oftel's activity. Within this coping culture, the approach to consumer complaints was wholly reactive (a feature criticized by a 1993 National Audit Office report, which argued that the reactive style sometimes caused breach of licence conditions to go undetected (NAO 1993: 2)). Success in handling complaints was seen by the relatively junior staff concerned in terms of the rapidity with which cases were disposed of (by putting them back to the firm complained against, moving the issue to another part of the organization or brokering a solution through a good offices role). As so commonly occurs with front-line public service cultures, CRS staff felt ignored and despised by the staff officers and generals elsewhere in the organization and poorly informed about what was going on.[17] For example, a CRS Team Leader declared, 'We are the last to know [about decisions and new policy developments] and the first to get an earful'.

As is the way with public bureaucracies, there was some element of the Cartesian-bureaucratic issue-processing style in the way Oftel responded to consumer complaints. Complaint-handling was routinized into standard operating procedures, with stock responses, standard logging systems and a bulky operating handbook ('the Bible'). Another commonly-observable feature of bureaucratic behaviour was that complaints coming directly to the DGT from peers or MPs on behalf of constituents were treated differently from the general run of complaints. For complaints coming directly to the DGT from such sources there was pressure for faster responses, a tendency for Oftel to go higher up the organizational hierarchy of the company involved to secure a solution, and the letters to the complainant were signed directly by the DGT ('*Doing Business with the DG*' *Oftel Office Notes* 1994). These DGT letters created precedents, subsequently defining the CRS line on particular topics.

However, just as important as the (rather superficial) Cartesian-bureaucratic approach to standardizing office routine over the handling of consumer complaints was an approach to following them up that relied almost exclusively on the bargaining-diplomatic style. As with the traditional Oftel approach to dealing with industry complaints discussed in the previous paragraphs, the formal enforcement and rule-making powers that were available to the organization as a response to consumer complaints about PTO behaviour were not used. Senior policy staff believed that a decision had been taken not to use these formal powers and the junior staff who handled complaints at the 'pointed end' of the organization were unaware that such powers existed at all. For instance, those staff do not seem to have known of the powers Oftel possessed under the 1992 Competition and Service (Utilities) Act 1992. That legislation empowered the regulator to oversee the development of internal customer complaints procedures by 'designated operators' and to issue formal determinations, or delegate the power to an arbitrator, over disputes between customers and designated operators concerning undue discrimination, undue preference, charges, billing disputes or deposits.[18] CRS staff incorrectly believed they had no formal powers to arbitrate or adjudicate. (EC legislation subsequently led Oftel to consider a more formal approach using arbitration, as discussed in the Epilogue to this book.)

Thus decision-making over responses to consumer complaints, while it was Cartesian-bureaucratic to some extent in a low-level procedural sense, consisted of informal negotiation rather than a systematic process in which formal sanctions were applied from time to time *pour encourager les autres* (in the 'responsive regulation' mode advocated by Ayres and Braithwaite (1992) and discussed further in Chapter Ten). Rather, CRS staff conceived their role as informal fixers, sometimes acting as go-betweens and honest brokers and sometimes seeking to act as educators, particularly for the OLOs who had developed less elaborate procedures than BT for handling consumer complaints and were less well-informed about Oftel's functions and responsibilities. The majority of cable operators were US companies without BT's public-service origins and the associated legacy of civil service-type routines for handling public complaints. That characteristic meant that cable companies were considered by CRS to be more willing to take Oftel's opinion on board and co-operate (while BT was less likely to admit to 'a fair cop' and more likely to adopt an 'attrition' approach to complaints), even if they lacked BT's experience.

Indeed, the preference for informal resolution of customer complaints was so strong that on occasion formal breaches of licence conditions were used to solve a problem, by agreement between Oftel and a licensee. For example, according to the CRS, free telecom connections were not permitted under the terms of the BT licence (Condition 17 prohibited undue preference in provision of service) but they were nevertheless sometimes resorted to as a goodwill gesture for aggrieved customers.

There was little sign of fundamental change in the position of the consumer complaint-handling function within Oftel over the period of our study, even though a series of managerial changes were made over the years (some in response to a 1993 National Audit Office report) in the form of upgraded IT facilities, increased attention to training and response times and the like. The NAO's (1993: 2) criticism of Oftel for failure actively to enforce the requirements on licensees to develop arbitration procedures and consumer codes of practice was followed up by Oftel in the form of greater emphasis on licensee's capacity to handle complaints internally. This reflexive philosophy was stated in *Oftel News* (December 1997: 5):

> It is the customer's own telecoms company which is best placed to resolve the complaint or the problem and it is in their interests to do so as competition increases and customers have more choice of supplier . . . We have a range of powers at our disposal to regulate the UK telecoms industry but these rarely have a direct bearing on individual dispute cases and were not really designed for use in these circumstances.

Thus (in classic autopoietic style) Oftel's response to the NAO's criticisms of its consumer complaints handling reinforced the semi-detached nature of this function within the organization (Clune 1992). What is perhaps surprising is that pressure to hive consumer complaints off into a free-standing organization with a clear consumer advocacy mission developed so late in the telecoms sector (subsequent to the period of our study, and commented on in the epilogue to this book). Such a separation had already occurred within telecoms in other countries, such as Australia, and within the UK regulatory tradition it was common for regulation and grievances to be handled in distinct organizations.[19] Indeed, even in telecoms Oftel was only directly responsible for handling grievances in England, since there were separate grievance-handling organizations (statutory committees) for the other countries of the UK. Even though such a separation might have served bureau-shaping ambitions for the policy-fixated part of Oftel, grievance-handling remained as a poor relation housed in the organization's garret (metaphorically speaking) for a remarkably long time.

Overall

Oftel's response to complaints largely consisted of attempts at informal resolution rather than throwing the book at PTOs for breach of licence conditions. As noted in the last chapter, such behaviour reflected a more general tendency for softly softly approaches to enforcement, commonly noted in other studies and commentaries on business regulation in the UK and some other countries (see, for example, Vogel 1986; Cranston 1979; Hawkins and Thomas 1984; Yeung 1998).

How can we account for the apparent preference for co-operative negotiations and informal solutions over strict enforcement? At one level, motives and opportunities for such behaviour were built into the legal framework of the regime. The DGT's duties to enforce licence conditions set out by the 1984 Telecoms Act gave him wide discretion to deal with licence contraventions without formal enforcement proceedings. The elaborate obstacle course that Oftel faced in enforcement of licence conditions, briefly described in Chapter Two (see Figure 2.1), provided an incentive for the regulator to prefer an administrative method of enforcement over a judicial method involving clear offences and routine application of sanctions for breach (see Gist 1990: 35–6 for the claim that the telecoms regime was deliberately designed to encourage such a preference and Ellison (1994) for a criticism of Oftel for failure to use the 'judicial method'). Beyond the legal structure of motives and opportunities were factors built into the culture and configuration of the regulatory space, particularly in the sixth age of telecoms regulation when BT possessed much greater expertise and experience than Oftel over the interpretation of licence conditions. In bilateral negotiations over compliance between Oftel and BT (cf. Hutter 1997: 13–14), BT could exert powerful influence and Oftel lacked credible sanctions to back up its negotiating position (Gist 1990: 50).

Oftel's preference for informal accommodation in response to complaints seems better explained by such factors than as an effective compliance approach to enforcement of licence conditions. A compliance approach denotes a strategy of obtaining compliance by mostly co-operative or educative responses to violations by regulators, with only occasional use of formal sanctions if admonitions or informal bargains fail to obtain compliance (Hutter 1997: 14–15). Evidently no such strategy was ever contemplated for the handling of consumer complaints. ('The famous line about protection from breaches in the licence? Let's face it, it would take a PTO starting World War Three to get Oftel after them,' was the acerbic comment of one member of CRS.) Even for complaints from telecoms firms, the culture of accommodation seems to have been firmly entrenched, Oftel's capacity and authority over the rules of the game was limited and its heavy weaponry very difficult to deploy.

There were however signs of change during the period of our study. While consumer complaint handling seemed likely to remain in some form of the bargaining-diplomatic style of issue-processing (even though office procedure had some features of the Cartesian-bureaucratic style), Oftel's response to complaints by telecoms firms showed some signs of a move towards a more Cartesian-bureaucratic style in a substantive sense. This change matched the changing culture and configuration of the regulatory space as the sixth age of telecoms regulation gave way to the seventh, and new players challenged the older bilateral style of informal bargaining between BT and Oftel.

CONCLUSION

None of the episodes discussed in this chapter is a pure or unambiguous specimen of the bargaining-diplomatic style of issue-processing. Although the middle and later stages of the FTC saga might at first sight seem to be wholly dominated by that style, at least one of the key participants (Don Cruickshank) did not acknowledge that what was going on was bargaining in a substantive sense. The handling of consumer complaints involved elements of a Cartesian-bureaucratic style in a formal sense as the casework moved through the office, even though the substantive decision activity seems to have been wholly bargaining-diplomatic in style. Indeed, in some cases those decisions seem to have been taken in ignorance of, or without reference to, the formal rules of the game and the legal powers and duties of the players. As suggested earlier, the handling of complaints from telecoms firms showed signs of being in transition from a process entirely dominated by the bargaining-diplomatic style to a hybrid of the Cartesian-bureaucratic and bargaining-diplomatic one.

The episodes considered in this chapter indicate some of the variety in the bargaining-diplomatic style, as discussed in Chapter Six. The FTC episode contains a clear specimen of the second variant of that style, with explicit deals being struck between contending parties, accompanied by the tactical behaviour associated with formal bargaining strategy – such as threats to escalate a dispute into other decision fora, linkage tactics, exchange of contradictory legal opinions, counter-proposals, cultivation and lobbying of third parties. That variant of the bargaining-diplomatic style was much less evident in the complaint-handling episodes. Rather what seems to have dominated those episodes is the first variant of the bargaining-diplomatic style. Here the negotiation works through a process of continuous mutual adjustment or informal agreement that may not even be recognized as bargaining and translates into generally-accepted ways of doing business, viewing the world and understanding the key terms of the regulatory trade.

These episodes bring out some of the positive and negative elements of the bargaining-diplomatic decision style in its different forms. The FTC involved heavy expenditure of emotion and organizational energy by Oftel in a bargaining process in which BT succeeded in extracting substantial concessions. The upshot was a licence condition considered by Oftel's own lawyers to be more cumbersome and less readily enforceable than some of the existing licence conditions it was intended to improve upon. For handling of business and consumer complaints over any sort of utility service, some element of the bargaining-diplomatic style is no doubt unavoidable and can often achieve a resolution that satisfies the complainant. The handling of business complaints in a bargaining-diplomatic style seems to have served sometimes to secure rapid dispute resolution with low transaction costs to the contending parties. Clearly the efficacy of such a style depended on its acceptance within the wider culture of the telecoms community and the extent to which BT was able to control the interpretation of its own licence conditions. The way consumer complaints were handled may also have served to provide quick and acceptable fixes in some cases, although the caseworkers' ignorance of the formal powers available to Oftel may have limited the bargaining leverage they were able to bring to bear. In addition the cultural wall between the grievance-handling function and what were perceived as the higher-level regulatory work of the organization also limited its overall intelligence and bargaining leverage.

We might conclude that the softer form of the bargaining-diplomatic decision style is pervasive and unavoidable in the regulatory process (even if often unrecognized, but cf. Reichman 1992), since the meaning of key terms is subject to a continuous process of cultural negotiation in practice. The harder form of the bargaining-diplomatic decision style seems difficult to deploy effectively for a regulator with limited experience and resources facing an entrenched dominant operator. Yet it often seems to dominate the regulatory process *faute de mieux*.

Part V

Lessons learnt

10 Regulatory science, regulatory policy and possible regulatory futures

Loud cackle, little egg.

Old Proverb

The preceding chapters have given an account of a particular era of UK telecoms regulation as perceived from the inside of the regulatory vehicle rather than from a helicopter viewing the action from above. Our observations were made during a period of transition, in which Oftel sought to adapt itself and the regime to a seventh era of telecoms regulation involving multilateral competition, in contrast with the public monopoly of the fifth age and the regulated private duopoly of the sixth. In this short closing chapter we reflect on what we have learned, going beyond our understanding of the UK telecoms sector during the time of our study to some broader issues.

As noted in the first chapter, three main themes have run through our analysis of UK telecoms regulation in this study. First, we noted ways in which organizational and broader cultures (sometimes in tension) regulated regulation, shaping what and how issues were perceived, defining meanings and cognitive boundaries, keeping rival attitudes and beliefs in tension, and mediating change. Second, we highlighted Oftel's position inside a broader regulatory space within which it was constrained by other key actors. The power of other actors – telecom firms, government departments, user groups – was not static and it was a product not just of legal power, but also informal authority deriving from experience, information, organizational resources and legitimacy in a broader sense. Third, we noted some of the different decision styles in which policy was processed, as it went through the telecoms regulatory issue-machine. Our treatment of those styles was necessarily selective, but our argument was that there was no single all-purpose style that was either observable in practice or desirable in theory, since all of the three main decision styles – Cartesian-bureaucratic, adhocratic-chaotic and bargaining-diplomatic – have both strengths and weaknesses.

These three themes are inter-linked. Culture and interdependent relations within the regulatory space seem to have been just as important as instrumental considerations in shaping the decision style in which issues were processed. For example, stress on a bargaining-diplomatic style in some cases reflected culture more than legislative authority (as with complaint-handling, discussed in Chapter Nine) and at other times was a product of Oftel's dependence on others for information or authority (as with the Fair Trading Condition, discussed in Chapters Eight and Nine). Interdependence within the regulatory space may sometimes be shaped by cultural perceptions about the appropriate authority and legitimacy of particular actors and, indeed, how space is constructed is itself a product of culture.

Academics reporting a research study are characteristically (and properly) asked three questions by those trying to assess the significance of their work: 'tell me about it . . . '; 'so what?'; and 'where to from here?'. The previous nine chapters have attempted to answer the first question. The following three sections of this chapter offer some brief and speculative ideas about the other two. First we draw on what we have learned from this 'inside' study of telecoms regulation to assess received theories of regulation and comment on the state of the art in regulatory science. Second, and relatedly, we reflect on the implications of our study for the design of regulatory processes and institutions. Third, we discuss possible futures for telecoms regulation, considering in particular the issue of whether the seventh age of regulation is likely to be succeeded by an eighth, and if so what such an eighth age might look like.

RE-FRAMING REGULATORY SCIENCE?

Three implications for regulatory science more generally could be drawn from this study. They concern the notions of regulatory interdependence and of responsive regulation and the idea of using shifting balances as an alternative to the conventional hierarchical conceptions of control.

Regulatory interdependence

Our study chimes strongly with those theories of political science generally, and regulation in particular, which emphasize the interdependence of the various public and private actors within policy domains and regulatory spaces (Doern and Wilks 1998). Such theories cast doubt on empirical or normative conceptions of regulators as all-powerful within their regulatory domains. Economists have long recognized that regulators commonly possess less information about the regulatory domain than regulatees. An interdependence conception of regulation can go further, in suggesting it is only information which can be unevenly divided among participants in the regulatory space, but also formal authority (deriving from legal instruments) and informal authority (deriving from experience and information).

It was already well known from other external studies that BT possessed not only key information, but also formal authority to veto licence amendments proposed by Oftel (requiring reference to a third party, the MMC). Our inside study also demonstrates the importance of *informal* authority possessed by BT over interpretation of licence conditions, which locked Oftel into informal and ineffective processes of licence enforcement, and rendered the meaning of regulatory law contingent upon these relationships of authority. An inside perspective also reveals the extent to which Oftel's activities were monitored by the DTI, with which Oftel nominally maintained an arms length relationship. Insiders considered that the influence of the DTI made it virtually impossible for Oftel to develop or sustain initiatives at odds with the DTI view. Indeed, in the one case which we observed where Oftel policy threatened to undermine DTI policy (the Fair Trading Condition, discussed in Chapter Nine) the DTI became a major player in a policy process within Oftel's jurisdiction. Finally, the study brings out some of the historical changes shaping the nature of interdependent relations within the regulatory space as explained in Chapter Five.

Rethinking responsive regulation

One received view or influential academic recipe for contemporary regulatory reform is summarised in the title of Ayres and Braithwaite's (1992) well-known book *Responsive Regulation: Transcending the Deregulation Debate*. They suggest several ways in which the effectiveness of social or economic regulation can be enhanced while reducing the extent of heavy-handed state intervention. Others have used the label *Smart Regulation* (Grabosky and

Gunningham 1997) to denote similar ideas. Our study of UK telecoms regulation in the mid 1990s suggests some scepticism about some of the assumptions that underpin the *Responsive Regulation* recipe. The central assumption of that approach is the idea that agencies which regulate responsively have lurking beneath their benign exteriors a big gun, the capacity to exercise traditional regulatory fiat, and that this capacity can be used to support the development of less interventionist forms of regulation in the shadow of the threat of decisive intervention and heavy penalties (Ayres and Braithwaite 1992: 161). The basic idea is one of a pyramidal structure within which enforced self-regulation and negotiated compliance are seen as the most desirable forms, and can be effective precisely because the iron regulatory fist lies beneath the velvet self-regulatory glove.

We did observe that Oftel sought to promote less interventionist rule-making models (for example with customer codes of practice) and deployed informal negotiative methods for licence enforcement (discussed in Chapter Nine). Such behaviour did not arise because Oftel was following the script advocated by the *Responsive Regulation* school (cf. Wilks 1998: 156–7); rather a mixture of ingrained cultural preferences and lack of formal authority prevented Oftel from draconian intervention. Regulatees knew quite well that Oftel lacked the capacity to escalate regulatory technique or enforcement methods. Because Oftel could only require two firms (BT and Kingston) with dominant positions in the market to draw up codes of practice it chose not to use that formal power at all and instead relied on moral suasion or coaxing to persuade all firms into drawing up such codes. The capacity to change the rules, to extend the ambit of the mandatory customer codes, resided with the DTI. And, as noted above, informal approaches to licence enforcement during the sixth age of telecoms regulation, and much of the seventh, were a product of the fact that BT had the lion's share of interpretive authority over licence conditions. Even if Oftel had been able to bring formal enforcement actions, it was encumbered by lengthy procedural processes requiring costly and time-consuming litigation before any formal sanctions could take effect. There was no enforcement pyramid and no credible threat of escalation. Even where Oftel was given formal authority to resolve consumer disputes, under 1992 legislation, no attempt was made to use the new formal authority to support the development of a credible enforcement pyramid, and the potential benign big gun approach was left unexplored, as shown in Chapter Nine.

Those who advocate the *Responsive Regulation* recipe could be expected to respond to such observations by declaring the telecoms regulation system of the mid 1990s to be a poorly-designed regime that precisely demonstrates the need for better arrangements linking self-regulation and negotiated compliance to legislative capacities and a readily usable sanctions escalator. But such a response would overlook some of the conditions that may make the regime we observed more typical of regulation in Parliamentary systems of government than the *Responsive Regulation* recipe allows for. One (as noted earlier) is that the preference for informality and the bargaining-diplomatic style we observed seemed to be rooted in culture as much as formal institutional capacity, and change in the latter does not necessarily change the former. The other is that the built-in reluctance in Parliamentary systems to create the kind of 'governments in miniature' common among US federal agencies is likely to dilute the autonomous escalator capacity in both rule making and enforcement considerably. EU developments, to be discussed below and in the Epilogue, might conceivably alter this pattern; but until or unless they do, there seem to be formidable obstacles in the way of the *Responsive Regulation* model in all but the most exceptional cases.

Shifting balances and limits to control

In fact our study suggests some of the difficulties facing *any* instrumental theory of regulation, whether positive or normative. It highlights the extent to which culture, bounded rationality in decision-making and shared capacity or interdependence limit freedom of manoeuvre for regulatory agencies. While it is theoretically possible (in some variant of Hood's (1976) perfect administration model) to conceive of regulatory authorities unencumbered by such limits, such models only demonstrate how unlikely such conditions are likely to be in practice. And to the extent that enforcement machines (Hood 1986: 205) which allow no scope for bureaucratic discretion in enforcement are possible for the type of regulation discussed here, such machines are notorious for their over-inclusiveness, lack of responsiveness, and tendency to provoke unanticipated responses by their human targets.

Instead of the metaphor of a ladder or pyramid underlying the *Responsive Regulation* recipe, we would be more inclined to place the emphasis on an alternative metaphor of a pair of scales or a servomechanism built on pent-up forces in tension. To the extent that regulatory regimes are steerable at all, in the sort of political/institutional conditions sketched out above, it seems to be by the judicious or opportunistic manipulation of tensions among the different actors in the regulatory space. Such an insight is far from new – the underlying model has been spelt out by Andrew Dunsire (1978; 1996) in what he calls the collibration model of control, to which we have referred in earlier chapters. Such a view of how to obtain leverage within regulatory systems seems more feasible on the basis of our study than the demanding politico-institutional conditions needed for the *Responsive Regulation* recipe to operate. Indeed, as discussed in Chapter Two, institutional economics analysis of the UK telecoms regimes suggests the arrangements were designed precisely to ensure that no-one was in overall control (Levy and Spiller 1996). Government was constrained in its capacity to reverse key policies by the issuance of licences, Oftel was constrained in its capacity to make policies by the licensee consent/MMC reference requirements, and in enforcement by the requirement of judicial proceedings, and the DTI retained various powers to prevent capture of Oftel by BT. From a regulatory space perspective we observed a few key actors located close to the centre of the space by virtue of the resources they commanded. But the constellation of the actors in the space could be used to obtain extra leverage by actors like Oftel, as we saw in Chapters Seven and Nine.

In line with this perspective, the potential to shift the balance of power within the regulatory space provides an indirect mechanism of regulatory reform. Obvious targets for such a balance-shifting strategy are the capacity of BT to veto licence modifications, and the capacities of the DTI to veto or refer to the MMC licence modifications. In principle such changes in the formal resources held by the key actors would reduce the need for Oftel to operate in the bargaining-diplomatic style as in the FTC case, discussed in Chapter Nine (see Scott, Hall and Hood 1997) but even then the culture of accommodation would need to change as well.

In fact, Ayres and Braithwaite (1992: Chapter 3) themselves add to their ladder recipe for responsive regulation an idea for reconfiguring regulatory space by giving public interest groups authority to enforce regulatory rules alongside public bureaucracies.[1] Potential effects of such a move applied to telecoms regulation would be to dilute the bilateral enforcement relationship between Oftel and BT. Relative resourcing of actors in policy space is likewise a method of changing policy balance that has been recognized by Dunsire (1996) and has some potential application to telecoms regulation. Attempts to reconfigure the space, which occurred after the completion of our study, are discussed in the Epilogue.

REGULATORY POLICY, PROCESSES AND INSTITUTIONS

The limits of rational regulation

As we noted in Chapter Six, regulatory agencies (and all public bureaucracies) are expected to demonstrate the rationality of their decision processes, and Oftel was no exception to this rule. Nevertheless, as we saw in the last four chapters, issues were processed in practice in several different decision styles, and an issue might shift from one style to another at different points of a policy cycle. It is tempting to assume that the Cartesian-bureaucratic approach is invariably the most appropriate one for regulatory decision-making and that any departure from such a decision style is to be deplored. In fact we found both positive and negative policy outcomes for each of the decision styles. This observation suggests that a Cartesian-bureaucratic decision style may in some conditions not only be unfeasible but also less effective than some of the alternatives. The Cartesian-bureaucratic decision style can produce policy fiascos if it is based on a false consensus or unexamined assumptions that turn out to be flawed. In our discussion of numbering administration (in Chapter Seven) we saw that Oftel got into difficulty because of its assumption that the information it was passed on numbering, when it took over the task from BT, was accurate and sufficient to form the basis for a technical solution. As Oftel found, relying on a Cartesian-bureaucratic decision style in those conditions creates the risk of reaching ill-informed decisions efficiently. In the Price Control Review case study (also discussed in Chapter Seven) the DGT upset the orderly development of a Cartesian-bureaucratic process by going outside the models and parameters that Oftel's econocrats had worked out on the basis of previous PCRs by throwing in a new assumption that BT would out perform its own predictions. An adhocratic-chaotic decision style can make a creative input to policy making in some conditions, and the same goes for the bargaining-diplomatic style.

Routes to countering information asymmetry

As noted earlier, information asymmetry is one of the classic problems faced by regulatory agencies: the information problem faced by Oftel was not simply a deficit of information about the industry and the policy domain, but also the difficulty of accessing and using effectively the information it did have, and knowing what to do with it. The first type of information problem was anticipated by the framers of the UK telecoms regulation regime in the early 1980s, and Oftel was consequently given formal powers to require information to be provided. These powers were little used in the sixth age of telecoms regulation, and though some use of those powers began to be made by Oftel in the seventh age, other, and arguably better methods were found to counter Oftel's information asymmetry problem. Oftel found ways of obtaining information from BT's emerging competitors. Not only did BT's competitors supply information about matters such as cost structures, pricing models and anti-competitive conduct, they also provided a way for Oftel to test information being supplied by BT or flush out new information. By developing instruments such as industry fora and working groups Oftel was thus able not only to increase the *quantity* of information it received, but also improve the *quality* and *reliability* of such information.

Regulatory accountability – the wrong problem problem

In Chapter Five we drew a familiar distinction between efficient and dignified forms of accountability. We found that what we call extended mechanisms of accountability, the day to day involvement of interested public and private actors in Oftel's activities, provided a more important check on Oftel's activities than those formal accountability mechanisms to which Oftel was subjected. The interdependence among the actors within the telecoms regulatory regime implies that power, and thus arguably a duty to give account for the exercise of that power, resided not just with Oftel, but also BT, the DTI and, to a lesser extent, other actors within the space. So a focus on accountability, which has exercised so many minds directed towards regulatory reform, would seem to be misdirected if it relates only to a single institutional actor (Wilks 1998: 152). A narrow regulatory reform focus on Oftel, so common to many of the analysts of UK-style regulation in the 1990s, seems to miss the point that the DTI and BT were just as deserving of being made accountable (Scott, Hall and Hood 1997). DTI accountability was hampered by the secrecy in which it conducted its telecoms activities. For instance, it did not give reasons for its decisions over licensing. In some senses BT was more accountable than any other actor within the regulatory space with accountability to the capital market, the consumers and the regulator (Scott 1993a), though a full assessment of these mechanisms would also require an evaluation of the quality of corporate governance processes on requiring senior BT management to account for itself (Wilks 1998; Braithwaite 1997). The general point is that if we are to avoid the wrong problem in debating accountability we need to consider the obligations on all the key actors – not just of the Of-type regulators – to account for their actions.

POLICY AND INSTITUTIONAL DYNAMICS IN TELECOMMUNICATIONS REGULATION

Finally we turn from 'so what?' to 'where to from here?' and consider three issues specific to telecoms regulation. First, what does the Oftel experience tell us about the rival merits of moving from a fifth to a seventh age of telecoms regulation directly, or moving through a sixth age or its equivalent? Second, does Oftel's survival into the seventh age represent policy success or the failure of an organization to self-destruct when the conditions for which it was created had disappeared? Third, will the seventh age of telecoms regulation give way to an eighth and, if so, what might that eighth age look like?[2]

The seventh age challenge – is a sixth age needed?

The seventh age of UK telecoms regulation, developing at the time of our study, involved a shift from a regulated duopoly to a wider market. The shift from monopoly to some form of competition in telecoms is widely observable across the world.[3] But is it necessary to have a sixth age as a launching-pad for a seventh, or would it be possible to launch out of a fifth age monopoly into a seventh age competitive structure?

In New Zealand the reform process skipped the sixth age altogether, with a state monopoly privatized simultaneously with the removal of legal barriers to entry. Few sectoral regulatory rules were adopted and no Oftel-type regulator established (Flood 1995; Bollard and Pickford 1997). The result, according to an official report into the liberalized New Zealand telecoms sector, was that the dominant incumbent, the privatized New Zealand Telecom was, in effect, the regulator for the sector, since it had the power to determine the conditions of entry to the market for other companies by virtue of its infrastructure, information and experience (Commerce

Commission 1992). The responsible Government department, the Ministry of Commerce, provided some counterweight to that power, but its threats to intervene were not sufficiently credible to induce New Zealand Telecom to provide access to its infrastructure on reasonable terms. A judicial ruling (by the Privy Council, sitting in London) held that the general competition rules which, in the absence of more specific regulatory rules, governed telecoms in New Zealand, did not prevent New Zealand Telecom from using its market power to protect its revenues against the activities of new entrants (Scott 1998b). The New Zealand experience tends to support the observation of one Oftel insider that the transition from monopoly to competition 'is likely to require a phase where regulation (or the application of special rules) is more comprehensive than at either end of the spectrum'. (Barnes 1998: 232; see also Laffont, Rey and Tirole 1997; Webb and Taylor 1998).

The experience reported in this book suggests there is some value not just in the development of sectoral rules requiring dominant incumbents to provide fair and reasonable access to their infrastructure, but also in creating a regulatory institution which can develop authority and expertise, somewhat independently of both the dominant incumbent and the government. Moreover the presence of a regulatory authority capable of resolving at least some disputes among participants in the liberalizing market, *ex ante*, may slow, if not eliminate, a process of juridification marked by a growing involvement of lawyers, legal values and the courts in decisions which had previously been taken on the basis of commercial or administrative values (Scott 1998a). Accordingly, while it is evidently possible to move directly from a fifth to a seventh age of telecoms regulation without the institutional apparatus set in the UK for the sixth age, that apparatus has substantial merits as well as drawbacks.

The dynamic conservatism problem: should Oftels self-destruct?

In the first flush of thinking about UK utility privatization in the 1980s, Oftel and the other regulators that were modelled on it were seen by some as transitional measures 'to hold the fort until competition arrives' mainly by checking the monopolists' power over pricing through RPI–x price controls, and creating the conditions for competition to develop. Such a vision suggests that the ultimate test of success for sectoral regulators like Oftel is their ability to self-destruct once their transitional task has been achieved and the free market cavalry has arrived (OECD 1997: Chapter 1; cf. Cave 1997). One of us has observed that market liberalization has been accompanied by processes of proceduralization, meaning that the trend towards ever more detailed rules and sector specific institutions is reversed, giving way to greater emphasis on procedural over substantive rules, and towards more general rules and general (as opposed to sectoral) regulatory institutions (Scott 1998b). The study reported in this book indicates a shift to greater emphasis on process (discussed in Chapter Seven) and more general rules (discussed in Chapters Eight and Nine). However, through reinventing itself as a competition authority Oftel appears to have evaded, temporarily at least, the fate of the successful sector-specific authority – extinction.

That pattern does not seem to have occurred everywhere. For instance, in Australia the Australian Telecommunications Commission (AUSTEL), established to regulate a telecommunications duopoly established in 1989, was abolished when the market was fully liberalized (at least as matter of law) in 1997, with its economic regulation functions transferred to the general competition authority, the Australian Competition and Consumer Commission (ACCC) (Reuters, 27 June 1997). Some residual standard-setting and consumer protection functions were transferred to a new authority. There are certainly plausible arguments in favour of such a move. A general rather than sector-specific competition authority can build up across-the-board expertise in the application of competition rules, and avoid the difficulties Oftel faced when it tried to apply the Fair Trading Condition to BT (as discussed in Chapter Nine). The fact of less routine and focused contact between a general competition authority and the dominant incumbent in any one market sector, may also reduce the risk that such a regulator might be captured, either by dominant incumbent or by the interests of new entrants (Makkai and Braithwaite 1995). Furthermore, a competition authority is less likely to seek to extend its jurisdiction through the sort of turf battles in which Oftel engaged over broadcasting, or to have issues dumped on it because the regulator appears to be conveniently placed to perform a new task, as happened to Oftel with numbering administration.

On the other side of the argument, however, we have seen that even with developed and specialized expertise in telecoms, Oftel found it difficult enough to monitor and apply rules within a single sector, with which a general purpose competition authority would be even less well equipped to grapple. So it might be argued that Oftel's response to reinvent itself as a sector specific competition authority was the appropriate one (Cave 1997). The ACCC's complaint in Australia that AUSTEL had been applying bastardized versions of competition rules, rather than real competition law, may be less applicable to Oftel in the UK since the appointment of an Expert Advisory Committee on Fair Trading demonstrated its capacity to hold Oftel to what it saw as correct application of competition rules, at least on the occasion of the first reference to the Committee.

Perhaps the chief significance of institutional choice for contemporary telecoms regulation – sectoral regulator or general competition authority – is symbolic. Retention of a sectoral regulator signals a belief that telecoms continues to possess special features, notably the continuing power of a dominant incumbent, which marks it out in regulatory terms from the general world of business and commerce. Conversely the displacement of the sectoral regulator's role by a general competition authority suggests a commitment to less sector-specific intervention in the market by government. If symbolism is the key, Oftel's survival need not automatically count as evidence of dynamic conservatism involving failure of its original mission.

Towards an eighth age? Supranational regulation, global providers?

Finally, are we seeing the emergence of an eighth age of telecoms regulations, going beyond the Shakespearean seven-ages analogy? To assess this possibility we need to look at the political and economic forces affecting telecoms internationally. The World Trade Organization secured the agreement of 69 countries to a policy of telecoms liberalization in 1997 (Scott 1998b). The European Union adopted legislation in 1996 to secure the substantial liberalization of the EU telecoms sector by 1998. The UK experience, as discussed in this book, suggests that even with strong political commitment and considerable resource and expertise devoted to independent regulation, the path to liberalization is far from smooth. National regulatory authorities have to deal not only with the informal authority, experience and informational advantages possessed by dominant incumbents, but also with the ambivalence of powerful central government authorities (for financial or political reasons), as with the sixth age of telecoms regulation in the UK.

So if there is to be an eighth age of telecoms regulation, it seems likely that it will involve more internationalized regimes constraining domestic arrangements. Such supranational attempts at control are far from problematic, since they are demanding both in terms of legitimacy and resources on both sides, and institutional structures are often poorly developed (Hood, Scott *et al.* 1999: Chapter 8). One effect of such a process could be a shift in power from Oftel to the DTI, as it is the latter which has primary responsibility for ensuring compliance with EC requirements.[4] The responsibility of government departments, rather than national regulatory authorities, for implementation of EC and WTO policies, may mean such a pattern develops more generally.

In Chapter Five we noted that where Oftel failed to enforce rules allowing market access for new entrants the supra-national bureaucrats in the European Commission were decidedly reluctant to intervene. But aggressive international telecoms companies, pursuing their ambitions to be global providers, and often unconstrained by domestic conventions of informality of the kind we observed in the sixth age for the UK, are likely to pursue all strategies available to open up markets where the commitment to liberalization is ambivalent. Among the steps such firms can take are the litigation route, challenging the behaviour of firms or public authorities in the courts, or the multilateral governance route, appealing to supranational authorities such as the European Commission and the WTO. The problems of achieving rapid market liberalization in practice, especially in response to international regulatory *diktats*, suggests the supranational authorities are likely to be drawn into disputes with increasing frequency. It may be too that once the inevitably limited capacity of general authorities like the European Commission and the WTO becomes apparent, there will be increased demands for specialized supranational regulatory institutions.[5] If the seventh age of UK telecoms regulation involved a reconfiguration of the regulatory space by the entry of new industry players, internationalizing the regulatees, the eighth age could see a further reconfiguration of the public authorities, internationalizing the regulators, either through creation of new institutions or through a considerably enhanced structure for co-ordination of domestic institutions.

Epilogue

OFTEL'S FOURTH LIFE STAGE? NEW DIRECTOR-GENERAL, NEW LABOUR, NEW RULES OF THE GAME

Our fieldwork was concluded in December 1997, but of course life went on in the world of telecoms regulation. New policy issues emerged, old issues were revisited and Oftel continued to change.[1] A number of important institutional changes occurred also, largely a product of the election of a Labour Government in 1997 and its implementation of various reform commitments.

Don Cruickshank was, apparently at his own request, not re-appointed at the end of his five year term as DGT in 1998. His successor, appointed by the President of the Board of Trade, was someone with a civil service background (including experience within the DTI) who had recently worked in the private sector.

One of the first things the new DGT did was to introduce a root and branch review of Oftel's organizational structure with the aid of management consultants. The outcome of this process was the reorganization of the office into just two major Directorates, one for Regulatory Policy and the other for Compliance. Announcing the reorganization the DGT said 'A key finding of our review was that the cumbersome 10-branch structure was not conducive to flexible, agile responses to emerging issues. This could hinder us in our objective of protecting consumers'. (Oftel Press Release 74/98).

Evidently the creative tension doctrine that Cruickshank and other top brass in Oftel had used to justify the branch/project group structure was being modified by the new DGT. But our study suggests that Oftel was far from sclerotic in responding to emerging issues in its previous life-stage, and the difficulties Oftel had in protecting consumers, discussed in Chapter Nine, appeared to us more attributable to a cultural reluctance to treat consumer issues as seriously as those of competition.

The DTI also embarked on a number of reforms of the utilities regulators in general, and of Oftel in particular. The Government announced its intention to legislate to make the protection of consumer interests the single primary duty of the utilities regulators, including Oftel (DTI 1998a: Conclusion 3.1). This step could be interpreted as a matter of symbolic politics, since, as we have seen in earlier chapters, Oftel already interpreted its somewhat diffuse duties as a mission to seek 'The best possible deal for consumers, in terms of value quality and choice'. Indeed, a new statutory duty is unlikely to resolve the contradictions among 'value, quality and choice', and is not sufficiently precise to give more power to third parties challenging the regulator for failure to carry out the newly defined duty, for example by means of judicial review.

Perhaps going a little beyond symbolic politics, the Government proposed to establish an independent statutory Telecommunications Consumer Council, outside Oftel, to take on the bulk of the consumer complaints handling previously carried out by the CRS within Oftel, and act as a professional advocate for the interests of telecommunications users of all types (DTI 1998a: Conclusion 3.2; DTI 1999).[2] This development chimes with our finding that the handling of consumer complaints tended to be a poor relation within Oftel as against policy work, in spite of the 'Best possible deal . . .' mantra (Scott, Hall and Hood 1997; see also Hansard Society 1996 Recommendation 15). The creation of this new organization may well put more pressure on Oftel to treat consumer complaints in ways that differ from its traditional informal bargaining-diplomatic style. A new TCC will, inevitably, act a magnet for consumer issues in telecoms generally, and this modest reconfiguration of the players in the regulatory space may be an example of the kind of marginal balance-shifting discussed in the final chapter.

The DTI also committed itself to greater transparency in its relationships with the regulatory offices, and in particular the publication of ministerial statutory guidance on social and environmental objectives (DTI 1998a: Conclusion 2.1). The right to provide guidance enhances the formal powers of the DTI but it seems unlikely that such published guidance will become the sole mechanism of influence for the DTI. Indeed, it seems hard to predict whether the outcome will be more transparency over the scope and limitations of the regulators' independence of policy judgement, or continuing use of informal methods of influence as prevailed for forty years in the nationalized industry era, and into the sixth and seventh ages of telecoms regulation.

The DTI also accepted that reliance on bilateral licence modification procedures for the adaptation of regulation rules in the telecommunications sector could no longer be regarded as appropriate for a liberalized telecommunications sector (DTI 1998c; cf. Scott, Hall and Hood 1997; Long 1995: xiii). Pressure for this change has come in part from the EU, with the Licensing Directive of 1997 (97/13/EC) requiring a shift away from individual licence conditions towards more general rules, and with a general EC preference for transparent, open and objective secondary rule making in telecommunications. The new regime proposed by the DTI would permit Oftel to make licence modifications affecting a class of licensees, even where some of the licensees object, without their consent and without a reference to the Competition Commission (which replaced the Monopolies and Mergers Commission under the Competition Act 1998). This change mirrors the reforms to the licence modification procedure in the Gas Act 1995 (criticized by Scott 1997) and dilutes a crucial part of the formal checks and balances architecture of the sixth age of telecoms regulation, as discussed in Chapter Two. How much difference it will make in practice to BT's capacity to influence rule making processes remains to be seen.

A further change proposed by the government is the clarification of the relationship between regulatory offices and the Competition Commission (CC, formerly MMC) in areas where licence modification procedures will continue to be relevant, as with changes to the price control on BT. The extent of the current duty on regulators to follow MMC recommendations in relation to a proposed licence modification is a matter of debate (Scott 1997; Graham 1997). The government has announced that it does not intend to require CC approval for every licence modification, but where a licence modification is referred CC approval will be required for the licence modification which the regulator finally decides to make (DTI 1998a: Conclusion 7.14). In practice Oftel has always indicated in the past that it would follow MMC recommendations on licence modifications where a reference had been made, so this change is unlikely to have any effect on Oftel's practice.

The DTI seemed keen to steer the utilities regulators, including Oftel, into more use of formal regulatory powers. In parts of the market where competition had not been achieved the government declared that regulators should use their existing formal powers to set standards, and that it intended to give to all regulators powers to impose monetary penalties for failure to meet such standards (DTI 1998a: Conclusions 3.7., 3.8). Since there are many UK consumers with little or no choice of telecoms supplier, it would appear that Oftel would have plenty of scope to exercise such powers and that the power to levy financial penalties would create a basis for *Responsive Regulation* strategies as discussed in the last chapter. But it remains to be seen whether the accommodation culture would be radically changed in practice, and some ambiguity in the Government's stance is demonstrated by the DTI's approval for Oftel's less interventionist approach in competitive markets, based on publication of comparative performance indicators (CPIs) (DTI 1998a: Conclusion 3.9).

The Government also proposed modest institutional reforms for all the regulatory offices including Oftel. The previous absolutist structure of a single DGT formally exercising all the statutory powers was to be replaced by a 'small executive board' comprising a chairman and two others (DTI 1998a: Conclusion 7.1; cf. Hansard Society 1996: Recommendation 5), a structure not so different from the *troika* which in practice dominated Oftel during the period of our study. Oftel would further be required to 'consult on, publish and follow a code of practice governing [its] consultation and decision making processes' (DTI 1998a: Conclusion 7.3). Again, this proposal seems unlikely radically to change existing practice, since as we have seen, Oftel in practice went far beyond its statutory obligations over consultation in this third life stage and Oftel had a rather good track record in setting out and following its own procedures (Scott, Hall and Hood 1997). Equally the Government proposal that Oftel should be under a statutory duty to publish reasons for its decisions (DTI 1998a: Conclusion 7.5) would simply formalize existing practice.[3]

The Fair Trading Condition introduced into BT's licence in 1997 (discussed in Chapters Eight and Nine), and subsequently incorporated into other PTOs' licences, is likely to become redundant when the Competition Act 1998 comes into force in the year 2000, which will enhance Oftel's powers over anti-competitive conduct. The substantive rules of the new legislation are similar to those incorporated in the FTC, having been based on the EC Treaty competition rules, but the new procedural powers will greatly increase Oftel's capacity for formal enforcement, since it will be entitled to collect information in dawn raids on company premises, and to apply substantial financial sanctions directly without need for a court order. Third parties will also gain the right to secure damages for harm caused by anti-competitive conduct directly through an application to the Court, without the need for an initial Oftel order (Yeung 1998). Other legislative cross-winds likely to affect telecoms regulation include the government's proposal to pass a Freedom of Information Act, and the passage of the Human Rights Act 1998, which is likely to require an enhancement to the formality of regulatory procedures which lead to the application of sanctions.

As some of the comments above have suggested, there is less to some of this package of reforms than meets the eye. The two key questions for Oftel's fourth life-stage after the Cruickshank era seem be whether its regulatory style will change towards a *Responsive Regulation* approach with the new sanctions available to it (instead of the elaborate obstacle course over licence enforcement built into the sixth age regime, as discussed in Chapter Two) and how Oftel will relate to the other actors in the regulatory space as reconfigured by this package of reforms. Whether a DGT coming from the DTI will be more amenable to DTI pressure than Cruicksank remains to be seen, and whether a diminished role for BT at the centre of the regulatory space (by dilution of its bilateral veto power over licence modification and exposing it to financial penalties directly imposed by Oftel) will radically change entrenched ways of working also remains to be seen. It will require a future generation of Oftel-watchers to assess how these changes played out in practice in Oftel's fourth age.

POSTSCRIPT

After the completion of the manuscript two further sets of proposals for change were published. The DTI and the DCMS published a paper giving the government's response to the consultation on the 1998 Green Paper (DTI 1998). This new paper, Regulating Communications: The Way Ahead – Results of the Consultation on the Convergence Green Paper (London, 1999), announced that a number of important changes would be made to the regulatory framework established by the Telecommunications Act 1984. First, the Government will introduce a procedure for licensees to appeal to the courts against decisions of the DGT on grounds of either fact or law (para. 3.44). Second, while acting on its earlier commitment to simplify the licence modification procedure, the Government proposed to consider replacing licences with a system of general authorizations (para. 3.49). This proposal was to be the subject matter of further consultation, but Oftel indicated in its response that it was in favour of this change. The new appeals system may be expected to constrain Oftel further in its decision-making, shifting the balance towards licensees. However, as noted in Chapter 5, unsuccessful appeals against regulatory decisions may bolster the legitimacy and power of the regulator. The shift to a system of general authorisations is likely to shift BT away from the centre of the regulatory space, and strengthen the hand of Oftel more generally in making changes to the regulatory rules.

In September 1999 Oftel consulted on *Proposed New Dispute Resolution Procedures for Fixed Telecommunications* (London: Oftel). This consultation proposes both new arbitration procedures for dealing with customer complaints in respect of all fixed telecoms services (whether provided by PTOs or systemless service providers) and that Oftel will use powers of determination to resolve disputes over the provision of services by PTOs exercising Significant Market Power to other telecoms companies. Oftel's proposals are that customers of all fixed telecommunications service providers should be entitled to refer outstanding disputes to independent arbitration, and that in the case of PTOs exercising Significant Market Power (currently BT and Kingston Communications) Oftel would reserve to itself the power to settle disputes with other telecoms companies by determination. The proposed arbitration procedures would appear to involve the development of powers which were given to Oftel by legislation in 1992 (discussed in Chapter Nine).

However, the consultation document makes no mention of those statutory powers, but rather purports to implement requirements laid on the UK government by the EC Revised Voice Telephony Directive of 1997. Most curiously these new procedures are to operate alongside the existing dispute resolution procedures (discussed in Chapter Nine) rather than provide an integrated and more responsive basis for encouraging compliance by firms with regulatory norms (as proposed in Chapter Ten). It may be that the consultation does not represent an attempt by Oftel to move towards a culture with would provide more effective and responsive dispute resolution, but rather the minimum formal steps necessary to show compliance with EC requirements, with little serious belief that this will effect cultural and operational change from the practices described in this book.

Notes

1 Ducts, poles and holes in the ground: the inner world of telecommunications regulation

1 The understanding of the role of culture here is similar to the Goffman concept of framing, as it is deployed by Manning (1992: 259–61) to indicate how organizational decisions in agencies are patterned but not determined in terms of 'what information is sought, or seen as relevant and significant, and what such information conveys for organizational actions'.

2 The archaeology of a regulatory regime

1 The privatization of BT was carried out largely for financial reasons. The Cabinet settled on the policy in 1982 to free BT from Treasury control, enabling it to make investments on a scale that the Treasury would not have approved under a public ownership regime (Baker 1993: 78). For the Treasury, the attraction of BT privatization was that it would raise revenue and reduce public debt in the year of sale, a key policy objective. In a classic instance of the mingling of different streams of policy (Kingdon 1984), these hard financial objectives chimed with broader political objectives, such as reduction of the power of public sector labour unions, and fitted with the Thatcher government's enthusiasm for 'roll-back-the-state' rhetoric (Moon, Richardson and Smart 1986: 341).

2 Ellison (1994) says that the DTI considered giving the regulatory powers to the OFT but rejected the idea on the grounds that OFT might be swamped with telecoms work. The OFT had been set up with what appeared to be a full raft of regulatory powers, including rule-making, issuing of licences (for consumer credit), monitoring and the application of sanctions. In practice, the DTI had functioned as the senior partner in the regulatory regime. OFT was heavily constrained in its power to initiate new rules independent of other bodies, its statutory rule-making powers had rapidly fallen into disuse, and commentators concluded that OFT's powers to oversee the development of self-regulatory codes of practice initiated by industry trade associations in practice became 'the major regulatory "output" of the agency' (Ramsay 1989: 281).

3 Though Carsberg did act against convention by establishing the practice of publishing the advice which he gave to ministers.
4 This power of the Secretary of State is set down in s.47(3) of the Telecommunications Act 1984 and is in addition to the more specific ministerial power to give directions to the director-general in respect of matters affecting national security (s.94). It is an indication of the extent to which this power has remained very much in the background of relations between Oftel and the DTI that senior Oftel staff told us that our description of it 'badly overstates the Secretary of State's powers'.
5 A newspaper article headed 'The firm that means Mcjobs for the boys' referred to a 'religiously updated alumni list detailing the current job and telephone number of 5,000 former members of the consultancy' as McKinsey and Co's most important, though private publication, and 'probably the world's best contact list'. *The Observer* 29 June 1997, p6).

3 Peculiar place, peculiar culture: organizing and structuring the regulatory office

1 However, one BT insider said that if Oftel were ever to move out of London, for example to cut office costs, some of BT's offices would be likely to move too since the physical proximity was too useful to lose.
2 At a 1997 Oftel workshop to introduce civil service norms to those from non-civil service backgrounds, the participants were asked, 'How many of you consider yourself to be civil servants?'. Only half of the group raised their hand.
3 For example, changes in budget allocation and tighter cost allocation meant it became harder for the DTI to absorb the cost of carrying the administrative functions for Oftel as it had done in the first and second of Oftel's life-stages.
4 For example, from 1997, Oftel was able for the first time to set its own pay scales and reward effort or initiative with variable pay awards (subject to Treasury agreement).
5 But it must be noted that the word hierarchical was used in more than one way. Some saw central control as stronger in Oftel than in the DTI because the personal responsibilities of the DGT interlinked with the non-routine nature of most of Oftel's activity made vertical or horizontal decentralization of responsibility more problematic.
6 Though such an attitude contrasts with the general tendency of Oftel's top brass to deny that such a decision style was widespread within the organization, as discussed in Chapter Six. And, as will be shown later, the creative tension doctrine of the branch/project team relationship started to change towards the end of Cruickshank's tenure as DGT.
7 Secondees from city law firms were first recruited by Oftel in 1993 in an attempt to improve the quality of Oftel's staff. By 1997 there were eight of them (PAC 1998, Annex A), but in Oftel they worked as generalists leading projects and dealing with policy problems, rather than as lawyers.

8 To discourage a 'gradist' mentality among Oftel staff, official policy was to replace grade numbers with job titles, so Branch Heads were no longer called Grade 5s. But staff remained well aware of fine distinctions in status and grading since it had an important affect upon the way they could work and interact.

9 The annual Management Plan was a device that went back to the mid-1980s, but Don Cruickshank turned it from a surface exercise into an active instrument of managing Oftel, publishing the plan and even having public consultation (in 1998) about what should go into it.

10 These networks were mainly office-based and did not involve such phenomena as the Japanese bureaucratic tradition of collective drinking in the office late into the night. The only pale shadow of that practice was a regular drink in a local pub after work, which caused tensions within one branch because the pattern of participation was seen to be linked to status and influence, even affecting who was allocated what work.

11 Because general civil service training courses were seen as ill-matched to Oftel's needs, it was deemed necessary to Oftelize the staff training programme and a training officer was appointed in 1995. By 1997 she had become two and a half people.

12 Personal contacts linked with the meetings culture, in the sense that who was able to say what in a meeting was affected by the way individuals were networked, in particular to senior managers. For example, on one occasion a legal secondee was able to argue vigorously against the collective opinion of the legal branch about a licence modification because she had the personal status of close links to the DDG in another project.

13 A DTI observer saw this feature as a key difference in the decision-making style between the DTI and Oftel. 'Oftel staff always have to say "No, we must ask Don," when asked for a decision by DTI' but he, by contrast, could make a decision without referring to his boss so long as he told his superior what he had done.

14 In this project we were only able directly to observe meetings that took place within Oftel (with BT and other companies visting Oftel) and not the meetings occurring outside Oftels' offices, so it is not possible to tell if behaviour was different at meetings conducted in other locations.

15 Though records were often in the form of 'Notes' produced some time after the event.

16 Meetings varied in part according to the nature of the refreshments that accompanied them. Working meetings had coffee and biscuits; people worked with their jackets off and sleeves rolled up, talking as they drank their coffee in an atmosphere that was generally good natured and constructive. Other meetings were too tense to permit food to be consumed even if it had been ordered. Still other meetings, for example those with the various ACTs, might include a full buffet lunch and a great deal of the work was carried out during the conversation whilst it was eaten. Internal lunch time seminars held for the staff also included sandwiches, providing one of the few opportunities within Oftel for striking up casual acquaintances – a useful element in building personal networks. Later, however, much of this catering came to an end as a result of tighter financial constraints.

17 This RAD filter applied to all the meetings we observed and was BT's official policy; but the DGT told us that some of his meetings with senior BT staff were not observed by RAD.

18 Wright (1994: 2) comments that '[f]or an anthropologist reading this [organizational studies] literature there are moments of recognition closely followed by the discovery of familiar ideas used in disconcertingly unrecognizable ways'.

4 'Oftel, *c'est moi*': the role of the DGT

1 Cruickshank himself preferred radio, and in particular Radio 4's *Today* programme since interviews could be given live on new policy statements simultaneously with release of information to the London Stock Exchange, reducing the risk of breaches of security affecting trading in shares. An early morning interview got Oftel's view into the media before BT and the rest could launch pre-emptive media strikes.

2 Wilks and Doern (1998: 384–5) explain that the development of the Commission style regulation in the United States during the progressive era was a response to the problem that appointments to key administrative posts were, and remain, essentially political. Though single-person agency heads were supported by some in the early policy debates, the argument was rejected on the grounds that it would not be acceptable to have regulatory bodies controlled by either a Democrat or a Repbulican alone. They continue:

> This detracts somewhat from the idea that the British single-person regulator is somehow departing from the U.S. ideal. The British regulator may find his or her job unduly personalized, but, since the UK does not have a 'spoils system', he or she is a non-party political figure . . . This reasoning rather supports the status quo, in which single-person regulators hold statutory authority as individual office-holders, and are able to act with decisiveness, consistency and transparency.

3 Or, in the less colourful language of a senior DTI official, the DTI's ability to 'give advice on the political impact or consider regulatory consistency' even for matters which fell outside ministers' specific responsibility.

4 Cruickshank's own comment on our claim was that the position was 'Just the opposite! I gave the DTI a *de facto* veto'.

5 One Oftel branch head talked enthusiastically to us about the efficacy of 'fuss with threats' as a tactic for dealing with the DTI. A senior DTI official said that he and his Oftel opposite number periodically 'try to hose down our respective sides when they get hot and bothered. It is partly personality, partly turf wars and partly because practice has grown up that is just not supported by primary legislation . . . We share some policy interests but we feel that other policy is all our own – and so we get frustrated when we find someone else is parking their tent (*sic*) on our lawn . . .'

6 A feature of the Cruickshank era in Oftel, as noted in Chapter Two, and noted by many of our respondents in both the DTI and Oftel. One fast-stream civil servant, impeccably groomed himself, graphically testified to the improvement in the quality of Oftel staff and its place in the bureaucratic pecking order over that period:

> Oftel used to be in that dreadful red-brick building on the Holborn Viaduct. It had endless corridors in civil service green paint and walls that were peeling. It had chairs – like that one [pointing to a metal framed chair] – covered in tie-dyed nylon from the 1960s. It was dreadful. Full of people in grey shoes and petroleum cloth suits covered in dandruff. They were all 'techies', economic as well as technical, or benighted managers who hadn't got a hope in hell of getting a job anywhere else . . .

7 Though a senior DTI official contested the claim that Oftel did the work on the telephony aspects of radio spectrum. It was often difficult to match the DTI and Oftel versions of events.

8 Given the long debate about the possibility of making any determinate policy-administration dichotomy in public administration (Appleby 1949), that stereotype is more problematic even for orthodox government departments than it might at first sight appear.

9 In fact the DDG was in Oftel for only six years.

10 This DTI claim matched neither the perceptions or practices of recruitment of branch heads within Oftel. At this time at least one branch head had been recruited direct from British Telecom, another from a senior position in a local authority. We were unable to discover whether such external appointments are effectively invisible in the wider Whitehall or whether they somehow develop a presence out of neccessity. We may speculate that an Oftel entirely staffed by appointees from outside Whitehall would have a markedly different relationship with the DTI.

11 A common perception within Oftel was that only the DDG, DGT and a senior policy advisor were privy to the overall strategic picture.

12 Cruickshank himself commented on our draft manuscript that there was very little that was *important* that was outside the direct sphere of his knowledge and intervention and marked up his view that complaint handling was *not* a regulatory role. But this comment begs the question, what is important amongst the regulatory office's activities? It is certainly true that Cruickshank had a substantial direct role in major licence condition modifications, such as the Price Control Review (discussed in Chapter Seven) and the Fair Trading Condition (discussed in Chapters Eight and Nine), and also in less central or even trivial policies such as how to deal with hotel phone pricing (discussed in Chapter Eight) but the implicit claim that the high profile licence modifications were more important than routine bureaucratic tasks, for example in maintaining the legitimacy and effectiveness of the organization, is questionable.

5 Oftel in space: interdependence and accountability

1 These criteria became Condition 13.5A.5 of BT's licence.
2 On this second occasion Oftel had to force the issue to an MMC reference in 1995 (MMC 1995), which resulted in the introduction of a new and usable licence condition in 1996.
3 Not all companies participated in the CCA committee, although they generally associated themselves with the CCA line. 'Free-rider is not a bad term, but they more or less trust us to get the answer right' according to one member.
4 Perhaps this frustration was not relayed to the CA, as the CA comment was 'Oftel did not seem to mind' when the CA failed to meet deadlines.
5 Consumer groups were also selective about participation in the various panels and working groups established by Oftel, but this was often presented as a matter of principle, because of concerns that their capacity to speak out would be compromised.
6 See the numbering administration case study in Chapter Seven.
7 Oftel's decisions were challenged in a (surprisingly) limited number of cases brought before the courts, in the form of two applications for judicial review and one ordinary action in the Commercial Court; but the DTI had been challenged twice by BT over its implementation of EC Directives affecting BT (Scott 1998a).
8 See also the description of Oftel's defence of a judicial review action of the Fair Trading Condition in Chapter Nine.

6 Regulatory decision styles

1 It is difficult to measure the scale of Oftel's regulatory output, in terms of documents, with precision. An analysis of the organizational web site shows 41 publications by Oftel in 1996 (including statements, orders, consultation documents, bulletins and reports) and 84 such publications for 1997 and 87 press releases for 1996 and 99 press releases for 1997. The increase in numbers of publications from 1996 to 1997 may partially reflect a shift towards both greater openness and formality, rather than in increase in the quantity of decision-making *per se*.
2 90 per cent of all the 217 investigations conducted by Oftel between the beginning of 1995 and the end of December 1997 into particular practices which were allegedly having an anti-competitive effect on the UK market were in response to complaints from companies within the industry (NAO 1998: 3).
3 Including contributions from social psychology, anthropology, political science, organizational sociology and management science.
4 But during a review of Oftel by the National Audit Office, more than 75 per cent of industry respondents surveyed rated Oftel's legal and technical expertise as either good or very good – in sharp contrast to their views on Oftel's commercial awareness or appreciation of the problems faced by firms (NAO 1998: 30).
5 One lawyer in the Oftel team, drafting the licence modifications for the price control, admitted she could not understand the reason behind many of the clauses in the licence. As Oftel had a stated policy of removing

redundant and excessive conditions from the operator's licence, the lawyer's job of deciding what to leave in and what to leave out did not easily fit the Cartesian-bureaucratic style.

6 Though we must report that at least two of Oftel's very senior staff ultimately came to recognize the variety of decision-making styles which we observed, and gave considerable assistance to us in characterizing the conditions under which different styles might be used and/or be effective.

7 Price controls and numbering administration: Cartesian-bureaucratic issue-processing episodes

1 Headline from the *Daily Telegraph* 2 July 1996.

2 NB this table does not show changes to the elements of service within the price cap, other price constraints associated with the price control or services to which no price constraint applied. Details can be found in Burns (1994).

3 The proportion of BT's services subject to the control was a product of the basket of services to which the price control should apply. In theory Oftel was aiming to include in the basket those aspects of BT's service which were not subject to effective competition.

4 Or, in a much-quoted phrase from regulation guru Stephen Littlechild, 'holding the fort until competition arrives'. But despite this policy more of BT's revenue and services was price-controlled in 1996 than 1984, even though competition had increased over that period (Xavier 1995).

5 However, according to one team member 'A lot of really small decisions went straight to the DG because everyone wanted him to sign them off'.

6 But, according to one Oftel staff member, 'There are draconian penalties if a licensee fails to comply with Section 53 so it is only used as an escalation tool, and then very rarely'.

7 This view finds support in an independent economic analysis of BT's performance, suggesting that BT had a 'relatively high return [on capital employed] compared to other utilities' (Lapsley and Kilpatrick 1997: 99).

8 Headline from The *Daily Telegraph* 18 April 1995.

9 Residential lines in the UK had increased from 42 per cent penetration in 1972 to 92 per cent in 1995/6 (Oftel data), and demand for numbers was augmented by new technologies (notably fax and later mobile phones), new services like freephone and premium-rate numbers. There was also a huge growth in business lines with direct-dial personal numbers rather than a company switchboard, plus dedicated lines for data etc.

10 He also urged them to obtain the numbering data base from the incumbent operator 'as soon as possible, even if you don't do anything with it yet' to prevent Telekom from seeding blocks of numbers (behaviour that was observable in a number of countries) to inhibit competition before it began.

11 TNAB comprised representatives of key licensees (BT, Mercury, Kingston Communications, Cellnet and Vodafone), user groups (notably the Telecommunications Managers Association and the Telecommunications Users Association) and local government.

12 The Conventions were described in Condition 34B of BT's Licence as 'a set of principles and rules published from time to time by the Director after consultation with interested parties who are members of the Telecommunications Numbering Advisory Body, and if deemed appropriate, end-users'.

13 The quality of BT's information was of limited value because (among other things) it was organized on a regional basis. But why had Oftel assumed it would be otherwise?

14 The pyjamas are mentioned in a report in the *Independent* ('Dial 01 for Confusion', 13 March 1995) and is possible that this article is the source of the legend.

15 Senior Oftel staff claim that this formula was not misleading, as it left open the possibility of further code changes for existing users after consultation should the overlay solution be rejected. The widely quoted words of the DGT from an Oftel press release were: 'Customers can be confident that after Phoneday no new changes to their numbers will be imposed upon them. In the longer term, customers will have a choice between 01 and 02 for new numbers'. Oftel Press Release, 7 March 1995. See for example the report in the *Daily Telegraph* ('Phone Users to be Given Their Say' 9 March 1995).

16 Oftel continued to be extremely vulnerable to attack by Parliamentary committees on the numbering issue. The Trade and Industry Select Committee published a further highly critical report in 1999 (Trade and Industry Committee 1999).

8 Regulating anti-competitive conduct and not regulating hotel phone pricing: adhocratic-chaotic issue-processing episodes

1 Headline from *The Times* 8 December 1994.

2 The first meeting with OLOs over the FTC proposal was held only in September 1995, some nine months after the original consultation paper, and even then only a small number of OLOs were directly represented, including two mobile phone operators, two cable companies, Mercury, Ionica and Worldcom. They offered some information (though their intervention was not considered 'decisive' by a senior Oftel official, in contrast to the role they played in contributing information to the PCR described in the last chapter) and acted as allies for Oftel over FTC, for example in lobbying the DTI in an attempt to persuade it that the FTC was necessary.

3 His letter further warned that 'it is not Oftel's responsibility to consult on options available to ministers' (*Letter of 29 November 1994*).

4 Headline from an article in the *Mail on Sunday* 9 June 1996.

5 However, as the spread of mobile phones reduced general customer dependency on hotel equipment, the greater would be the amount of fixed costs to which each call on hotel equipment would need to contribute.

6 In this previous decision round, Oftel seems to have been provoked into action over hotel phone prices by a critical article in the *Daily Telegraph* in 1990 ('Hotels Give Guests a Hang-Up with Unfair Phone Charges', 1 August 1990). On this occasion Oftel concluded that telling customers

how much they would be charged for making calls from a hotel room phone was an adequate solution. From the file records it is evident that Oftel took two approaches to the issue. First, it considered promoting changes to the voluntary Booking Code for hotels (run by the British Tourist Authority), to include information about telephone charges, but concluded that public disquiet was insufficient to merit such a measure (*Memo 2 August 1991*). Second, it made changes to the Branch Systems General Licence (BSGL) which were incorporated in the succeeding Telecommunications Service Licence (TSL) to provide a power to require licensees to provide information about charging for payphones and remote payment payphones (such as those in hotel rooms). This change was apparently seen as a bureaucratically neat solution to the problem.

7 Paras 66–7, published by Oftel in October 1992.

8 An approach which could be termed regulatory 'bargaining within the shadow of the law' (Lewis 1985) in socio-legal jargon.

9 Although tariff information was obviously a consumer issue, TSOs had no legal powers of enforcement if no tariff was displayed beside a public payphone, since that requirement was imposed by the DGT under the 1984 Telecoms Act. They could only act if tariff information was displayed but inaccurate, using powers such as those they possessed under the 1987 Consumer Protection Act.

10 As noted in Chapter Six, institutional memory within Oftel was largely carried through individuals and when they moved on the memory was lost. The memory problem was exacerbated by the absence of records of telephone and other conversations so even when files were available for reference, they were often incomplete or skeletal.

Remarkably, Oftel returned once more in 1998 to the issue of regulation of hotel phones, proposing amendments to the TSL to require display of charges at bedsides – *Oftel Statement payphone regulation in the UK – the way forward Oftel's conclusions for payphone regulation in the UK* (March 1999) para. 2.13.

9 Complaint handling, licence enforcement and anti-competitive conduct II: bargaining-diplomatic issue-processing episodes

1 But it was far from a pure Prisoner's Dilemma game, since the potential for intervention by other parties, notably the DTI, meant it was not wholly bilateral (See Baird, Gertner and Picker 1994: 43–5).

2 Headline from *Evening Standard* 27 July 1995.

3 Such a reference could be made either by the DGT under s.13 of the Telecommunications Act 1984 or by the Secretary of State under the Fair Trading Act 1973.

4 For example, Oftel made an Order under Condition 17 in March 1997 (Oftel Press Release 10/97) which effectively stopped BT from offering below-cost service to customers returning to it from a competing operator.

5 BT's argument was that there was no mechanism to ensure consistency with EC law (i.e. no right of appeal).

6 The concessions made by Oftel at this meeting were to hand over a draft 'sunset clause' providing that the FTC would expire in 2001 or

at the point when legislative instruments with the same or better effect were introduced, and to indicate how the advisory panel would be included in a redraft of the FTC.

7 Don Cruickshank, a former company executive, believed the BT Board was not being properly advised about the FTC and later said he had been genuinely baffled as to why a well-informed BT Board would even consider rejecting the FTC.

8 Cruickshank often stated, publicly and privately, that he refused to use side letters under any circumstances.

9 As the Epilogue to this book will relate, the consumer complaint function was eventually earmarked for total separation from Oftel after the period of our study.

10 A Public Accounts Committee Report found that 90 per cent of Oftel's investigations into anti-competitive conduct originated from industry complaints (Public Accounts Committee 1998, para. 5).

11 Statutory powers to enforce licence conditions were used in the early 1990s to require cable TV companies to comply with their obligations to complete their networks according to the specified timetable (Oftel 1991: para. 2.2). The DGT also twice invoked Condition 13 of BT's licence to determine interconnection terms with MCL and issued directions over cross-subsidies adversely affected competition (BT Licence Condition 20B.15 and Oftel Press Release 19/97).

12 Even though this equipment had been obsolete for more than a decade in the mid 1990s, BT continued to charge equipment rental for hard-wired phones, claiming that its billing system could not identify them, and charged customers a fee to change out of hard-wired phones into modern jack and socket phones. Only if the phones were damaged or inoperable was the changeover made automatically and free of charge.

13 When there was no competition aspect that could be detected, Oftel staff tended towards the presumption that no breach of licence was involved.

14 Our observation of the Oftel enforcement style is at variance with the analysis of Steven Vogel (1996: 91), who described the regime established in the UK in 1984 as 'a much more formal and legalistic (juridical) variety of regulation'. Whilst the new regime did involve the writing down of procedures in legislation, our analysis suggests that space was left for the operation of the regime in a style much influenced by the informality of the fifth age of telecoms regulation.

15 Though BT had insisted from the outset of the sixth telecoms era in 1984 that all relations between itself and Oftel (indeed all regulators) be channelled through the 'commissars' in a specialist Government Relations Department (later re-named Regulatory Affairs Department). Oftel staff perceived this approach as a defensive strategy and one that made it difficult to develop good working relations with the BT staff actually engaged in commercial decision-making.

16 Between 1987 and 1997 total annual Oftel customer contacts (not all of which were complaints, since the boundary line between a complaint and a search for information or advice tends to be uncertain) ranged from a low of 23,415 in 1993 to a high of 41,393 in 1991 (Oftel annual reports and internal data).

17 Admittedly, Don Cruickshank made a visit to CRS mandatory for new Oftel staff during their induction period, to raise the profile of consumer issues within the organization. But such changes did not in practice change the lowly status and semi-detached nature of CRS within Oftel.

18 See TA 1984 s27E, as amended by CS(U)A 1992 s4 and TA 1984 s27F,G,I, as amended by CS(U)A 1992 ss5,6,7. The Secretary of State rather than Oftel had the power to designate operators which had at least 25 per cent of the market for voice telephony within an area (TA 1984 s27L as amended by CS(U)A 1992 s10), and BT and Kingston Communications were so designated in 1992 (Competition and Service (Utilities) Act 1992, Designation Order 1992 (SI no 1360)).

19 For example, in the UK gas sector complaints were largely handled by the Gas Consumers' Council, completely separate from the regulatory functions of the Office of Gas Supply (Ofgas).

10 Regulatory science: regulatory policy and possible regulatory features

1 There are not many existing examples of such tripartism in enforcement in the UK, apart from the enforcement provisions under the Unfair Terms in Consumer Contracts Regulations 1999, which the Government has amended so as to authorize consumer groups to share enforcement authority with the Office of Fair Trading.

2 A full review of future issues would require an evaluation of the effects of convergence of telecommunications with broadcasting and IT, arising out of the possibilities created by digitalization of data. Because the issue of convergence was outside of the scope of the research for this book, for pragmatic reasons, we do not address that issue in these concluding remarks. A useful approach to this broader question is provided by Melody (1997a).

3 The exception to this is for those regimes where government policy is to promote investment in and development of telecommunications facilities through mechanisms which preserve monopolistic characteristics, such as franchising and Build Operate Transfer (BOT).

4 Linked to this responsibility has been a marked increase in statutory rule making and licence modifications initiated not by Oftel but by the DTI. See for example Oftel press release 40/98, indicating that the DTI was introducing a new statutory instrument and new licence conditions into PTO licences to comply with the requirements of the EC Revised Voice Telephony Directive (1997).

5 The European Commission has considered such a move (NERA/Denton Hall 1996), but concluded that the necessary political will among the Member States is lacking. If the creation of effective liberalized telecommunications markets is a serious ambition of the EU and the broader international community, then experience may require a change of heart.

Epilogue

1 Some of the major policy developments can be tracked using press releases and publications on the OFTEL web-site http://www.oftel.gov.uk. This Epilogue concentrates on organizational issues.
2 The government decided not to pursue the possibility of replacing statutory consumer representation through industry funded ombudsman offices of the type developed in Australia (DTI 1998a: Conclusion 3.4).
3 Though the government consulted on new institutional models for the converged broadcasting and telecommunications sectors, it apparently intended to retain the ITC and OFTEL as separate regulatory organizations rather than replacing them with a new single communications regulator in the near future (DTI 1998b: Chapter 5).

Glossary

ACT Statutory Advisory Committee on Telecommunications.

ADC Access Deficit Contribution – payment made by interconnecting PTOs to BT, under terms of BT's licence (as amended in 1991) to compensate BT for the costs of providing access via its local loop infrastructure to its customers.

BDB British Digital Broadcasting – licensee for provision of digital broadcasting services.

BT British Telecommunications plc – public limited company created by the privatization (1984–92) of a publicly owned corporation, British Telecommunications.

CA Consumers Association – private association which, *inter alia,* monitors consumer markets and lobbies for consumer-friendly policies.

CC Competition Commission – public body which will replace the MMC under the Competition Act 1998.

Condition 17 Condition in BT's licence prohibiting undue preference and undue discrimination.

Condition 18A Condition introduced to BT's licence in 1996 which prohibits abuse of dominant position and restrictive agreements, and creates various procedures for the application by Oftel of these prohibitions (known as the Fair Trading Condition (FTC)).

CPIs Comparative Performance Indicators – non-statutory scheme established by Oftel for collecting comparative data on service levels from PTOs.

CRS Consumer Representation Section – division of Oftel charged with handling complaints about PTOs.

CS(U)A 1992 Competition and Service (Utilities) Act 1992 – legislation enhancing certain of the DGT's powers over consumer complaints.

DCMS Department of Culture, Media and Sport – government department responsible for *inter alia* broadcasting policy.

DDG Deputy Director General.

DG IV Directorate General IV of the European Commission responsible for application of competition policy.

DG XIII Director General XIII of the European Commission responsible, *inter alia*, for telecommunications policy.

DGT Director General of Telecommunications, appointed under the TA 1984.

DIEL Statutory advisory committee on the needs of Disabled and Elderly People.

DOE Department of the Environment – government department responsible, *inter alia*, for oversight of local authorities in England (replaced by Department of Environment, Transport and the Regions after 1997 general election).

DTI Department of Trade and Industry.

Duopoly Review process by which DTI decided to abandon the MCL-BT duopoly in basic telecommunications services (1991–2) and licence other PTOs.

EU/EC European Union/European Community.

FCC Federal Communications Commission – US independent regulatory commission for telecommunications and broadcasting.

FTC Fair Trading Condition – see Condition 18A.

GATT General Agreement on Tariffs and Trade.

GPO General Post Office – public corporation established in 1969 to operate UK postal and telecommunications services until BT was split from it in 1981.

ICAS Interconnection and Accounting Separation – term used to describe the policy process (1992–5) by which rules in BT's licence governing interconnection were revised and requirements added requiring the publication of accounts showing its various services separately as part of the post-duopoly liberalization process.

ITC Independent Television Commission – public body charged with regulation of UK broadcasting sector.

MCL Mercury Communications Ltd – subsidiary of Cable and Wireless plc created in 1982 to act as competitor to BT and subsequently absorbed into a new company, Cable and Wireless Communications.

MMC Monopolies and Mergers Commission – public body charged with investigating (at the request of the OFT, DTI or utilities regulators, such as Oftel) matters referred to it under competition or utilities legislation and making recommendations.

NAO National Audit Office – public body responsible for audit and value for money (VFM) audit of public bodies in England and Wales, reporting to Parliament.

NAU Numbering Administration Unit – section within Oftel created in 1994 to manage the UK National Numbering Plan.

NCC National Consumer Council – public body responsible for developing independent policies and lobbying on consumer protection matters.

NCC Day National Code Change Day (1995) also known as phONEday.

NRAs national regulatory authorities.

Number Portability regulatory requirement that customers moving from one PTO to another be able to retain the same phone number.

OFT Office of Fair Trading – Non-ministerial government department established by Fair Trading Act 1973 charged with monitoring UK markets for compliance with competition and consumer protection laws.

Oftel Office of Telecommunications – non-ministerial government department established by TA 1984 charged with regulation of UK telecommunications sector.

OLOs Other licensed operators – term used to refer to UK PTOs other than BT.

PAC Public Accounts Committee (House of Commons).

PCR Price Control Review – process by which Oftel modified BT's licence to maintain and adapt RPI – x price control on BT's prices.

PhONEday see NCC Day.

PSTN Public Switched Telephone Network – network providing services to the general public.

PTO Public Telecommunications Operator licensed under TA 1984.

RAD Regulatory Affairs Department – the division of BT responsible for managing contacts with Oftel and the DTI.

RPI–x formula applied to BT for control of prices, based on increase in the retail price index less a figure (x) to reflect efficiency gains to be achieved by BT.

SATRA South African Telecommunications Regulatory Authority.

SPL Self-Provision Licence – class licence permitting and applying certain conditions to the operation of certain telecommunications facilities such as private branch exchanges (PABX).

TA Telecommunications Act 1984 – main legislation governing provision and regulation of telecommunications in the UK (amended by the CS(U)A 1992).

TACS Telecommunications Advisory Committees – statutory committees established under TA 1984 to advise Oftel.

TISC Trade and Industry Select Committee (House of Commons).

TMA Telecommunications Managers Association.

TNAB Telecommunications Numbering and Addressing Body – advisory body for the UK Numbering Conventions, made under BT's PTO licence.

TSL Telecommunications Service Licence – class licence permitting and applying conditions to the operation of privately run telecommunications systems for advanced services.

TSOs Trading Standard Officers – local authority staff responsible for monitoring and enforcement of consumer protection laws.

UKREP UK Permanent Representation to the European Union – part of the British government responsible for co-ordinating UK input in to EC policy making.

USO Universal Service Obligations.

WTO World Trade Organization.

Bibliography

Alvesson, M. (1993) *Cultural Perspectives on Organisations*, Cambridge: Cambridge University Press.

Appleby, P.H. (1949) *Policy and Administration*, AL: University of Alabama Press.

Armstrong, M. ed., (1990–) *Communications Law and Policy*, Melbourne: Butterworths.

Armstrong, M., Cowan, S. and Vickers, J. (1994) *Regulatory Reform. Regulation of Economic Activity*, Cambridge, MA: MIT Press.

Ayres, I. and Braithwaite, J. (1992) *Responsive Regulation – Transcending the Deregulation Debate*, Oxford: Oxford University Press.

Bagehot, W. (1963) *The English Consititution*, London: Fontana (originally published 1867).

Bailey, F. (1969) *Strategems and Spoils: a Social Anthropology of Politics*, Oxford: Blackwell.

Baird, G., Gertner, R.H. and Picker, R.C. (1994) *Game Theory and the Law*, Cambridge, MA: Harvard University Press.

Baker, K. (1993) *The Turbulent Years: My Life in Politics*, London: Faber.

Baldwin, R. and McCrudden, C., (eds), (1987) *Regulation and Public Law*, London: Weidenfeld and Nicolson.

Baldwin, R., Scott, C. and Hood, C. (1998) 'Introduction' to *Reader on Regulation*, Oxford: Oxford University Press.

Bardach, E. and Kagan, R.A. (1982) *Going by the Book – The Problem of Regulatory Unreasonableness*, Philadelphia: Temple University Press.

Barnes, F. (1998) 'Regulating telecommunications' in D. Helm and T. Jenkinson (eds) *Competition in Regulated Industries*, Oxford: Oxford University Press.

Bernstein, M. (1955) *Regulating Business by Independent Commission*, New Jersey: Princeton University Press.

Black, J. (1997) 'New institutionalism and naturalism in socio-legal analysis: institutionalist approaches to regulatory decision making', *Law and Policy* 19: 51–93.

—— (1998) 'Talking about regulation', *Public Law* [1998]: 77–105.

Bradley, K. (1992) *Phone Wars – The Story of Mercury Communications*, London: Random Century.

Braithwaite, J. (1997) 'On speaking softly and carrying big sticks: neglected dimensions of a republican separation of powers', *University of Toronto Law Journal* 47: 305–61.

Bollard, A. and Pickford, M. (1997) 'Utility regulation in New Zealand', in M.E. Beesley (ed.) *Regulating Utilities: Broadening the Debate*, London: Institute of Economic Affairs/London Business School.

Bovens, M. and t'Hart, P. (1996) *Understanding Policy Fiascoes*, London: Transaction.

Braybrooke, D. (1974) *Traffic Congestion Goes Through the Issue Machine: A Case Study in Issue Processing, Illustrating a New Approach*, London: Routledge and Kegan Paul.

Brunnsson, N. (1989) *The Organization of Hypocrisy: Talk, Decisions and Actions in Organizations*, Chichester: Wiley.

Bryan-Brown, M. (1995) 'Reforming telecoms competition rules', *Consumer Policy Review* 5: 121–6.

Burns, P. (1994) *Discriminatory Pricing and Accounting Method in the UK Regulated Industries*, London: Centre for the Study of Regulated Industries.

Cave, M. (1997) 'The evolution of telecommunications regulation in the UK', *European Economic Review* 41: 691–9.

Chapman, R.A. and Greenaway, J.R. (1980) *The Dynamics of Administrative Reform*, London: Croom Helm.

Clune, W.H. (1992) 'Implementation as autopoietic interaction of autopoietic organizations' in G. Teubner and A. Febbrajo (eds) *State, Law and Economy as Autopoietic Systems – Regulation and Autonomy in New Perspective*, Milan: Guiffre.

Coates, K. (1999) 'Regulating the telecommunications sector: substituting practical co-operation for the risks of competition', in C. McCrudden (ed.) *Regulation and Deregulation*, Oxford: Oxford University Press.

Coen, D. and Willman, P. (1998) 'The evolution of the firm's regulatory affairs office', *Business Strategy Review* 9: 31–6.

Cohen, M.D., March, J.G. and Olsen, J.P. (1972) 'A garbage can model of organizational choice', *Administrative Science Quarterly* 17: 1–23.

Commerce Commission (1992) *Telecommunications Industry Inquiry Report*, Wellington: New Zealand Commerce Commission.

Corry, D., Souter, D. and Waterson, M. (1994) *Regulating Our Utilities*, London: Institute of Public Policy Research.

Corwin, R.G. (1983) *The Entrepreneurial Bureaucracy: Biographies of Two Federal Programs in Education*, Greenwich, CT: JAI Press.

Cranston, R. (1979) *Regulating Business – Law and Consumer Agencies*, London: MacMillan.

Daintith, T. (1997) *Regulation* in *International Encyclopedia of Comparative Law* Vol XVII, Chapter Ten, Tübingen: Martinus Nijhoff.

Day, R. and Klein, P. (1987) *Accountabilities*, London: Tavistock.
DTI (1984) *Notes to Clauses, Telecommunications Act 1984*, London: House of Commons (Oftel Library).
—— (1991) *Competition and Choice: Telecommunications Policy for the 1990s*, Cm 1461, London: HMSO.
—— (1998a) *A Fair Deal for Consumers: Modernising the Framework of Utility Regulation*, Cm 3898, London: HMSO.
—— (1998b) *Regulating Communications: Approaching Convergence in the Information Age*, Cm 4022, London: HMSO.
—— (1998c) *Licence Modification Procedure: Proposed Changes to the Telecommunications Act 1984*, London: Department of Trade and Industry (http://www.dti.gov.uk/public/frame8.html.).
—— (1999) *Consumer Councils: The Response to Consultation*, London: Department of Trade and Industry.
Dezalay, Y. (1991) 'Territorial battles and tribal disputes', *Modern Law Review* 54: 792–809.
Diver, C. (1982) 'Engineers and entrepreneurs: the dilemma of public management', *Journal of Policy Analysis and Management* 1: 402–6.
Doern, B. (1998) 'The interplay among regimes: mapping regulatory institutions in the United Kingdom, the United States and Canada', in B. Doern and S. Wilks 1998.
Doern, B. and Wilks, S. (eds) (1998) *Changing Regulatory Institutions in Britain and North America*, Toronto: University of Toronto Press.
Douglas, M. (1985) 'Introduction' in J.L. Gross and S. Rayner (eds) *Measuring Culture: A Paradigm for the Analysis of Social Organization*, New York: Columbia University Press.
—— (1990) 'Risk as a Forensic Resource', *Daedalus* 119: 1–16.
Dowding, K. (1995) 'Model or metaphor? A critical review of the policy network approach', *Political Studies* XLIII: 136–58.
Downs, A. (1966) *Inside Bureaucracy*, Boston: Little Brown.
Dunsire, A. (1978) *The Execution Process, ii, Control in a Bureaucracy*, Oxford: Martin Robertson.
Dunsire, A. (1996) 'Tipping the balance: autopoiesis and governance', *Administration and Society* 28: 299–334.
Edelman, M. (1964) *The Symbolic Uses of Politics*, Urbana: University of Illinois Press.
Ellison, I. (1994) Conference Speech at 'Ten Years of the Telecommunications Act 1984' Conference, at Waldorf Astoria Hotel, London, March 1994.
Everitt, C.W. (1931) *The Education of Jeremy Bentham*, New York: Columbia University Press.
Flood, C. (1995) 'Regulation of telecommunications in New Zealand – faith in competition law and the Kiwi share', *Competition and Consumer Law Journal* 3: 199–221.
Foreman-Peck, J. and Millward, R. (1994) *Public and Private Ownership of British Industry 1820–1990*, Oxford: Clarendon Press.

Foster, Sir Christopher D. (1992) *Privatization, Public Ownership and the Regulation of Natural Monopoly*, Oxford: Blackwell.

—— (1994) *Natural Justice and the Process of Natural Monopoly Regulation*, London: Centre for the Study of Regulated Industries.

Fuller, L. (1978) 'The forms and limits of adjudication', *Harvard Law Review* 92: 353.

Gerth, H.H. and Mills, C.W. (eds) (1948) *From Max Weber*, London: Routledge.

Gist, P. (1990) 'The Role of Oftel', *Telecommunications Policy* 14: 26–51.

Grabosky, P. and Braithwaite, J. (1986) *Of Manners Gentle: Enforcement Stategies of Australian Business Regulatory Agencies*, Melbourne: Oxford University Press.

Grabosky, P. and Gunningham, N. (1997) *Smart Regulation*, Oxford: Oxford University Press.

Graham, C. (1995) *Is There a Crisis in Regulatory Accountability?*, London: Centre for the Study of Regulated Industries.

—— (1997) 'Regulatory responses to MMC decisions', in P.Vass (ed.) *CRI Regulatory Review 1997*, London: Centre for the Study of Regulated Industries.

—— (1998) 'The office of telecommunications: a new competition authority?', in Doern and Wilks 1998.

—— and Prosser, T. (1991) *Privatising Public Enterprises*, Oxford: Oxford University Press.

Grint, K. (1997) *Fuzzy Management*, Oxford: Oxford University Press.

Hague, D.C., MacKenzie, W.J.M. and Barker, A. (1975) *Public Policy and Private Interests*, London: Macmillan.

Hancher, L. and Moran, M. (1989) 'Organizing regulatory space', in L. Hancher and M. Moran (eds) *Capitalism, Culture and Regulation*, Oxford: Oxford University Press.

Hansard Society (1996) *The Report of the Commission on the Regulation of Privatised Utilities*, London: Hansard Society/European Policy Forum.

Hawkins, K. and Thomas, J.M. (1984) 'The Enforcement Process in Regulatory Bureaucracies', in K. Hawkins and J.M.Thomas (eds) *Enforcing Regulation*, Boston: Kluwer-Nijhoff.

—— (eds) (1989) *Making Regulatory Policy*, Pittsburgh: University of Pittsburgh Press.

Helm, D. (1994) 'British utility regulation: theory, practice and reform', *Oxford Economic Review* 10: 17–39.

Heclo, H. (1977) *A Government of Strangers: Executive Politics in Washington*, Washington: Brookings Institution.

Heclo, H. and Wildavksy, A. (1974) *The Private Government of Public Money*, London: Macmillan.

Henshall, N. (1992) *The Myth of Absolutism: Change and Continuity in Early Modern European Monarchy*, London: Longman.

Hills, J. (1986) *Deregulating Telecoms*, London: Frances Pinter.

Horn, M.J. (1995) *The Political Economy of Public Administration, Political Economy of Institutions and Decisions*, Cambridge: Cambridge University Press.

Hood, C. (1976) *The Limits of Administration*, London: Wiley.

—— (1986) *Administrative Analysis*, Sussex: Wheatsheaf Books.

—— (1998) *The Art of the State*, Oxford: Oxford University Press.

—— and Dunsire, A. (1981) *Bureaumetrics: The Quantitative Comparison of British Central Government Agencies*, Farnborough: Gower.

—— and Scott, C., James, O., Jones, G. and Travers, T. (1999) *Regulation Inside Government*, Oxford: Oxford University Press.

Hunt, A. (1997) 'Regulation of telecommunications: the developing EU framework and its impact on the United Kingdom', *European Public Law* 3: 91–115.

Huntley, J.A.K. and Pitt, D.C. (1990) 'Judicial policymaking: the Greeneing of US telecommunications', *International Review of Law and Economics* 10: 77–100.

Hutter, B. (1997) *Compliance: Regulation and Environment*, Oxford: Oxford University Press.

Keeling, D. (1972) *Management in Government*, London: Allen and Unwin.

Kingdon, J.W. (1984) *Agendas, Alternatives and Public Policies*, Boston: Little Brown.

Laffont, J-J., Rey, P. and Tirole, J. (1997) 'Competition between telecommunications operators', *European Economic Review* 41: 701–11.

Lawrence, P.R. and Lorsch, J.W. (1967) *Organization and Environment: Managing Differentiation and Integration*, Cambridge, Mass: Harvard University Press.

Lapsley, I. and Kilpatrick, K. (1997) *A Question of Trust; Regulators and the Regulatory Regime for Privatised Utilities*, Edinburgh: Institute of Chartered Accountants of Scotland.

Levy, B. and Spiller, P.T. (1996) *Regulation, Institutions and Commitment*, Cambridge: Cambridge University Press.

Lewis, R. (1985) 'Insurers' agreements not to enforce strict legal rights: bargaining with government and in the shadow of the law', *Modern Law Review* 48: 275–304.

Littlechild, S. (1983) *Regulation of British Telecommunications' Profitability*, London: HMSO.

Litz, R.A. (1995) 'Self-inflicted capture: an exploration of the role of self-deception in regulatory enforcement', *Administration and Society* 26: 419–33.

Long, C.D. (1995) *Telecommunications Law and Practice*, London: Sweet & Maxwell.

Loughlin, M. and Scott, C. (1997) 'The regulatory state', in P. Dunleavy, A. Gamble, I. Holliday and G. Peele (eds) *Developments in British Politics 5*, London: Macmillan.

Lynn, J. and Jay, A. (1981) *Yes Minister*, London: British Broadcasting Corporation.

Machado, N. and Burns, T.R. (1998) 'Complex social organization: multiple organizing modes, structural incongruence, and mechanisms of integration', *Public Administration* 76: 355–85.

Majone, G. (1994) 'The rise of the regulatory state in Europe', *West European Politics* 17: 77–101.

Makkai, T. and Braithwaite, J. (1995) 'In and out of the revolving door: making sense of regulatory capture', *Journal of Public Policy* 12: 61–78.

Maloney, W.A. and Richardson, J. (1996) *Managing Policy Change in Britain: The Politics of Water*, Edinburgh: Edinburgh University Press.

Manning, P. (1992) ' "Big bang" decisions: notes on a naturalistic approach' in K. Hawkins (ed.) *The Uses of Discretion*, Oxford: Oxford University Press.

March, J.G. and Simon, H.A. (1958) *Organizations*, New York: Wiley.

March, J.G. and Olsen, J.P. (1989) *Rediscovering Institutions*, New York: Free Press.

March, J.G. and Olsen, J.P. (1979) *Ambiguity and Choice in Organisations*, 2nd edn, Bergen: Universitetsforlaget.

Marsden, C. (1997) 'Convergence or coexistence? Television and telecommunications policies diverge in the convergence debate', *Journal of Information Law and Technology* 1997(3) (internet) at http://elj.warwick.ac.uk/jilt/wip/97_3mars/default.htm.

Meidinger, E. (1987) 'Regulatory culture: a theoretical outline', *Law and Policy* 9: 355–86.

Melody, W. (1997a) 'Designing a workable telecom regulatory structure for 21st century information societies', in W. Melody (ed.) *Telecom Reform* Lyngby: Technical Institute of Denmark.

—— (1997b) 'On the meaning and importance of "independence" in telecom reform', *Telecommunications Policy* 21: 195–9.

Melville, A. (1994) 'Power, strategy and games: economic regulation of a privatized utility', *Public Administration* 72: 385–408.

Mintzberg, H. (1983) *Structure in Fives: Designing Effective Organizations*, Englewood Cliffs, NJ: Prentice Hall.

MMC (1993a) Monopolies and Mergers Commission Report on *Gas*, Cm 2314, London: HMSO.

—— (1993b) Monopolies and Mergers Commission Report on *British Gas Plc – Gas Act 1986*, Cm 2315, London: HMSO.

—— (1995) Monopolies and Mergers Commission Report on *Telephone Number Portability*, London: HMSO.

Moon, J., Richardson, J. and Smart, P. (1986) 'The privatisation of British Telecom: a case study of the extended process of legislation', *European Journal of Political Research* 14: 339–55.

Moore, M.H. (1995) *Creating Public Value*, Cambridge, MA: Harvard University Press.

Nader, L. and Nader, C. (1985) 'A wide angle on regulation: an anthropological perspective', in R. Noll (ed.) *Regulatory Policy and the Social Sciences*, Berkeley, CA: University of California Press.

National Audit Office (1993) *The Office of Telecommunications: Licence Compliance and Consumer Protection*, HC 529, London: HMSO.

—— (1996) *The Work of the Directors General of Telecommunications, Gas Supply, Water Services and Electricity Supply: National Audit Office*, HC 645, London: HMSO.

—— (1998) *Countering Anti-Competitive Behaviour in the Telecommunications Industry*, HC 667, London: HMSO.

NERA/Denton Hall (1996) *Issues Associated with the Creation of a European Regulatory Authority for Telecommunications*, Report for the European Commission (DG XIII).

Neustadt, R.E. (1961) *Presidential Power*, New York: Wiley.

Neunreither, K. (1998) Review article 'Political parties and interest representation in the European Union', *Government and Opposition* 33(2): 261–7.

Nicholson T. (1994) 'Institution building: examining the fit between bureaucracies and indigenous systems', in S. Wright (ed.) *Anthropology of Organisations*, London: Routledge.

Noll, R.G. (ed.) (1985) *Regulatory Policy and the Social Sciences*, Berkeley, CA: University of California Press.

OECD (1997) *The OECD Report on Regulatory Reform, Volume 1: Sectoral Studies*, Paris.

Oftel (1985) *Annual Report to 31 December 1984*, London: HMSO.

—— (1991) *Annual Report to 31 December 1990*, London: HMSO.

—— (1993) *Annual Report to 31 December 1992*, HC 718, London: HMSO.

—— (1994) *A Framework for Effective Competition*, London: Oftel.

—— (1995a) *Annual Report to 31 December 1994*, HC 340, London: HMSO.

—— (1995b) *Doing Business with Oftel*, London: Oftel.

—— (1995c) *Beyond the Television, the Telephone and the PC*, London: Oftel.

—— (1995d) *Effective Competition: Framework for Action*, London: Oftel.

—— (1995e) *Fair Trading in Telecommunications*, London: Oftel.

—— (1996) *Pricing of Telecommunications Services from 1997*, London: Office of Telecommunications.

—— (1997a) *Annual Report to 31 December 1996*, HC 37, London: HMSO.

—— (1997b) *Improving Accountability; OFTEL's Procedures and Processes*, London: Oftel.

Ogus, A. (1994) *Regulation: Legal Form and Economic Theory*, Oxford: Oxford University Press.

Parry, R., Hood, C. and James, O. (1997) 'Reinventing the Treasury: economic rationalism or an econocrat's fallacy of control', *Public Administration* 75: 395–415.

PAC (1998) *Sixty-Fourth Report of the Public Accounts Committee* Session 1997–8, HC 842.

Peltzman, S. (1976) 'Towards a more general theory of regulation', *Journal of Law and Economics* 19: 211–40.

Peters, T.J. and Waterman, R.H. (1983) *In Search of Excellence*, New York: Harper Row.

Perrow, C. (1984) *Normal Accidents*, New York: Basic Books.

Pitt, D.C. (1980) *The Telecommunications Function in the British Post Office*, Farnborough: Saxon House.

Prosser, T. (1997) *Law and the Regulators*, Oxford: Oxford University Press.

—— (1999) 'Theorising utility regulation', *Modern Law Review* 62: 196–217.

Pugh, D.S. and Hickson, D.J. (1976) *Organizational Structure in its Context*, Farnborough: Saxon House.

Ramsay, I. (1989) *Consumer Protection: Text and Materials*, London: Wiedenfeld and Nicolson.

Reichman, N. (1992) 'Moving backstage – uncovering the role of compliance practices in shaping regulatory policy', in K. Schlegel and D. Wiesburd (eds) *White-Collar Crime Reconsidered*, Boston MA: Northeastern University Press.

Rose-Ackerman, S. (1978) *Corruption: A Study in Political Economy*, New York: Academic Press.

Schaffer, B. and Lamb, G. (1981) *Can Equity Be Organized?*, Farnborough: Gower.

Schwarz, M. and Thompson, M. (1990) *Divided We Stand*, Hemel Hempstead: Harvester Wheatsheaf.

Scharpf, F.W. (1994) 'Games real actors could play: positive and negative coordination in embedded negotiations', *Journal of Theoretical Politics* 6: 27–53.

Schultz, R. and Doern, G. B. (1998) 'No longer "Governments in Miniature": Canadian sectoral regulatory institutions', in Doern and Wilks 1998.

Scott, C. (1993a) 'Privatisation, control and accountability', in J. McCahery, S. Picciotto and C. Scott (eds) *Corporate Control and Accountability*, Oxford: Clarendon Press.

—— (1993b) 'Regulating the liberalised telecommunications sector', *International Journal of Regulatory Law and Practice* 1: 185–92.

—— (1995) 'Changing patterns of European community utilities law and policy: an institutional hypothesis', in J. Shaw and G. More (eds) *New Legal Dynamics of European Union*, Oxford: Oxford University Press.

—— (1997) 'Regulatory discretion in licence modifications: the *Scottish Power* case', *Public Law* 1997: 400–9.

—— (1998a) 'Juridification of regulatory relations in the UK utilities sectors' in J. Black, P. Muchlinski and P. Walker (eds) *Commercial Regulation and Judicial Review*, Oxford: Hart Publishing.

—— (1998b) 'The proceduralization of telecommunications law', *Telecommunications Policy* 22: 243–54.

—— (1997) Hall, C. and Hood, C. (1997) 'Regulatory space and institutional reform: the case of telecommunications' in P. Vass (ed.) *CRI Regulatory Review 1997*, London: Centre for the Study of Regulated Industries.

Scott, W.R. (1995) *Institutions and Organizations*, Thousand Oaks: Sage.

Shearing, C. (1993) 'A constitutive conception of regulation', in P. Grabosky and J. Braithwaite *Business Regulation and Australia's Future*, Canberra: Australian Institute of Criminology.

Sieber, S. (1981) *Fatal Remedies*, New York: Plenum.

Souter, D. (1995) 'A stakeholder approach to regulation', in D. Corry, D. Souter and M. Waterson, *Regulating Our Utilities*, London: Institute of Public Policy Research.

Thatcher, M. (1993) *Examining Explanations of Public Policy Making: Industrial Policy in Britain and France in the Case of the Telecommunications Sector 1969–1990*, D.Phil Thesis, University of Oxford.

Trade and Industry Select Committee (1996) *Third Report*, Session 1996–7 (Telecommunications Regulation) HC 254.

—— (1999) *Fifth Report*, Session 1998–9 (Numbering Administration).

Veljanovski, C. (1987) *Selling the State*, London: Weidenfeld and Nicolson.

—— (1991) 'The regulation game' in C. Veljanovski (ed.) *Regulators and Markets – An Assessment of the Growth of Regulation in the United Kingdom*, London: Institute of Economic Affairs.

—— (1993a) *The Future of Industry Regulation in the UK*, London: European Policy Forum.

—— (1993b) 'The power of the regulator' in *But Who Will Regulate the Regulators?*, London: Adam Smith Institute.

Vickers, J. and Yarrow, G. (1988) *Privatisation: An Economic Analysis*, Cambridge, Mass: MIT Press.

Vogel, D. (1986) *National Styles of Regulation*, Ithaca, NY: Cornell University Press.

Vogel, S.K. (1996) *Freer Markets, More Rules; Regulatory Reform in Advanced Industrial Countries*, Ithaca, NY: Cornell University Press.

Webb, M. and Taylor, M. (1998) 'Light-handed regulation of telecommunications in New Zealand: is generic competition law sufficient', *International Journal of Communications Law and Policy* Issue 2 (http://www.digital-law.net/IJCLP/).

Wigglesworth, W.R.B. (1997) 'The role of information in telecom regulation', in W. Melody *Telecom Reform*, Lyngby: Technical Institute of Denmark.

Wilks, S. (1998) 'Utility regulation, corporate governance and the amoral corporation' in Doern and Wilks 1998.

—— and Doern G.B. (1998) 'Conclusions' in Doern and Wilks 1998.

Williams, B. (not dated) 'Facing up to the regulator', *The Manager* (BT Internal Publication).

Wright, S. (1994) *The Anthropology of Organizations*, London: Routledge.

—— (1998) 'The politicization of culture', *Anthropology Today* 14: 7–15.

Xavier, P. (1995) 'Price cap regulation for telecommunications', *Telecommunications Policy* 19: 599–617.

Yeung, K. (1998) 'Privatizing competition regulation', *Oxford Journal of Legal Studies* 18: 581–616.

—— (1999) 'Private enforcement of competition Law' in C. McCrudden, (ed.) *Regulation and Deregulation*, Oxford: Oxford University Press.

Index